Handbook of

PENTECOSTAL

CHRISTIANITY

Handbook of

PENTECOSTAL

CHRISTIANITY

Edited by Adam Stewart

NIU
PRESS

DeKalb

Design by Julia Fauci

Library of Congress Cataloging-in-Publication Data

Handbook of Pentecostal Christianity / edited by Adam Stewart.

   p.   cm.

ISBN 978-0-87580-672-3 (paperback : alk. paper)

ISBN 978-1-60909-047-0 (electronic version)

1. Pentecostalism. I. Stewart, Adam.

BR1644.H36 2012

270.8'2—dc23

2011034257

For Becky and Alasdair

Contents

Handbook of

PENTECOSTAL

CHRISTIANITY

A Brief Introduction

❧   With its more than five hundred million estimated adherents worldwide, Pentecostalism is claimed by approximately one in every thirteen people and one in every four Christians on the planet, making it one of the largest and fastest-growing religious movements in the world. While its roots are deeply embedded in the Protestant revivalism of nineteenth- and twentieth-century Anglo-America, Pentecostalism is now predominantly a movement of the Global South and is growing at an exponential rate on the continents of Africa, Asia, and South America. Although many of the most important histories of Christianity written during the last few decades tend to gloss over Pentecostalism (if they even mention it), there is little doubt that the past century will be remembered within the annals of Christian history as the century that catapulted Pentecostalism onto the world stage, significantly altering the face of global Christianity. This movement has been the single largest contributor to the transformation of Christianity from a religion of primarily Europeans and their descendents to a religion predominated by Asian, African, and Latin American adherents.

Pentecostalism has emerged from the last one hundred years as an established fixture on the North American religious landscape and has been transformed into an indomitable religious and cultural force in many other parts of the world, which means it is now more important than ever before to understand this dynamic religious movement. When North Americans think of Pentecostalism, however, their minds are often flooded with images of snake-handling preachers, people convulsing at the altar of a church, or televangelists pleading for money on late-night television. While scenes such as these form a real and important part of the Pentecostal tradition, they only tell part of the story. This book provides a corrective to the image of Pentecostalism that is often found within American popular culture by presenting a more complete picture of the movement in America and around the world.

Pentecostalism, like Methodism and Mormonism, is in a very real sense an "American" religion. Much of the movement's early momentum came from the unique culture and personalities of late nineteenth- and early twentieth-century America. The Wesleyan Holiness movement and African American religion in the United States—in addition to the Americans Charles F. Parham, William J. Seymour, William H. Durham, Charles H. Mason, and Ambrose J. Tomlinson—were responsible for giving shape to the early Pentecostal movement. Despite these important American influences, scholars of global Pentecostalism such as Allan Anderson remind us that the beginning of Pentecostalism cannot be isolated to a single, monogenetic source of origination in the United States. Rather, the existence of other early Pentecostal missions and revivals that predated, existed simultaneously, or emerged subsequently but independently of early American Pentecostal centers means that Pentecostalism is best understood as a truly global, polygenetic religious movement with multiple points of origination. The study of Pentecostalism, then, is important both because of the significance it holds for understanding twentieth-century American religious history and because of the role it plays and will continue to play in the lives of hundreds of millions of people in virtually every other country in the world.

There exists little consensus regarding exactly how to define Pentecostalism as a result of its diverse global expressions. Most scholars, however, agree that there are at least three major branches within the movement. Classical Pentecostals attend churches sharing historical roots with the Holiness, Reformed, and Oneness Pentecostal denominations formed during the first few decades of the twentieth century in North America. Charismatics are members of non-Pentecostal denominations and include Anglicans, Baptists, Eastern Orthodox, Lutherans, Methodists, Presbyterians, and Roman Catholics who, beginning primarily in the 1950s, adopted Pentecostal theology and spirituality but decided to remain intentionally within and "renew" their existing denominations. Neo-Pentecostals—also sometimes called Neo-Charismatics, Independent Charismatics, and Proto-Pentecostals—include nondenominational and independent Christians all over the world who have adopted some aspects of Pentecostal theology and spirituality, but who are not affiliated with either classical Pentecostal or traditional Christian denominational bodies. Some scholars use the term "Renewalists" to refer to all three of these groups of Christians. For the sake of consistency, however, this book most commonly uses the terms

"Pentecostal" or "Pentecostalism" to refer to the three as a whole, while the terms "classical Pentecostal," "Charismatic," and "Neo-Pentecostal" are used to identify the individual segments of the larger, global Pentecostal movement.

THE PURPOSE OF THIS BOOK

This book was written with two primary objectives in mind: first, to assist college, university, and seminary instructors who are faced with the task of introducing their students to Pentecostalism and, second, to serve as a compact companion for general readers who are interested in learning more about Pentecostalism. The increased scholarly interest in this religious movement has created a need for a concise, interdisciplinary text that can help instructors from various disciplinary backgrounds introduce their students to the wide array of necessary events, ideas, and figures that form its basic vocabulary. While the book adopts a reference-style format, it is not intended to function as an exhaustive dictionary or encyclopedia of Pentecostalism. A number of excellent texts with this objective have already been written. Also, the book does not pretend to be a comprehensive historical introduction to Pentecostalism. There is likewise an assortment of worthy texts that do this very well. Rather, this handbook is designed to provide the student or general reader interested in exploring Pentecostalism with a resource that does not currently exist: a volume of concise essays written by leading Pentecostal scholars who explain some of the most important concepts that are needed to gain an introductory understanding of the history, theology, practices, and contemporary forms of global Pentecostalism.

SELECTION OF ENTRIES

The fifty entries in this book were written by twenty-four scholars originating from five continents, writing from disciplinary perspectives as diverse as anthropology, biblical studies, black church studies, history, religious studies, sociology, and theology. With any book containing a necessarily limited number of topics intended to introduce such a large and diverse subject, there is bound to be disagreement regarding what are the most important and the merely peripheral concepts to be considered. The editor arrived at the final list of entries contained here through a lively exchange with a number of scholars from around the world. This process ensured that feedback was received from scholars inhabiting diverse sociocultural contexts and constituting multiple denominational and theological positions within (and outside of) Pentecostalism. While the tentative list initially sent out for comment was adapted significantly as a result of the excellent advice provided by a number of helpful colleagues, in the end, the terms were selected by the editor and any limitation of the book's purview is solely his responsibility.

The reader will notice that the entries in this book are weighted more heavily toward understanding North American, classical Pentecostalism. This decision was driven by practical rather than ethnocentric concerns. As this book is being published and distributed by an American university press, it is more likely to see greater use in North American classrooms and to be read by individuals living in the United States and Canada. The inclusion of topics—and, more important, authors—originating from other continents mitigates a North American myopia as much as possible in a book of this modest size.

The main objective was to cover topics and figures in Pentecostalism that most instructors would consider essential in any basic introduction. These topics primarily include Pentecostal origins and historical development, some of the early leaders, important beliefs and practices, and a survey of Pentecostalism on the various continents. After these were assigned, attention was given to topics either that are sometimes neglected in other introductions (such as Native American Pentecostalism and women) or that represent emerging areas of Pentecostal research (such as Godly love and suffering). Since the intention from the time of its inception was to limit the text to fifty terms, the coverage of this second group of entries is only representative of the diversity of worthy topics that could be explored

THE PERSPECTIVES OF THE AUTHORS

In this text, the deliberate aim is to address topics and include approaches that are of interest to scholars and students inhabiting different institutional spaces: outsiders to the Pentecostal tradition who predominate in public universities and insiders who are found in higher concentrations within Pentecostal colleges and seminaries. Forty of the book's fifty entries are written from what could be considered a broadly critical perspective, while ten of the book's entries—namely, the entries written on the Acts of the Apostles, baptism of the Holy Spirit, exorcism, healing, hermeneutics, Holy Spirit, initial evidence, salvation, spiritual gifts, and suffering—are written from a largely normative perspective. This allows the outsider reading this book to see the ways in which Pentecostals themselves both describe and understand their own tradition and gives the insider the equally valuable advantage of considering the tradition from a more critical point of view. It is in the spirit of fostering greater collaboration in the interdisciplinary study of Pentecostalism, and expanding the current boundaries of our understanding and analysis of Pentecostalism, that this book synthesizes the insights of scholars who adopt both critical and normative perspectives in the study of Pentecostalism.

A Sample Course Outline

Below is a suggestion for a thirteen-unit course outline intended to help instructors imagine how this book might be used in the classroom. The first units present a historical introduction to Pentecostalism. Other aspects of the movement are then considered in a roughly chronological order.

UNIT I—Pentecostal Origins, Part I—Holiness Movement, Keswick Movement, Azusa Street Mission and Revival

UNIT II—Pentecostal Origins, Part II—African American Pentecostalism, Native American Pentecostalism, Revival, Origins

UNIT III—Early Leaders—Charles Fox Parham, William Joseph Seymour, Charles Harrison Mason, Ambrose Jessup Tomlinson, William Howard Durham

UNIT IV—Early Women Leaders—Women, Hebden Mission, Aimee Semple McPherson, Pandita Sarasvati Ramabai

UNIT V—Early Pentecostal Theology—Full Gospel, Salvation, Healing, Baptism of the Holy Spirit, Eschatology

UNIT VI—Early Theological and Practical Developments—Dispensationalism, Ecclesiology, Finished Work Controversy, Oneness (Apostolic) Pentecostalism, Snake Handling

UNIT VII—Global Pentecostalism Part I—African Pentecostalism, Asian Pentecostalism, Latin American Pentecostalism

UNIT VIII—Global Pentecostalism Part II—North American Pentecostalism, European Pentecostalism, Australian Pentecostalism

UNIT IX—Mid-century Developments—Latter Rain Movement, Charismatic Movement, Televangelism

UNIT X—Pentecostal Perspectives on the Bible—Acts of the Apostles, Initial Evidence, Hermeneutics

UNIT XI—The Person and Work of the Holy Spirit—Holy Spirit, Spiritual Gifts, Glossolalia, Prophecy

UNIT XII—Aspects of Pentecostal Spirituality— Spirituality, Exorcism, Suffering

UNIT XIII—Contemporary Concepts and Issues—Academic Societies, Globalization, Godly Love, Neo-Pentecostalism, Word of Faith Movement

Fifty Topics

Academic Societies

MARTIN W. MITTELSTADT

✖ Pentecostal academic societies did not emerge until the final quarter of the twentieth century. In the short period since that time, however, at least one academic society committed to Pentecostal research has been established on every continent. The Society for Pentecostal Studies (SPS), founded in 1970, is the oldest, and it materialized from the vision of three aspiring Pentecostal academics: William Menzies (Assemblies of God), Vinson Synan (Pentecostal Holiness Church), and Horace Ward (Church of God [Cleveland, Tennessee]). Its first annual meeting coincided with the sixth Pentecostal World Conference in Dallas, Texas, which was sponsored by the Pentecostal Fellowship of North America (PFNA). The meeting initially drew 139 registrants and concluded with 108 charter members. Although the society functions "to serve the church world by providing an authoritative interpretation of the Pentecostal Movement," SPS leadership made a courageous migration away from the PFNA and became a separate entity in 1975 (Society for Pentecostal Studies 2010).

Members settled on the name "Society for Pentecostal Studies" rather than the "Society of Pentecostal Scholars" in order to stimulate academic rigor in the study of Pentecostalism and not limit involvement to only Pentecostal academics. Originally, SPS members were required to adhere to the PFNA's Statement of Faith, which excluded many African American and Hispanic American Pentecostals, whose denominations had been denied membership in the PFNA; Oneness scholars, who could not align with Trinitarian language; and Charismatics, many of whom did not subscribe to the classical Pentecostal doctrine of speaking in tongues as initial evidence of the baptism of the Holy Spirit. This requirement was eventually removed in order to promote more diversity within the

SPS, but still others voiced concern that a North American body might exert too much interpretative influence upon the larger global Pentecostal movement. The diversity of past presidents indicates the efforts made by SPS members to be inclusive; over the course of forty years, the presidential list demonstrates diversity in gender, ethnicity (including African Americans, Hispanics, and Canadians), as well as denominations and traditions (with links to Oneness, Roman Catholic, Presbyterian, and Episcopalian traditions). The society continues to hold annual meetings that are generally focused on a common conference theme, featuring plenary speakers together with presenters and respondents on an ever-increasing range of themes including Asian/Asian American concerns, biblical concerns, Canadian Pentecostalism, Christian ethics, ecumenism, history, missions and intercultural studies, philosophy, practical theology/Christian formation, religion and culture, and theology. The SPS also sponsored two extensive ecumenical dialogues between Roman Catholics and Pentecostals and between classical and Oneness Pentecostals. In 1979, the society launched its first issue of *Pneuma: The Journal of the Society for Pentecostal Studies*, now recognized for premier academic contributions not only among Pentecostals and Charismatics but also among students and scholars from all traditions. Like the society, *Pneuma*—currently published three times a year—continues to grow in denominational, ethnic, and international diversity, thereby reflecting the ever-increasing global dynamic of twenty-first-century Pentecostalism. Still on North American soil, the recently formed Canadian Pentecostal Research Network examines issues related to the study of Canadian Pentecostalism. A number of symposia have led to monographs focusing on histories of Canadian Pentecostalism and to the establishment of the *Canadian Journal of Pentecostal-Charismatic Christianity.*

In Europe, several organizations materialized to address specific issues relating to Pentecostalism on that continent. The European Pentecostal Theological Association (EPTA), founded in 1979, exists for "the promotion of Pentecostal learning, ministerial training and theological literature, and the fostering of exchange and cooperation between member institutions" (European Pentecostal Theological Association 2010). Like members of the SPS, EPTA members strive to address a multiplicity of languages, cultures, and traditions within the European context. Unlike the SPS, the EPTA includes only Pentecostal members and serves primarily the concerns of Pentecostal education. In 1981, the society began quarterly publication of the *EPTA Bulletin*, and in 1996, the EPTA transitioned to an annual publication renamed the *Journal of the European Pentecostal Theological Association (JEPTA)*. In the same year, a second association named the European Pentecostal Charismatic Research Conference (EPCRA) initiated an international, interdenominational, and interdisciplinary exchange among academics and lay people on the study of Pentecostal and Charismatic movements. Finally, the most recent European society—chartered in 2004 as the European Research Network on Global Pentecostalism (GloPent)—now acts as a network for researchers with particular interest in African, Asian, and Latin American Pentecostalism. GloPent consists of an ambitious steering group of scholars from the University of Birmingham, England, Vrije Universiteit in Amsterdam, and the University of Heidelberg. The network encourages membership of scholars from any European university, and by way of the Hollenweger Center for the Interdisciplinary Study of Pentecostal and Charismatic Movements in Amsterdam publishes *PentecoStudies: Online Journal for the Scientific Study of Pentecostalism and Charismatic Movements.*

In Asia and Australia, various societies with national, regional, and/or international ambitions include Asia Charismatic Theological Association (ACTA); Asia Pacific Theological Association (APTA), which publishes the *Asian Journal of Pentecostal Studies*; Asian Pentecostal Society; Australasian Pentecostal Studies, which publishes *Australasian Pentecostal Studies*; Conference of Pentecostal Theologians—India; Japan Society for Pentecostal Studies; and Korean Pentecostal Society, which publishes the *Journal of Korean Pentecostal Theology*. From Africa, recent groups to emerge include the Ghana-based Centre for Pentecostal and Charismatic Studies and the Pentecostal Theological Association of Southern Africa (and their journal entitled *Pneumatikos*). Moving to Latin America, the Comisión Evangélica Pentecostal Latinoamericana (CEPLA) serves under the World Council of Churches and addresses fundamental challenges facing the Pentecostal movement in Latin America. Since 1990, researchers continue to focus upon the historical roots of the Pentecostal faith and to respond to the increasing demand for discipleship, ministerial formation, and ecumenism. Given the recent surge in global Pentecostalism, immediate research requires scholarly analysis of national and regional identities, histories, theologies, and praxes, thus highlighting the need for growth in Global South scholarship. Unfortunately, distance and cost impediments sometimes force these organizations to scale back the frequency of their conference meetings and publications.

A final noteworthy society, Pentecostals and Charismatics for Peace and Justice (PCPJ), does not exist primarily along geographic lines but, rather, "to encourage, enable, and sustain peacemaking and justice-seeking as authentic and integral aspect[s] of Pentecostal & Charismatic Christianity, witnessing to the conviction that Jesus Christ is relevant to all tensions, crises, and brokenness in the world" (Pentecostals and Charismatics for Peace and Justice 2010). PCPJ publishes *Pax Pneuma: The Journal of Pentecostals & Charismatics for Peace and Justice* and seeks to provide resources for local chapters to participate in Jesus-shaped, Spirit-empowered peace with justice.

As Pentecostal academic societies uphold their mission statements, the future of Pentecostal research and praxis looks bright. First, by fulfilling their mission, Pentecostal students and scholars will enlarge their personal and academic identity through rigorous dialogue among peers. Indeed, Pentecostal scholars shape each other and contribute much to the historical and theological identities of Pentecostals now into their second century of existence. These scholars in turn help shape the exegetical, historical, sociocultural, and theological self-awareness not only in their academic but also in their ecclesial communities. Second, Pentecostal academic societies no longer remain on the fringe of scholarship. The efforts of Pentecostal societies launch many young scholars into careers that not only shape the Pentecostal tradition but also offer contributions to the larger academy and the church universal. By way of example, consider recent developments in the Evangelical Theological Society (ETS), and the American Academy of Religion (AAR). In 1999, the ETS affirmed a session under the leadership of Paul Elbert and James Shelton entitled "Charismatic Themes in Luke-Acts." Meetings continued at ETS for five years and stimulated important dialogue between Pentecostal and evangelical scholars. Turning to the AAR, although a formal request for a Pentecostal track was rejected in 1984, current generation Pentecostals under the direction of James K. A. Smith and Amos Yong recently received entry as the "Pentecostal-Charismatic Movements Consultation." Inaugurated in 2007, the consultation is currently in its second three-year term.

References and Suggestions for Further Reading

European Pentecostal Theological Association. 2010. http://www.eptaonline.com.

Hunter, Harold D. 2002. "International Pentecostal-Charismatic Scholarly Associations." In *The New International Dictionary of Pentecostal and Char-ismatic Movements*. Revised and expanded edition, ed. Stanley M. Burgess and Eduard M. van der Maas, 795–97. Grand Rapids, MI: Zondervan.

Pentecostal-Charismatic Theological Inquiry International. 2010. http://www.pctii.org.

Pentecostals and Charismatics for Peace and Justice. 2010. "Our Mission." http://pcpj.org.

Society for Pentecostal Studies. 2010. http://www.sps-usa.org.

Spittler, Russell P. 2002. "Society for Pentecostal Studies." In *The New International Dictionary of Pentecostal and Charismatic Movements*. Revised and expanded edition, ed. Stanley M. Burgess and Eduard M. van der Maas, 1079–80. Grand Rapids, MI: Zondervan.

Acts of the Apostles

ROGER J. STRONSTAD

The Acts of the Apostles, the fifth book in the New Testament canon, holds a privileged place within the Pentecostal tradition. It is in the book of Acts that we find mention of the disciples being filled with the Holy Spirit and the subsequent operation of the various gifts of the Holy Spirit among the disciples. Both occurred on the day of Pentecost, from which modern-day Pentecostals get their name. The Acts of the Apostles is the only continuation narrative, or "part two" book in the New Testament. Part one is, of course, the Gospel of Luke. Considered as the two-part unified narrative, which it is, the two books are usually identified as Luke-Acts. In this regard, Luke-Acts is more like the Old Testament narrative 1 and 2 Chronicles than it is like the separate New Testament Letters, 1 and 2 Corinthians. The Acts of the Apostles extends the narrative about "all that Jesus did and taught" (Acts 1:1), by implication to all that Jesus continues to do and teach through his Spirit-baptized followers and their Spirit-baptized converts. Luke-Acts, therefore, is a two-book narrative of the history of salvation united in literary genre, history, and theology.

Acts reports the progress of the disciples' triumphant, though often persecuted, witness about Jesus from Jerusalem to Rome. This witness begins on the first post-Easter day of Pentecost in Jerusalem, when about three thousand were added to the church, and concludes in Rome about thirty years later, when Paul, though bound in chains, preached and taught "about the Lord Jesus Christ with all boldness and without hindrance" (Acts 28:31). Historically, Acts also functions as the continuation narrative for each of the other Gospels—Matthew, Mark, and John. This is because Luke's history about Jesus as Savior is also their history, and their history about Jesus assumes the fulfillment of the "great commission" with which each Gospel ends (Mt 28:16–20; Mk 16:14–18; Jn 20:19–23). Therefore, although Acts is separated from Luke in the New Testament canon by the Gospel of John, it rightly stands as the continuation narrative not just for Luke but for all four Gospels and also as the bridge and introduction to the many New Testament epistles that follow, beginning with Paul's epistle to the Romans.

Acts is the only history of the apostolic church to be found in the New Testament. It is the only eyewitness report about the spread of the gospel. From Acts 16–28 there are several so-called "we" passages. These identify the author as a participant in the narrative action. If Acts had not been written, it would be impossible for later generations of New Testament readers to reconstruct the history of the apostolic church from the letters of Paul and the other writers of the books of the New Testament.

The writer of Luke-Acts in the "we" passages identifies himself as a participant in some of the action in Acts. However, he nowhere names himself. In this respect Luke-Acts is like the historical books of the Old Testament, which are also written anonymously. Because the author does not identify himself, Luke-Acts differs from the letters of the New Testament. In these letters the author identifies himself in the salutation (for example, Paul, an apostle) and his identity gives the letter a personal authority that is lacking in the Old and New Testament historical books.

Though Luke-Acts is an anonymous two-volume document, testimony from the early church is that Luke is the author. This identification of Luke as the author of the Gospel that bears his name and of the Acts of the Apostles is supported by evidence within the New Testament. For example, the author of the "we" passages is an occasional companion of Paul. On Paul's second evangelistic tour, the "we" passages indicate that the author joined Paul at Troas (Acts 16:11ff). He then accompanied Paul to Macedonia, and he remained behind in Philippi when Paul moved on to Thessalonica. The writer rejoins Paul toward the end of Paul's third evangelistic tour and travels with him from Philippi to Jerusalem. Finally, the writer of Luke-Acts accompanies Paul from Caesarea to Rome.

When Paul is in Rome one of his companions is Luke. In Paul's letter to the Colossians he identifies Luke as "the beloved physician" (Col 4:1). About the same time that Paul writes to the church in Colossae, he also writes to a certain Philemon. In this letter he identifies Luke as a fellow-worker (Phlm 24). Several years later Paul writes to Timothy and describes Luke as a faithful or loyal companion (2 Tm 4:11).

This combined evidence from Acts and the relevant letters of Paul witnesses to Luke being the author of Acts, and hence, also of the Gospel that bears his name. Christians came to this conclusion early in the history of the church. For example, the fourth-century historian of the early church Eusebius of Caesarea, in his *Ecclesiastical History*, identifies Luke as the author of two books, the Gospel and the Acts of the Apostles. Thus, the internal evidence (Acts and Paul's letters) and the external evidence (*Ecclesiastical History* by Eusebius) consistently witness to the Lukan authorship of Luke-Acts. Little more can be said of Luke except that he has a thorough knowledge of the Greek language translation of the Old Testament, which is called the Septuagint (abbreviated LXX). This knowledge of the Old Testament in Greek makes it possible that Luke was a Hellenistic—or Greek-speaking—Jew.

When Luke actually wrote his history about the origin and spread of Christianity cannot be established with certainty. Several factors imply, however, that he wrote in the early sixties of the first century. We know the earliest possible date. Luke has traveled with Paul to Rome, and he concludes his history with a reference to Paul's two-year-long house arrest in that city. This means that Luke-Acts could not have been written before 62/63 CE.

The pastoral letters of Paul (1 and 2 Tm and Ti) imply that Paul was released some time after his imprisonment in Rome. At this time Luke is still a companion of Paul (2 Tm 4:11), but he reports nothing of Paul's activities later than his Roman imprisonment. Further, in 64 CE a fire burned through large parts of the city of Rome. The emperor, Nero, blamed the Christians in the city for the fire and martyred many of them. Luke is silent about this persecution of Christians by Nero. Luke is also silent about the revolt of the Jews in Judea against the Romans in 68–70 CE. The Romans soon crushed the revolt, destroying the Temple in Jerusalem in 70 CE. Luke's silence about these events needs to be measured by his interest in contemporary history. For example, in Acts 18:1 he reported that the emperor Claudius had expelled the Jews, including Aquila and Priscilla, from

Rome (49 CE). Since Luke is silent about the last years of Paul's ministry and silent about events within the empire such as Nero's persecution and, later, the destruction of the Jewish Temple, it is reasonable to conclude that Luke-Acts was written later than Paul's imprisonment in Rome but before Nero's persecution of Christians in Rome. Therefore, Luke probably wrote Luke-Acts sometime in the years 62–64 CE.

The Bible is written in a variety of literary forms. In the New Testament the most common form is the letter. Paul, James, Peter, John, and Jude all wrote letters to individual churches, groups of churches, or individuals. The book of Hebrews identifies itself as a "word of exhortation" or written sermon (Heb 13:22). The last book in the New Testament identifies itself as a revelation or an apocalypse (Rv 1:1). In contrast, the first five books in the New Testament are written as historical narrative. The church classifies the books of John, Matthew, Mark, and Luke as "good news," or Gospels, and Luke's second book as the Acts of the Apostles. Luke, however, classifies both his books—the Gospel and the Acts—as historical narrative. At the beginning of his first book, Luke identifies what he has written to Theophilus by the Greek word *diegesis*, which means "account" or "narrative" (Lk 1:1), and which, therefore, identifies both the Gospel of Luke and the Acts of the Apostles as historical narrative. At the beginning of Acts he retrospectively identified his first book by the Greek word *logos*, which means "account, chronicle, or scroll."

Eusebius identifies Luke's two books by two terms. The first is the Greek word *historesen*, which means "written account," "narrative," or "history." Later, Eusebius identifies both Luke and Acts by the Greek word *praxeis*. This word is usually translated into English as "acts." *Praxeis*, or Acts, is the traditional title of Luke's second book. Clearly, the evidence of these four terms is unanimous. Though the Gospel of Luke and the Acts of the Apostles have different titles in the English Bible, separately and together Luke-Acts is historical narrative, history, or acts. This would make Luke, their author, the first historian of the church.

Like the books of 1 and 2 Samuel, 1 and 2 Kings, and 1 and 2 Chronicles found in the Old Testament, Luke-Acts also contains a unified theological narrative. Luke's theological perspectives about God, Jesus, and the Holy Spirit do not change from one book to the other. Since Lukan studies began in the 1970s it has become increasingly common to consider Luke a theologian as well as a historian. As part of this shift toward recognizing Luke's theological interests, it is more appropriate to discuss Luke as an independent theologian, when, for example, comparing the theology of the Gospel of Luke with the theologies of Matthew and Mark, or when comparing the theology of Luke-Acts with the theology of Paul's epistles. In other words, Luke-Acts contains theological content that is unique to these books.

It is important to note that Luke-Acts is set in the two cultures in which Christianity emerged and spread, both the Jewish and the Greco-Roman cultures. In the Gospel and Acts 1–12, Luke's readers find themselves in the world of Judaism. This is the world of the Pharisees and of the synagogues, of righteousness by law-keeping, of messianic expectations, of Jewish feasts, and of the religious and political hierarchy in Jerusalem and at the Temple. But Paul's missionary activity (Acts 13–28) brought Christianity into direct contact with Roman officials and Roman law. For example, when Barnabas and Paul travel through Cyprus, they are brought before the proconsul, Sergius Paulus (Acts 13:7). Later, in Philippi, Paul and Silas are accused by its citizens of "advocating customs that are not lawful for us as Romans" (Acts 16:21). In Thessalonica, Paul and Silas are accused of acting "contrary to the decrees of the emperor" (Acts 17:7). When Paul travels to Corinth he meets Aquila and Priscilla, who along with other Jews had earlier been expelled from Rome itself by the emperor Claudius (Acts 18:2). The later chapters of Acts contain many further contacts between the history of early Christianity and the Greco-Roman world.

Luke-Acts is also selective history. Luke makes no attempt to write a complete history of Jesus, his apostles, or the spread of the gospel throughout the Roman world. For example, Luke reports that about 120 disciples in Jerusalem await the arrival of the day of Pentecost (Acts 1:15). These disciples include the apostles; Mary, the mother of Jesus; and the brothers of Jesus. Of these 120 disciples, Luke tells his readers nothing more about Mary (where she lived, when she died, or her role in the early church, for example). He tells us nothing about the brothers of Jesus, except James (briefly), who is not mentioned again until the Jerusalem Council (Acts 15). Of the twelve apostles Luke says nothing, except about the inner circle, namely, Peter, James, and John. Luke mentions James and John only briefly. In contrast, Luke reports extensively about Peter in Jerusalem, Samaria, and Judea.

Luke tells his readership nothing about the church in Galilee, where the gospel first appeared, and he tells his readers nothing about the spread of the gospel to Egypt, though he reports about Apollos, a Christian from Alexandria in Egypt (Acts 18:24–28). In time Peter will write to Christians

in the province of Pontus, Cappadocia, and Bithynia (1 Pt 1:1). Luke, however, is silent about the evangelization of these provinces. Further, Paul
writes letters to the churches in Rome, Colossae, and Laodicea (Rom 1:1;
Col 1:1, 4:15–16). From Luke we know nothing about how, when, or by
whom the churches in these cities were founded. He is very selective when
he chooses information that conforms to and advances his purposes in
narrating the spread of the gospel.

It is interesting to note that Luke writes as a teacher. His historical and
theological interests are more than mere private interest or indulgence.
He writes to instruct his patron Theophilus, and everyone else who reads
his history, about the things God has accomplished through the apostles.
Luke uses Old Testament terminology adapted from the Septuagint, the
Greek translation of the Jewish Scriptures redacted in the third and second
centuries BCE, using phrases such as "filled with the Holy Spirit." This
Old Testament terminology communicates theological connotations that
every reader of Luke's narrative who is also familiar with the Old Testament would understand.

Luke teaches most directly when he reports the direct teaching of Jesus
and his disciples. For example, Luke teaches Theophilus and his later readers about the Holy Spirit by reporting the teaching of Jesus about the Holy
Spirit. Jesus taught that the Father would give the Holy Spirit to those who
ask him, that is, to those who pray (Lk 11:13). Thus, leading up to the
day of Pentecost, the disciples are in prayer (Acts 1:14, 15). When Peter
and John later go to Samaria, they pray that believers there might receive
the Holy Spirit (Acts 8:14–15). Jesus identified this promised gift of the
Holy Spirit as the disciples being "baptized in the Holy Spirit" (Acts 1:4–5;
compare 11:15–17). Finally, Jesus states that the purpose for the Holy
Spirit to come upon the disciples is so that they might receive power for a
worldwide witness (Acts 1:8). And so, by reporting the teaching of Jesus,
Luke himself teaches: (1) disciples can pray to receive the Holy Spirit; (2)
this reception of the Spirit is their Spirit baptism; and (3) the purpose of
this Spirit baptism is vocational, that is, it is for witness or service.

Luke also teaches about the Holy Spirit by reporting the teaching and
preaching of the disciples of Jesus. For example, by applying the Joel
text to the outpouring of the Holy Spirit on the day of Pentecost, Peter
makes three primary points: (1) that this pouring forth of the Spirit is the
promised "last days" gift of the Spirit (Acts 2:17a); (2) that it is potentially
universal—crossing all age, gender, and socioeconomic boundaries—and

is available from generation to generation (2:17b–18, 39); and (3) that it is the pouring forth of the Spirit of prophecy (2:17b–18). Following the outpouring of the Spirit upon the household of Cornelius (Acts 10:44–48), Peter explains to the church in Jerusalem that Cornelius's reception of the Holy Spirit is after the pattern of Pentecost (Acts 11:15) and that it is a Spirit baptism (Acts 11:16). By reporting the teaching or preaching of Peter, Luke himself teaches: (1) Spirit baptism results in the gift of tongues-speaking, and (2) this is a pattern for disciples who are baptized in the Holy Spirit.

Luke writes a carefully crafted narrative about the origin and spread of the gospel. He gives both Luke and Acts a common thematic structure. But the book of Acts can also be outlined independently of the gospel, which would highlight other nuances in the meaning of the Acts narrative. For example, the interpreter may outline the second book according to the geographic pattern of Acts 1:8; thus, Jerusalem (chapters 1–7), Samaria and Judea (chapters 8–12), and to the ends of the earth (chapters 13–28). Or the interpreter can divide Acts according to Luke's two primary heroes; thus, Peter (Acts 1–12) and Paul (Acts 13–28). The interpreter can emphasize the work of the Holy Spirit; thus, the origin of the charismatic community (Acts 1:1–2:41), the acts of the charismatic community (Acts 2:42–6:7), and the book's major section, namely, the acts of the six charismatic disciples, Stephen and Philip (charismatic deacons), Barnabas and Agabus (charismatic prophets), and Peter and Paul (charismatic apostles) (Acts 6:8–28:31). Each of these approaches (and others) to outlining either Luke-Acts or Acts alone has its own inherent logic. Thus, each makes its own contribution to a better understanding of the message of Acts.

References and Suggestions for Further Reading

Liefeld, Walter L. 1995. *Interpreting the Book of Acts.* Guides to New Testament Exegesis. Grand Rapids, MI: Baker Books.

Marshall, I. Howard. 1992. *The Acts of the Apostles.* New Testament Guides. Sheffield: Sheffield Academic Press.

Martin, Ralph P., and Peter H. Davids, eds. 1997. *Dictionary of the Later New Testament and Its Developments.* Downers Grove, IL: InterVarsity Press.

Parsons, Mikeal C. 2007. *Luke: Storyteller, Interpreter, Evangelist.* Peabody, MA: Hendrickson.

Powell, Mark Allan. 1991. *What Are They Saying about Acts?* Mahwah, NJ: Paulist Press.

African American Pentecostalism

LEWIS BROGDON

The origin and growth of early American Pentecostalism are heavily indebted to African religious practices and spirituality. Its roots can be traced back to nineteenth-century enslaved Africans, who mixed elements of African culture with elements of Protestant Christianity to form what African American scholars refer to as slave religion. African religious practices such as the ring shout, dreams, visions, trances, drums, healing, and belief in spirits or the spirit world were commonplace in slave religion and later became integrated into the Christian milieu of American Protestantism through the Wesleyan Holiness movement. These practices empowered and sustained enslaved Africans as they resisted centuries of oppression and formed a new identity as children of the God of liberation. The genius and power of slave religion rested in its ability to sustain community amid difficulties of slavery and death.

One of the most important early influences on African American Holiness-Pentecostalism, Bishop Charles Harrison Mason, tried to maintain the spirituality he witnessed among enslaved Africans (Clemmons 1996, 4). Mason knew firsthand the value of this brand of spirituality. African practices from slave religion were carried over into black Holiness Methodist and Baptist Churches, causing a great deal of contention between blacks who desired to distance themselves from what they believed were pagan, superstitious practices and blacks who believed these were authentic expressions of spirituality. Zora Neal Hurston's study of the "sanctified church" (African American churches that incorporate African religious content) supports this vital link between elements of African spirituality and the pneumatological traditions of black Holiness-Pentecostalism. The sanctified church sought to revitalize elements of religion that were brought over from Africa and found that some blacks cleaved to these practices as a protest movement or critique within the black community against highbrow African American churches (Hurston 1981, 104–7).

The emergence of the Holiness movement is important in the history of Pentecostalism because of the growing belief in a second (post-salvific) blessing. The origins of this belief can be traced to John Wesley's views of Christian perfection in Methodism. Wesley's view of perfection claims that one can have an experience with God where one is delivered from sin, is restored to the whole image of God, and loves God with all one's heart, soul, and mind. Wesley's views of perfection were revised as leaders within Methodism began articulating a new holiness or sanctification doctrine that led to the emergence of the Holiness movement. For example, John Fletcher, a contemporary of Wesley, pushed the doctrine of perfection to include also an experience he referred to as a baptism of burning love—a baptism of the Pentecostal power of the Holy Ghost, also a baptism of the Holy Ghost and fire. Some Holiness preachers referred to this second blessing experience as "entire sanctification." By 1870, the Holiness movement was employing Pentecostal language to describe the experience of sanctification. In many respects, the second blessing doctrine of the Holiness movement is foundational to the doctrine of the "baptism of the Spirit" that was developed by Charles F. Parham, and which set the stage for the emergence of Pentecostalism with its own distinct second blessing doctrine.

The Holiness movement was integral in the African American community because it provided a space to retain elements of African spirituality. African Americans with "spirit" tendencies and second blessing theological commitments created a stir among black Methodists and Baptists who "clamored for acceptance by whites and assimilation into the American cultural mainstream" and as a consequence deemphasized "the power of religious experience" (Clemmons 1996, 17). Some blacks like Mason and Charles Price Jones were kicked out of denominational churches and began to establish separate churches that welcomed African practices such as shouting, drums, visions, and healing as well as beliefs in the second blessing or entire sanctification. Separate black Holiness denominations were founded in the late nineteenth century, including the Church of God in Christ, the Church of Christ (Holiness), and the United Holy Church. The importance of these African practices and the belief in sanctification was connected to the empowerment necessary to address the existential challenges of life in the Reconstruction age. Spiritual resources were valuable resources for blacks who continued to face monumental social challenges.

In 1906, a black Holiness preacher named William J. Seymour accepted a call from Mrs. Julia W. Hutchins, a former member of the historic Second Baptist Church, to serve a new Holiness congregation in Los Angeles, California. Having been exposed to Parham in Houston, Texas, who taught from Acts 2 that speaking in tongues is the evidence of receiving the "baptism of the Spirit," Seymour began preaching about this experience. After a month, a movement began with reports of healings, miracles, and people receiving the "baptism of the Spirit." People of all nationalities visited the church, experienced the baptism of the Spirit, underwent other spiritual awakenings including visions, and returned to their home churches spreading the Pentecostal message. Over time, news of these events in Los Angeles—which became known as the Azusa Street revival—began to impact people in Europe, Asia, Africa, and South America. The Azusa Street revival provided a national and international venue for people to experience elements of African spirituality in America.

For these reasons, some historians and scholars believe that the origin of the Pentecostal movement is the Azusa Street revival under William J. Seymour and, more important, that the spirituality of Azusa is African. For example, Leonard Lovett, beginning with the "latter rain" theory of Pentecostal history, argues that Pentecostalism's origin is linked more to the Azusa Street revival under Seymour than to Parham's evidential doctrine, because the Azusa Street revival propelled the movement from local to international acclaim (Lovett 1975, 125–40). One can reasonably conclude that modern-day Pentecostalism has roots in the spirituality of the black church and represents one of its major contributions to American Protestant and global Christianity.

However, there is another important layer to the significance of Azusa in the early years of Pentecostalism. Seymour's theological vision, demonstrated by his intentional insistence on inclusion, is an essential piece of this history. Douglas Nelson—followed by Iain MacRobert, Leonard Lovett, and Ithiel Clemmons—began emphasizing Seymour's distinct understanding of the "baptism of the Spirit." It is commonly believed that Seymour took Parham's teaching to Azusa without contextualizing or adapting it to his own view of God and the world. While no one can doubt Parham's influence, it does not preclude the process of internalization, adaptation, and reinterpretation that African Christians in America have done since the late seventeenth century. There are clues in both Seymour's teaching and his praxis that there were radical differences between him and

Parham in regard to the evidence and implications of being baptized in the Spirit. These clues represent not only the genius of a man who desired to transcend Jim Crow segregation but also Pentecostalism's opportunity to spearhead a movement with radical spiritual and social implications.

Douglas Nelson's unpublished dissertation on Seymour provides one of the first treatments of Seymour as a major theological influence in early Pentecostalism. For Nelson, the interracial character of Azusa was no accident but, rather, a product of Seymour's theological commitment to communal relationality. The first issue of his periodical, *The Apostolic Faith*, stated, "multitudes have come. God makes no difference in nationality, Ethiopians, Chinese, Indians, Mexicans, and other nationalities worship together" (Seymour 1997, 12). In addition to encouraging people of all nationalities to worship together, Seymour included women at every level of leadership. Actions of this nature reflect commitments and a theological vision of Pentecostalism. Even in the years before Azusa, Seymour was drawn to churches that were racially mixed. In Indianapolis and Cincinnati, he sought out and attended racially integrated churches. These actions are an extension of his theology. According to Ithiel Clemmons, "Seymour championed one doctrine above all others: there must be no color line or any other division in the Church of Jesus Christ because God is no respecter of persons" (Clemmons 1996, 51). One can interpret Seymour's insistence on human equality and relationality in community—in the midst of a society that gave absolute sanction to segregation and racism—as the real sign of the "baptism of the Spirit" and spiritual empowerment. In this sense, Seymour connected glossolalia (speaking in tongues) and koinonia (fellowship) in a manner that was entirely different from the way Parham and most other white Pentecostals connected them.

Seymour's theology is also influenced by the communal spirituality of the African American community. There are two reasons for this belief. First, as he was growing up in Louisiana Seymour was exposed to elements of slave religion that include black folk religion, Negro spirituals (which he loved), and visions. Second, his close relationship with Mason, who was devoutly committed to retaining the rich residue of slave religion, must have been influential to some extent on his thinking, teaching, and ministry. It is important to note that Mason employed the same inclusive and communal practices in the Church of God in Christ, for he ordained white ministers who then eventually broke away and formed the Assemblies of God. Seymour's beliefs about communal relationality resemble the communal spirituality of slave religion that was latent in various black Holiness churches.

Beyond its historical and theological importance, Azusa holds social significance as a product of the African American church with its emphasis on the power of religious experience and its distinct understanding of communal spirituality. One of Azusa Street's truly remarkable traits was its interracial nature during the era of Jim Crow segregation. During this time, American churches followed other institutions in practicing segregation. However, during the early years of Azusa, roughly between 1906 through 1911, blacks and whites from across America worshipped together in a black church with a black pastor. These events gave birth to the Pentecostal movement. Blacks and whites worshipped together without any special prohibitions governing interactions and there were no divisions at the altar where all sought to experience the Holy Spirit. Seymour received the baptism of the Spirit at the altar kneeling beside a white man. Frank Bartleman reported that "the color line was washed away in the blood of Jesus" (Bartleman 1980, 61). Whites who attended were startled by this practice and many reported life-changing experiences. In this sense, the Azusa Street revival offered Pentecostalism, as well as its Protestant counterparts, a new model for American churches to follow. There was potential at Azusa for a movement that would incite great social upheaval and spiritual transformation. Azusa could have impacted American society in a truly significant manner.

On the other hand, there is debate among historians about the significance and nature of Azusa's interracial environment. While some historians view its interracial nature as a witness of the power of Pentecostal experience and spirituality, others question if interracial worship means true racial equality, even intimating that the belief is a myth. They do so for two basic reasons. First, it is difficult to establish an interracial precedent when most contemporary Pentecostal movements did not reflect the interracial character supposedly portrayed in Azusa. Edith Blumhofer argues that "there was nothing intrinsic to early Pentecostalism that fostered racial inclusivism" and that the revival "could not hold the allegiance of its own enthusiasts, who broke away to form numerous rival congregations nearby, none of which was known to replicate the racial mix of the mother congregation" (Blumhofer 1994, 445). Second, the problematic actions of whites that led to the decline and eventual demise of the Azusa Street revival also cast significant doubt on Azusa's interracial composition. These include Clara Lum's taking Seymour's periodical *The Apostolic Faith* and its mailing list and relocating to Portland, Oregon; white clergy's withdrawing from Azusa and starting independent missions in other places; and two visits from prominent leaders Charles Parham and William Durham, during which they both tried to correct some element of Seymour's theology and take over the mission.

There is no doubt that the interracial element of the Azusa Street revival was significant, but it is equally clear that this vision failed to capture the imagination of early Pentecostals who were content to lapse into following dominant American social practices. It is apparent that, although Azusa initially represented the potential of Pentecostalism to transcend segregationist practices, the choice often made by white Pentecostals from 1911 and continuing past the 1970s—followed by black Pentecostals, to some extent—would be to exercise the gifts of the Spirit in segregated churches. This decision altered the trajectory of the movement throughout the remainder of the twentieth century and represented a shift away from its African spiritual roots to fundamentalist, evangelical, and American secular or capitalistic spirituality.

For most of the century, Pentecostalism among whites—and to some extent, blacks—regressed into exclusivist practices such as racism and sexism, which signified a rejection of its earlier inclusive vision. Denominational Pentecostalism is segregated, and incidents of racism influence the establishment of denominations, mission philosophies, as well as marital and dating relations. In addition, Pentecostal denominations regress in their support of women in ministry. The growing institutionalization of the movement, especially in its alignment with the fundamentalist and evangelical understandings of women's roles from the 1920s to the 1970s, led to the decline of women in ministerial positions. Most black Pentecostal denominations will follow the exclusive practices of their white denominational counterparts and exclude women from ordained positions in the church.

Pentecostal spirituality, characterized by the gifts of the Spirit in community, occupies a central place in Pentecostal denominations. However, because the movement aligns itself with fundamentalism and evangelicalism, the African emphasis on communal spirituality is replaced by an emphasis on individual spirituality. In this sense, the communal vision of Pentecostalism, articulated by Seymour, is lost within many American Pentecostal denominations. This allows many Pentecostals to avoid connecting spirituality to social realities. In slave religion, spirituality aided blacks in confronting and overcoming the evils of slavery, and for Seymour and Mason in black Holiness-Pentecostalism, spirituality aided them in confronting and overcoming segregation in the church. Denominational Pentecostal spirituality is confined to worship spaces and individualized experiences of empowerment. Particularly in black Pentecostal denominations, the loss of communal and social outlets results in a spirituality that empowers for worship in church but not for work in the world. With this brand of spirituality in place, many Pentecostals tolerate social injustices such as racism and sexism and, historically, have isolated themselves from social movements such as the civil rights movement.

In the contemporary era, popular Pentecostalism, characterized by televangelism, megachurches, and prosperity teaching, will thoroughly replace the African influence in Pentecostalism as leaders centralize individual success and wealth as the distinguishing marks of the Spirit-filled life. Important white and black figures such as Oral Roberts, Kenneth Hagin, Sr., Kenneth and Gloria Copeland, Jerry Savelle, Jesse Duplantis, John Avanzini, Marilyn Hickey, Fred and Betty Price, Keith Butler, LeRoy Thompson, Michael and Dee Dee Freeman, T. D. Jakes, Noel Jones, Creflo and Taffi Dollar, Eddie Long, and a host of others represent a brand of Pentecostalism that is far removed from its original vision of empowering and communal spirituality that effects change in society. Popular Pentecostalism is the dominant feature of American Pentecostalism in the last quarter of the twentieth century and makes significant inroads into African American churches and emerging Neo-Pentecostal black churches.

The challenge of twenty-first-century African American Pentecostalism in particular, and American Pentecostalism in general, could potentially rest on the decision of its leaders either to reengage its African roots and unearth empowering spiritual practices and communal spirituality or to continue to follow fundamentalist, evangelical, and even secular spiritualities.

References and Suggestions for Further Reading

Bartleman, Frank. 1980. *Azusa Street: The Roots of Modern Day Pentecost.* South Plainfield, NJ: Bridge Publishing.

Billingsley, Scott C. 2008. *It's a New Day: Race and Gender in the Modern Charismatic Movement.* Tuscaloosa: University of Alabama Press.

Blumhofer, Edith L. 1994. "For Pentecostals, a Move toward Racial Reconciliation." *Christian Century* 111(14): 444–46.

Clemmons, Ithiel C. 1982. "True Koinonia: Pentecostal Hopes and Historical Realities." *Pneuma* 4(1): 46–56.
———. 1996. *Bishop C. H. Mason and the Roots of the Church of God in Christ.* Bakersfield, CA: Pneuma Life.
Harrison, Milmon F. 2005. *Righteous Riches: The Word of Faith Movement in Contemporary African American Religion.* New York: Oxford University Press.
Hollenweger, Walter J. 1997. *Pentecostalism: Origins and Developments Worldwide.* Peabody, MA: Hendrickson.
Hurston, Zora Neale. 1981. *The Sanctified Church.* New York: Marlowe.
Lovett, Leonard. 1975. "Black Origins of the Pentecostal Movement." In *Aspects of Pentecostal-Charismatic Origins*, ed. Vinson Synan, 123–41. Plainfield, NJ: Logos.
MacRobert, Iain. 1988. *The Black Roots and White Racism of Early Pentecostalism in the USA.* New York: St. Martin's Press.
Nelson, Douglas. 1981. "For Such a Time as This: The Story of William J. Seymour and the Azusa Street Revival." Ph.D. dissertation, University of Birmingham.
Sanders, Cheryl. 1996. *Saints in Exile: The Holiness-Pentecostal Experience in African American Religion and Culture.* New York: Oxford University Press.
Seymour, William J., ed. 1997. *Azusa Street Papers: A Reprint of The Apostolic Faith Mission Publications, Los Angeles, California (1906–1908).* Foley, AL: Harvest.
Turner, William C., Jr. 2006. *The United Holy Church of America: A Study in Black Holiness-Pentecostalism.* Piscataway, NJ: Gorgias.

African Pentecostalism

ALLAN HEATON ANDERSON

Any description of "African Pentecostalism" depends very much on how "Pentecostalism" is defined, and here it will be described as those movements where there is an emphasis on the gifts and power of the Spirit, especially as manifested in healing, prophecy, and speaking in tongues. Some prominent expressions of Christianity in the sub-Sahara may be called "African Pentecostal" churches because of a particular emphasis common to churches that would otherwise be quite different. Divergent African churches emphasize the working of the Spirit in the church, particularly with ecstatic phenomena such as prophecy and speaking in tongues, healing, and exorcism. These phenomena have been characteristic of Pentecostalism throughout the world and are widespread throughout Africa, across a great variety of Christian churches. These include thousands of African-initiated churches or African Independent Churches (AICs) known collectively as "Spirit" or "spiritual" churches. There are two other types of churches that are now growing more rapidly than the older AICs: those churches of Western, "classical" Pentecostal origin and the new independent Charismatic churches and "ministries" that have arisen since the late 1970s and have now formed one of the most prominent features of the African religious landscape.

Pentecostal missionaries from North America and Europe arrived in 1907–1908 in South Africa, Angola, Liberia, and British East Africa, some of them from the Azusa Street revival in Los Angeles. In these regions at least, Pentecostalism of the "classical" variety can be traced. But in many parts of Africa, indigenous movements arose independently and often prior to classical Pentecostalism. The Assemblies of God has expanded in almost every African country, but there are now several African-initiated Charismatic churches (especially emanating from Nigeria) that have taken on the nature of denominations with church branches throughout the sub-Sahara. Given the significance of classical Pentecostal denominations throughout Africa, and the brave sacrifices made by their missionaries in remote parts of Africa, most of these missionaries have been well chronicled. African leaders of Pentecostal churches, however, tend not to appear as prominently in the literature, so here we will concentrate more on movements initiated by Africans.

Several churches arising in West African revivals connected (in the 1930s) with the Apostolic Church in Britain and the Yoruba evangelist Joseph Babalola are now enormous organizations throughout this region, but especially in Nigeria and Ghana. Some of them have historical links with revivals led in the 1910s by prophetic figures such as William Wade Harris, Garrick Sokari Braide, and Engenas Lekganyane. It is difficult to determine what Pentecostalism consists of in an African context. Not all these different churches should be labeled Pentecostal, and they do not always see themselves as such, for they are nowhere near a homogeneous whole. The variety, entrepreneurship, and creativity in African Christianity are remarkable. Careful observers of African Christianity, however, will admit that a great number of AICs are of a Pentecostal nature, and that these churches have been in the forefront of the contextualization of Christianity in Africa for over a century. Harvey Cox and Walter Hollenweger have both described the "Spirit" churches as "the African expression of the worldwide Pentecostal movement." The "Pentecostalization" of African Christianity can be called the "African Reformation" of the twentieth century, which has fundamentally altered the character of African Christianity, including that of the older churches. But the "Spirit" AICs might no longer be paradigmatic of African Pentecostalism, as they have been overshadowed by the enormous new churches that have sprung up in African cities more recently. Nevertheless, they are certainly an important expression of Pentecostalism, and no student of global Pentecostalism can afford to ignore them.

There are thousands of these churches throughout the sub-Sahara. Although they do not usually call themselves Pentecostal or Charismatic, many of these churches do consider themselves part of Pentecostal and Charismatic Christianity and exhibit similar theology and orientation. In southern Africa the majority of "churches of the Spirit" are known as Zionists, after the Chicago movement of John Alexander Dowie, and Apostolics, after the classical Pentecostal movement from which they emerged, the Apostolic Faith Mission. In East Africa and in parts of West Africa, they originated in African Pentecostal revivals and are called churches of the Spirit, and in western Nigeria they are known as Aladura (owners of prayer) churches, after a Charismatic prayer group that first formed in an Anglican church but was later influenced by classical Pentecostalism. The Spirit churches have much in common with classical Pentecostals, and their history is inextricably tied up with them. They practice gifts of the Spirit, especially healing and prophecy, and they speak in tongues. Because of these churches' Spirit manifestations, emphases, and experiences, most earlier studies misunderstood them or generalized about them and branded them syncretistic, post-Christian, and messianic. Unfortunately, these terms are still sometimes used pejoratively by other African Pentecostals, often because of misapprehensions and a lack of communication. Part of the problem that outside observers have had with the "churches of the Spirit" is that they have often been seen as accommodating the pre-Christian past and are linked with traditional practices such as divination and ancestor rituals. More recent studies have shown this to be an inaccurate view and certainly not how these churches see themselves.

Although there are clear affinities and common historical and theological origins shared by African and classical Pentecostals, the passing of time and the proliferation of AICs have accentuated the differences. Pentecostal AICs throughout Africa are often churches that emphasize healing through prophets. Many of these churches have few connections with classical Pentecostalism, and they have differences among them that are not common to all the churches. Included in some churches are external differences such as the use of healing symbolism including blessed water, many other symbolic ritual objects representing power and protection, forms of government and hierarchical patterns of leadership (sometimes including hereditary leadership, not unknown in Western Pentecostalism), the use of some African cultural practices, and the wearing of distinctive robes or uniforms. Some of these churches feature distinctly different approaches to African religions and culture, in their liturgy, healing practices, and each one's unique contribution to Christianity in a broader African context. This distinct and innovative approach often differs sharply from those who promote and are more heavily influenced by Western forms of Pentecostalism.

In several African countries, older independent churches and the newer Charismatic varieties form the majority of Christians, an important component of world Christianity. Pentecostalism is actively growing throughout Africa, which may indeed now be the most "Pentecostal" continent. This is particularly the case in countries such as Zimbabwe, Kenya, Nigeria, Ghana, Zambia, the Democratic Republic of the Congo, and South Africa, where 10–20 percent of the populations belong to classical Pentecostal and newer Charismatic churches. If the AIC Spirit churches and Charismatics in the older churches are added to these numbers, percentages are considerably higher. In Zimbabwe, South Africa, Kenya, the Democratic Republic of the Congo, Nigeria, Ghana, and Zambia, for example, 25–50 percent of the populations belong to these churches. Although these proportions are speculative and subject to interpretations of how "Pentecostal" is defined, they do give an indication of the strength of African Pentecostalism today.

REFERENCES AND SUGGESTIONS FOR FURTHER READING

Anderson, Allan. 2001. *African Reformation: African Initiated Christianity in the Twentieth Century*. Trenton, NJ: Africa World Press.

———. 2004. *An Introduction to Pentecostalism: Global Charismatic Christianity.* Cambridge: Cambridge University Press.

Cox, Harvey. 1995. *Fire from Heaven: The Rise of Pentecostal Spirituality and the Reshaping of Religion in the Twenty-First Century.* Cambridge, MA: De Capo Press.

Hollenweger, Walter J. 1997. *Pentecostalism: Origins and Developments Worldwide.* Peabody, MA: Hendrickson.

Kalu, Ogbu. 2008. *African Pentecostalism: An Introduction.* New York: Oxford University Press.

Asian Pentecostalism

CONNIE HO YAN AU

Asia is a vast continent, and just as social systems, culture, and language vary from country to country, so does Pentecostalism. A simplistic generalization does not do justice to the diversified nature of Asian Pentecostalism. Currently, serious scholarly work on Asian Pentecostalism focuses mainly on South East Asia (Chinese migrants in Malaysia and Singapore, Philippines, Indonesia, and Thailand), East Asia (China, Hong Kong, and Korea), and South Asia (India and Sri Lanka). However, most of these works were written by Western scholars basing their information on materials from missionaries and Western church publications instead of applying ethnographic methodologies such as fieldwork, case studies, and surveys. There are still plenty of research projects to be launched to fill historical, sociological, anthropological, and theological gaps concerning Asian Pentecostalism, and the primary investigators should be Asians. Furthermore, although some prominent Pentecostal denominations such as the Assemblies of God (AG) were started by Western missionaries, the majority of Asian Pentecostal churches were started by Asians. Some of the most successful of these Asian denominations are the many independent church networks with Pentecostal features in China, the Jesus Is Lord Church in the Philippines, the Pentecostal Mission in Hong Kong, and the Indian Pentecostal Church of God. There are also large Catholic Charismatic communities in India and the Philippines, where the El Shaddai movement has over seven million adherents.

These countries share some common features, which has allowed Pentecostalism to take root and rapidly develop. First, they all have colonial experience and, as a result, have been undergoing a national identity crisis for generations. Christianity entered these countries after colonialism (except in Korea where the colonizer, Japan, was not a Christian country), and was regarded as an alternative form of imperialist invasion. However, given its historical appeal among the poor, oppressed, and marginalized, together with its strong adaptability to local culture and openness to the spiritual dimension, Pentecostalism was generally accepted by the colonized masses. Particularly in the case of Korea, Pentecostalism became a source of strength to help the people cope with the severe political oppression and cruelty of the Japanese regime during the Korean revival in 1907.

Second, the oppression of women is a serious domestic and social problem in Asia. For instance, in China, Korea, and Taiwan, which have been influenced by Chinese culture, society is dominated by a strict patriarchal system based on Confucianism. Women are voiceless and powerless in both families and society. They are not entitled to equal rights in education, employment, or political involvement with men but are perceived to be useful for sexual satisfaction and child rearing. There are hundreds of cases involving the abandonment or murder of female infants, especially in small villages.

Like missionaries from other Christian denominations, Pentecostals have opened orphanages and rescue centers for prostitutes, but their distinctive contribution is that they brought spiritual and psychological empowerment to women through the experience of the baptism in the Holy Spirit and the accompanying charisms. Antoinette Moomau was an Apostolic Faith missionary in Shanghai and opened a center for prostitutes. She served three thousand women in 1908–1916, and most of them were baptized in the Spirit. In India, Pandita Ramabai's mission was launched to save the lives of young widows and female orphans. In these trampled lives and traumatized souls, the fire of revival was ignited and spread around central India in 1905–1907. Today it is common for Pentecostal churches in Asia to be headed by women.

Third, another type of oppression in Asia is the caste system. In India, the caste system is especially obvious as it has been justified by certain forms of Hinduism and is, therefore, embedded in society. The *Harijans* are people of the lowest caste who are considered untouchable, and they suffer extreme poverty and social segregation. These oppressed individuals, however, have become oppressors themselves, as they were tempted to create subcastes within their own caste. In communist China, a virtual caste system is formulated between government officials and ordinary people, as well as between rich and poor. Since the dictatorship of the Communist Party holds the ultimate political, legal, administrative, economic, and military authority of the whole country, many of the politically powerless and militarily unarmed general masses have been undergoing severe and unreported physical, financial, medical, sexual, psychological, and mental oppression. The opening of the economy for national and international trade since the 1980s seems to have lifted the country from the abyss of poverty, but it has also fostered an affluent middle class while the majority of the population is still struggling to survive in poverty. As the rich gain higher social status, cases of corruption among the rich and governmental officials increase, and the poor and ordinary people are the immediate sufferers. These differentiated social classes are a source of continuous oppression, discrimination, inequality, deprivation, and poverty, which can be inherited from generation to generation.

The emphasis on the power of the Holy Spirit and hope in the resurrected Jesus Christ in Pentecostalism lift up these traumatized souls by visible and tangible manifestations. Healing is the ultimate source of hope for physical and psychological restoration for Christians in the house churches in China for whom medical care is unaffordable. The experience of the baptism of the Holy Spirit confirms the value of their lives. This becomes a source of motivation to make a difference for their lives, and in some cases upward social mobility then occurs, terminating the cycle of poverty.

Fourth, Asian countries, mainly because of their strong dependency on fishing and agriculture, have generally created different forms of primal religion. They create different kinds of spiritual objects to worship in order to receive blessings of health, wealth, and protection in the workplace and during travel. Countries that have their roots in Confucianism emphasize ancestral veneration, which is a way to honor deceased senior family members and to remember their contributions to the family from generation to generation. Worshippers believe that, although the ancestors' bodies have passed away, their spirits are still actively involved in the material human world. They also believe that, since the dead have become spirits, they have divine power to fulfill the worshippers' requests, either for blessings in marriage, career, finance, and health or for bringing curses against enemies.

Chinese folk religion also incorporates the worship of historical warriors and national heroes as a way to seek physical empowerment, such as Guandi who, ironically, is worshipped by both police forces and triad groups (an international Chinese criminal organization).There are also spirits created from characters in ancient novels, such as the monkey king, Sun Wukong, who is one of the dominant characters of *Journey to the West*. This mythological story is about a Buddhist monk who is called by a goddess, Guanyin, to travel to the West (which is India) to collect a Buddhist text. Since it is expected that the monk will be attacked by evil spirits, Sun Wukong (a monkey), Zhu Bajie (a pig), and Sha Wujing (a bull) are sent by Guanyin to protect the monk with supernatural power. This novel vividly reflects the Buddhist and Daoist elements in Chinese folk religion and mythology. In countries such as Malaysia, Taiwan, and urban areas in China, where sorcery, witchcraft, and folk religions incorporated with Buddhist and Daoist practices are popular, spiritual encounters with both good and evil spirits are embedded in the culture. Given Pentecostalism's emphasis on the supernatural, it resonates strongly with Asian spirituality and culture possibly contributing to the movement's success in Asia.

Fifth, Asian culture has a strong element of utilitarianism and pragmatism. Many Asians expect real and concrete blessings instead of only cognitive and spiritual enrichment. They regard religion as a means to gain material welfare, health, good fortune, and security. Offering is primarily a means to acquire more blessing from the divine instead of self-dedication. Hence, the prosperity gospel presented by some Pentecostal preachers and the performance of healings attract those Asians who have suffered poverty and sickness. The most prominent phenomenon of Pentecostal utilitarianism is Yonggi Cho's preaching about the gospel of blessing during the devastation of livelihood after the Korean War. Because of this utilitarian, pragmatic mentality, Asian Pentecostals only selectively appropriated the American classical Pentecostalism brought by missionaries. When some doctrines are not considered useful or practical for their purposes, many Asian Pentecostals simply do not teach or practice them. This is the case of speaking in tongues as the initial physical evidence of the baptism of the Holy Spirit. This phenomenon is particularly obvious in regions such as Hong Kong and wealthy Asian cities, where capitalism and materialism are wedded with Christianity and where Pentecostals are generally middle-class and often focused on church growth.

Moreover, some Asian Pentecostal churches do not adapt some classical Pentecostal teachings and practices such as tongues and prophecy because they can prevent gaining recognition from evangelical and traditional churches. These churches adapt Western Pentecostalism into a more evangelicalized version. These two reasons lead to a trend of "de-Pentecostalization," which is not only a threat to Pentecostal identity, but also the traditional Pentecostal emphasis on missionization premised on the power of the Holy Spirit. The evangelicalization of Pentecostalism could also result in an entrepreneurial mentality to support church growth and expansion into other countries, leading to an Asian version of religious invasion and colonialism.

Sixth, throughout the last century, Pentecostal churches and organizations sent missionaries to Asia who were motivated by the urgency to preach the gospel before Jesus' expected imminent second coming, and who also confirmed the endowment of "missionary tongues" (the ability to speak in an unknown language for the purpose of evangelism). Many of these missions, however, were not firmly rooted in Asian culture and only made a small or short-term impact, mainly because they failed to contextualize the gospel effectively into the culture. This missionary history has resulted in conflicts between Western missionaries and their Asian coworkers. Asians tend to be relational and hence can be flexible when dealing with rules, whereas Westerners tend to follow written rules and agreements, which from an Asian perspective can be harmful to maintaining relationships.

Moreover, as far as Asians were concerned, missionary churches were functionally a rice-feeding center or charity that opened schools and orphanages, especially during the postwar period. Churches were "useful" for them, but they were not prepared to make significant commitments. When economic circumstances improved, especially since the 1980s when the four economic dragons Singapore, Taiwan, South Korea, and Hong Kong arose, the Western missionary churches experienced decline. Like other Christian denominations, Western Pentecostal churches also transplanted ecumenical problems from the West to Asia, which has caused considerable frustration for some Asian Pentecostals. For example, historically, Pentecostals from Canada, Finland, and the United States each worked in China, Hong Kong, Thailand, and Taiwan, but they worked independently of each other instead of formulating a centralized body. In Taiwan, for example, the AG is now supported only by the United States because the Pentecostal Assemblies of Canada ceased their involvement in 1994 after years of fruitless and financially challenging ministry, while the Finnish Pentecostal group is close to disappearing from the island. As a result, the AG in Taiwan has remained weak and marginalized by both traditional mainline Protestant and younger Neo-Pentecostal churches. Nevertheless, there are still strong Pentecostal denominational churches in Asia, such as the Grace Assembly in Singapore and the AG's Chinese division in Malaysia. These churches continue to follow AG fundamental doctrines, such as Spirit baptism evidenced by tongues.

Most of the successful and prominent Pentecostal churches in Asia are Asian-initiated, independent, and institutional churches. This is another manifestation of independency similar to the African Independent Churches. These churches are not controlled by foreign mission boards but are totally self-governed, self-supported, and self-propagated. They formulate their own liturgy and institute their own sacraments, based on their own hermeneutics of the Bible and theology within their own cultural context. An Asian Initiated Church (AIC) that has a well-formulated ecclesiastical structure and sacramental practices is the True Jesus Church, which is the largest Pentecostal denomination founded by Paul Wei in China in 1914. It keeps Sabbath on Saturday, practices foot-washing as a sacrament in addition to full immersion and the Eucharist, and has a Oneness or non-Trinitarian theology. It has expanded into South East Asia in countries like Malaysia, Singapore, Taiwan, Hong Kong, and to Chinese communities in North America. City Harvest Church in Singapore is another Chinese AIC, which is probably the largest independent Chinese church in Asia. The AICs gradually become denominations when they develop branches inside and outside the country, such as the largest Pentecostal denomination in Korea, Yoido Full Gospel Church (with roots in the AG), and the Jesus Is Lord Church in the Philippines.

Research on Pentecostalism within Asian aboriginal communities has been severely neglected despite its significance. For example, Taiwan is originally an island inhabited by tribal people, but since the migration of Han Chinese, especially the exile of the Nationalist Party after their loss in the civil war against the communists in 1948, the tribal people have been marginalized. They are usually deprived of educational and occupational opportunities. An aboriginal ministry founded by an AG pastor who is himself aboriginal, Yan Kim Lung, and his wife of Japanese origin, Yoko Maruyama, targets aboriginal women who work in bars as prostitutes and holds a prayer meeting in their workplace before they start work every evening.

In recent years, Asian Pentecostals have taken theological education more seriously. They seek to understand their Pentecostal experiences from a doctrinal, biblical, theological, and historical perspective. This reflects the fact that Asian Pentecostals are searching for, as well as confirming, their distinctive Christian identity. Moreover, like Pentecostals on other continents, Asian Pentecostals have been under constant critical challenges from evangelicals. Hence, theological education is a way to formulate Pentecostal apologetics as well as to equip Pentecostals to defend and protect their faith. Pentecostal theologians are becoming an increasingly significant voice in Asian Christianity. Asian Pentecostals see the need to develop a theology that is applicable and explainable to Asian Pentecostal experiences, rather than directly importing Western Pentecostal theology to deal with an Asian situation. Apart from the Bible colleges established by Western denominational churches like the AG, independent Charismatic churches have founded their own theological training schools. Chinese AG churches in Malaysia and Taiwan have organized theological conferences in recent years in order to investigate doctrines like Spirit baptism and charisms from a pastoral perspective. The speakers have primarily been Chinese Pentecostal theologians from Malaysia, Singapore, Hong Kong, and Taiwan. The Asia Pacific Theological Association (APTA) and Asian Pentecostal Society (APS) organize annual conferences to discuss issues that concern wider Asian communities from an academic perspective. The *Asian Journal for Pentecostal Studies* published by the APS is a platform for scholars, both Asians and non-Asians, to provide the latest theological, pastoral, hermeneutical, and historical ideas concerning Pentecostalism.

Asian Pentecostals have the potential to contribute to global Pentecostal communities theologically, experientially, and ecumenically. When their Pentecostal mother churches in the West are undergoing numerical, financial, and spiritual decline, these Asian churches continue to spread the Pentecostal message with powerful relevancy to local culture, both inside and outside their national borders. As Asian Pentecostalism continues to grow and mature, it will be a significant force within global Christianity.

REFERENCES AND SUGGESTIONS FOR FURTHER READING

Anderson, Allan, and Edmond Tang, eds. 2005. *Asian and Pentecostal: The Charismatic Face of Christianity in Asia.* Baguio City: APTS Press; Oxford: Regnum Books International.

Bergunder, Michael. 2008. *The South Indian Pentecostal Movement in the Twentieth Century.* Grand Rapids, MI: Eerdmans.

Ma, Wonsuk, William W. Menzies, and Hyeon-sung Bae, eds. 2004. *David Yonggi Cho: A Close Look at His Theology and Ministry.* Baguio City: APTS Press; Seoul: Hansei University Press.

Xi, Lian. 2010. *Redeemed by Fire: The Rise of Popular Christianity in Modern China.* New Haven, CT: Yale University Press.

Australian Pentecostalism

SHANE CLIFTON

Australian Pentecostalism is not, as is sometimes assumed, an American import. Instead, it is an indigenous movement inspired by the globalizing forces of revivalism at the turn of the twentieth century. Precursors of the movement can be found in the voluntarism and lay spirituality of democratized Christianity, which flourished in a nation of convicts and immigrants. It was within this historical context that the desire for holiness and revival sprang.

In 1906, Sarah Jane Lancaster ordered a pamphlet from England called "Back to Pentecost," and in 1908 she was baptized in the Holy Spirit and spoke in tongues. On New Year's Eve 1909, Lancaster (by then a fifty-year-old mother of five) opened Good News Hall, a faith mission in Richmond, Melbourne. The mission was launched with a prayer meeting that could not be stopped. For six weeks, Lancaster and the small community that gathered to pray experienced a "glorious revival" that continued night and day. Before long, she had gathered a congregation numbering in the hundreds, and such was the extent of this move of the Spirit that Lancaster and her husband moved their house to the upstairs floor of the hall, where they were to live for more than twenty years. Thereafter, Lancaster toured Australia preaching the "fourfold gospel"—Jesus saves, heals, baptizes in the Spirit, and is coming again. A network of churches was eventually established under the banner of the Apostolic Faith Mission, with Lancaster as the informal leader. Her primary influence upon Australian Pentecostalism was to come through the publication of the *Good News* journal, which was printed monthly and achieved a circulation of thousands.

Lancaster is something of a controversial figure. With an Adventist background, she was an annihilationist, rejecting the concept of eternal damnation. Her biblicist restorationism and suspicion of traditional creeds also saw her reject the doctrine of the Trinity—a term and concept she did not find in the Bible. Rather than follow Oneness Pentecostals in the United States, she developed a "binitarian" theology, arguing that God and the Holy Spirit were one and the same, while distinguishing and subordinating the Son to the Father. She was not, however, a dogmatic theologian, and she hoped for a nondoctrinal spiritual unity, one that could transcend doctrinal differences. For a short time such unity prevailed, but during the 1920s the influence of fundamentalist theology created difficulties. In the first place, there was increasing concern about her leadership, because she was a woman. To mollify such concerns she appointed male elders in her church, though she stood her ground as a female leader. To support her case, she published a series of articles by female evangelist Mina Ross Brawner, which set out a thoroughly egalitarian understanding of ministry, baptism in the Spirit, and gender relations. But it was the visit of Aimee Semple McPherson in 1922 that was to cause her the most difficulty. With her trip to Australia sponsored and promoted by Lancaster, McPherson arrived only to decide that she did not want to be associated with someone with whom she held "grave doctrinal differences." McPherson went elsewhere, and her ministry led to the founding of the Foursquare Church of Australia in 1923. Lancaster, meanwhile, continued her leadership of Good News Hall through the 1920s and early 1930s, but all of these issues gave rise to the formation of separate Pentecostal fellowships.

While Lancaster had promoted a loose-knit, informal, and unstructured ecclesiology (she did not even like the word "church"), the establishment of Pentecostal assemblies throughout the nation generated a need for more formal organizational structures. These institutional developments intended to help clarify the boundaries of doctrine (given that theology informs ecclesial identity and shapes ministry), facilitate education of pastors and leaders, and enhance the effectiveness of local and overseas mission. State-based fellowships were founded in the 1920s and 1930s (the Assemblies of God in Queensland, and the Pentecostal Church of Australia located in New South Wales and Victoria), and these came together in 1937 to form the national fellowship of the Assemblies of God in Australia (AGA). AGA's basis of fellowship, including a congregationalist form of governance, was noteworthy: "The Assemblies of God in Australia is a fellowship of Pentecostal Assemblies in voluntary co-operation, on terms of equality, as self-contained and self-governed Christian Assemblies, united for aggressive evangelism, unity, fellowship, order, discipline, and other purposes" (Assemblies of God in Australia 1943). Working together, the cooperative fellowship was to establish a Bible college (Commonwealth Bible College commenced in 1948 and continues today as Alphacrucis College), plant churches, and conduct overseas mission. Focusing especially on Papua New Guinea, AGA missionary efforts saw the planting of Pentecostal churches amid tribal communities and the creation of a nationally significant movement in that country. Of course, whatever the ideal of voluntary cooperation and local autonomy, "independence" is only ever relative. Disputes arose, for example, as AGA leaders prevented their churches from inviting guest speakers who held to British Israel teaching (which argued that the Anglo-Saxon race was descended from the ten northern tribes of Israel). There were also difficulties between the AGA and Pentecostal churches planted under the banner of the Apostolic Church of Australia. Founded in 1930, Apostolic churches were doctrinally similar to the AGA and preached a similar message but advocated a more hierarchical ecclesiology, grounded in the authority of apostles, prophets, and evangelists.

By the 1970s, while Pentecostal churches had accumulated more than fifty years of history, the movement as a whole remained a small and relatively obscure part of the larger Christian landscape in the country. This was to change with the outbreak of the Charismatic movement in the 1970s and 1980s as Pentecostal churches began to experience revival. David Cartledge's Assemblies of God church in the regional center of Townsville, for example, had the unprecedented experience of growing into a congregation of more than a thousand members—the first Australian so-called megachurch. Similar growth occurred in Charismatic

Pentecostal churches in most Australian cities, although this revival created a degree of tension within what had become a stable and conservative AGA executive. In particular, executive leaders in the movement were concerned about the Charismatic focus on "dancing, deliverance, and demons," and there were also fears about relationships that were forming with other churches, especially Roman Catholics, modernists, and liberals. The issue came to a head in 1977 when the pastor of the world's largest church, Korean Yonggi Cho, was the keynote speaker at the AGA national conference. His endorsement of Charismatics resulted in a change in leadership in the movement, with Adelaide megachurch pastor Andrew Evans being installed as the new general superintendent, a position he held for twenty years, after which time he handed the leadership on to Brian Houston (of Hillsong Church). In the three decades that followed, with an emphasis on Charismatic renewal and the implementation of church growth theory, the AGA grew from less than ten thousand to more than two hundred thousand members, with more than one thousand churches. Beyond the AGA, other Pentecostal/Charismatic movements were also founded. In Sydney in 1980, New Zealanders Phil and Christine Pringle started Christian City Church (now C3). With a congregation growing into the thousands, C3 planted churches throughout Australasia, eventually founding the C3 denomination, which now has more than 230 churches globally. In Brisbane, the Christian Outreach Centre was founded by Clark Taylor, and his megachurch also went on to establish related congregations internationally. From an obscure sect, Pentecostalism as a whole was to become, in terms of weekly attendance, the second-largest Christian movement in Australia.

In addition to the Charismatic movement, the arrival of Frank Houston from New Zealand in 1983 reshaped the AGA and Australian Pentecostalism more broadly. Initially Houston wanted nothing to do with the AGA, believing it had become too conservative and institutionally hidebound. He was also wary of congregational forms of government, preferring a more centralized model (similar, in fact, to that of the Apostolic Church). Convinced by Evans to join the AGA, Houston established the Christian Life Centre Church in Sydney, and his congregation soon numbered in the thousands. He was later to send Brian, his son, to plant Hills Christian Life Centre, which was to become the famous Hillsong Church, today boasting a congregation numbering in the tens of thousands. The influence of

Hillsong upon Australian Pentecostalism and beyond has been substantial. In the first place, through worship leaders and songwriters such as Geoff Bullock and Darlene Zschech, it has contemporized Pentecostal worship. Second, given the influence of Hillsong conference as well as Brian's appointment as president of the AGA in 1997, the church's leadership model came to be adopted by most AGA congregations. Sometimes labeled the Apostolic Revolution, this was a move away from congregational forms of local church government, with church leadership moving into the hands of the senior pastor and executive board. Recent decades have also seen moves away from local church autonomy, with "apostolic" leaders now overseeing multiple assemblies. Hillsong, for example, has three campuses in Sydney, as well as campuses in Brisbane, London, Kiev, Cape Town, Stockholm, and Paris, with one soon to be in New York, all of which come under the senior leadership of Brian Houston.

The influence of contemporary church models has also affected Pentecostal theology. Forms of prosperity teaching are common, although (at their best) the emphasis is not only on health and wealth but on a broader conception of human flourishing. The fourfold gospel has undergone revision, with moves away from the otherworldly emphasis of premillennial eschatology. This has facilitated a more explicit focus on the social mission of the church, relating the gospel to issues of local and global poverty and injustice. Traditional theologies of baptism in the Spirit have also been revised, with churches rewording their doctrinal statements to exclude reference to more controversial categories such as initial evidence. There remains a relatively pragmatic approach to doctrine—and a tendency to be suspicious of critical (labeled "negative") thinking and the more academic disciplines of theology. This suspicion, however, is also changing, as various Pentecostal Bible colleges, once unaccredited, have moved to offer recognized undergraduate and postgraduate degree programs.

REFERENCES AND SUGGESTIONS FOR FURTHER READING

Assemblies of God in Australia. 1943. United Constitution. Article 2(a).

Australasian Pentecostal Studies. 2010. http://webjournals.alphacrucis.edu.au.

Clifton, Shane. 2009. *Pentecostal Churches in Transition: Analysing the Developing Ecclesiology of the Assemblies of God in Australia.* Leiden: Brill.

Azusa Street Mission and Revival

ADAM STEWART

❤   The Azusa Street revival is one of the most important—though often misunderstood—events in the history of Pentecostalism. The revival has its origins in the ministry of William J. Seymour, an African American Holiness preacher who was influenced by early Pentecostal theologian and leader Charles F. Parham. While studying at Parham's Apostolic Bible Training School in Houston, Texas, in January and February of 1906, Seymour became deeply committed to Parham's novel teaching that there existed a "third blessing" following justification and sanctification that was known as the baptism of the Holy Spirit, evidenced by speaking in tongues, and that provided power for Christian service. The belief that one could be baptized in the Holy Spirit was hardly a new idea. As early as the 1850s, prominent leaders within the Holiness movement such as Phoebe Palmer and Asa Mahan had developed coherent doctrines of the baptism of the Holy Spirit (Dayton 1987, 87–89). The conviction that there existed three distinct blessings or experiences in the life of the believer, while certainly radical, was also not a new concept within the Holiness melting pot of ideas. Beginning particularly in the 1890s, leaders within a radical wing of the Holiness movement (including, most notably, R. C. Horner) suggested that there were three works of grace in the order of salvation: justification, sanctification, and the baptism of the Holy Spirit (Dayton 1987, 90, 95–100). Even the practice of speaking in tongues sometimes occurred during Holiness revivals in the decades preceding the emergence of Pentecostalism at the turn of the twentieth century. What made Parham's theology unique, distinct from the many Holiness teachings he drew upon, was the idea that the third blessing of the baptism of the Holy Spirit following justification and sanctification was only authentic if it was accompanied by the "Bible evidence" of speaking in tongues. The baptism of the Holy Spirit, the third blessing, and speaking in tongues, each on their own, added nothing new to late nineteenth-century Christian revivalism.

The specific arrangement of these three ideas, however, was one of the most polarizing combinations of Christian concepts to be developed in the twentieth century.

It was shortly after studying at Parham's school in Houston that Seymour was invited to assume temporary pastoral responsibilities in a small African American Holiness church located at 1604 East Ninth Street in Los Angeles, California. The current pastor, Julia W. Hutchins, was preparing to travel to Liberia to engage in missionary work and was looking for a replacement to watch over her church while she was away in Africa. Seymour promptly accepted the position and, with help from Parham, arrived in Los Angeles on 22 February 1906. Even though Seymour had yet to experience this new Pentecostal blessing for himself, his commitment to Parham's theology was such that he immediately began to share this new doctrine with the members of the congregation. As was the case among most Holiness adherents at the time, the members of Seymour's congregation believed there were only two works of grace leading to salvation. These were justification and sanctification, which served to provide, as earlier Methodists would write, the "double-cure" for sin. It is possible that when the members of Hutchins's congregation heard Seymour teaching about a third blessing of the baptism of the Holy Spirit evidenced by speaking in tongues, this reminded them of the earlier radical Holiness teaching that there existed three works of grace, which most members of the mainstream Holiness movement understood as heretical.

By referring to the baptism of the Holy Spirit as a third blessing, however, Seymour was not suggesting there existed more than two works of grace; he affirmed the Methodist two-stage understanding of the order of salvation. Rather, Seymour was proposing that the baptism of the Holy Spirit with the evidence of speaking in tongues was a completely different type of experience that could grant the believer a greater degree of power for Christian service, but which was in no way tied to the order of salvation (Jacobsen 2003, 70; Robeck 2006, 63). This theological nuance mattered little, as the new Pentecostal doctrine was a great offence to the many members of Hutchins's congregation who believed they had already experienced the baptism of the Holy Spirit and empowerment at the time of their sanctification. As a result, Hutchins and the leadership of the Holiness Church Association, to which the congregation belonged, promptly ejected Seymour from the church on 4 March 1906.

Fortunately for Seymour (who was now out of a job), two former parishioners, Edward and Mattie Lee, invited him to stay in their home until he could decide what to do next. Before long, Seymour had begun a small prayer group in the Lee residence, which was attended by a growing number of members from the church on East Ninth Street. Soon the group outgrew their space at the Lee residence, at which point they relocated to the home of Richard and Ruth Asberry at 214 North Bonnie Brae Street. Seymour's prayer meeting continued to attract more African Americans interested in his teaching on the new Pentecostal blessing. On Monday, 9 April 1906, after returning home from work complaining that he felt ill, Edward Lee asked Seymour if he would pray for him to overcome this illness. Seymour, as well as Lucy Farrow, a friend of Seymour's from Houston, Texas, laid hands on and prayed for Lee that he might be healed from this ailment. Lee then fell to the floor and spoke in tongues, thus, according to Parham's model, receiving the Pentecostal blessing of the baptism of the Holy Spirit.

Later that night, gathered at the Asberry home, Seymour shared the story of Edward Lee's experience, and within minutes others began to speak in tongues, experiencing the baptism of the Holy Spirit. Once the news of what was happening at the Asberry home began to spread throughout the city and the Holiness Church networks, the number of people hoping to witness or experience the baptism of the Holy Spirit for themselves swelled so great that the front porch of the Asberry home, which had been converted into a pulpit, collapsed under the weight of those gathered to watch and listen. Three days later, on 12 April 1906, Seymour also shared in the new Pentecostal experience. The need for a larger venue was apparent to Seymour, and by the next day he had secured the lease for a former African Methodist Episcopal Church that had suffered a fire and most recently had served as a storage facility. The new venue was located at 312 Azusa Street, which Seymour later named the Apostolic Faith Mission. It was 312 Azusa Street (despite the fact that the revival initially began in the Lee and Asberry homes) that Vinson Synan correctly identifies as "the most famous address in Pentecostal-charismatic history" (Synan 1980, ix). With this new location secured and news of the revival spreading rapidly throughout Anglo-American Holiness networks, Azusa Street began to draw large numbers of not only African Americans and other racialized minorities but also many whites, from all across the United States and around the world. The important symbolic role played by the Azusa Street

Mission within the early Pentecostal ethos and perhaps the paternalistic racism implicit among the white leadership of the movement are attested by the fact that, on three separate occasions, prominent white Pentecostal leaders attempted to wrest control of the mission from Seymour. These were Charles F. Parham in 1906, Florence L. Crawford in 1908, and William H. Durham in 1911.

The Azusa Street revival was exceptional, not only because of its new theology, unconventional origins, and sensational growth but also because of the multiracial composition of its congregation, which included African Americans, whites, Asians, Latinos, and Native Americans, as well as the fact that its African American leader, Seymour, played an important leadership role in introducing future leaders of many white Pentecostal denominations to the new Pentecostal doctrine and experience. Seymour, of course, played just as important a role in spreading the Pentecostal teaching to African American leaders such as Charles H. Mason, the founder of the largest Pentecostal denomination in the United States, the Church of God in Christ. The pioneering role that Seymour assumed in passing on the new Pentecostal teaching to prominent white Pentecostal leaders was unique given the racial tensions of the day. Despite these early innovations, by the beginning of 1909, the crowds at Azusa Street were beginning to dwindle, and Seymour was largely ignored or forgotten by the many white converts he had helped introduce to the new Pentecostal way. The Apostolic Faith Mission again became an almost entirely African American congregation.

Nonetheless, the sheer number of individuals from all over the world that Seymour and the Azusa Street revival were responsible for introducing to Pentecostalism in just three short years is nothing less than remarkable. Seymour did this not only through directly exposing people to Pentecostal teaching as they visited the mission but also, and perhaps chiefly, through the publication of the mission's periodical, *The Apostolic Faith*, which was distributed at no cost to readers all over the world. It would be difficult to overestimate the role that *The Apostolic Faith* played in extending Seymour's message beyond the confines of the city of Los Angeles. Through this periodical, interested Christians from all over the world were exposed to the thought of Seymour; Clara Lum, the journal's editor, who often contributed anonymously to the journal; and the testimonies and correspondence of countless others who attested to their experiences of the baptism of the Holy Spirit (Robeck 2006, 99, 105–6).

One of the critical blows that led to the eventual decline of both the Azusa Street revival and, concomitantly, Seymour's leadership within the emerging Pentecostal movement was the relocation of Clara Lum and *The Apostolic Faith* from Azusa Street in Los Angeles to a mission in Portland, Oregon, led by Seymour's former protégée Florence Louise Crawford in 1908. The reasons for Lum's departure from Azusa Street are unclear. Cecil Robeck argues it is possible Lum disapproved of Seymour's marriage to Jennie Evans Moore in May 1908. Her disapproval may have been based on the conviction either that marriage was a distraction from the work of Christian ministry or that sexual activity, even within the confines of marriage, could compromise one's sanctification. Both of these were not uncommon views within the Holiness and early Pentecostal movements. Robeck poses a more interesting and possibly more plausible reason for Lum's departure from Azusa Street, however, which is that Lum was in love with Seymour and felt spurned when he chose to marry Jennie Evans Moore. Regardless of the reasons for the move, the simple fact is that *The Apostolic Faith* was Seymour's lifeline to the burgeoning Pentecostal movement, through which the revival was publicized and funds were elicited.

With the periodical's relocation to Portland, Seymour and Azusa Street fell into obscurity. Seymour faithfully continued to minister to his small African American congregation until his death in 1922. His wife, Jennie, then took up leadership of the mission until 1930 when a new member of the mission, Ruthford D. Griffith, offered to take over the pastoral duties. By 1932, this transition of leadership resulted in Griffith's vying for control of the mission, a series of lawsuits, and the eventual demolition of the building at 312 Azusa Street. This forced the few remaining members to hold services once again at the Asberry home on 214 North Bonnie Brae Street (Robeck 2006, 320). And so, after twenty-six years, the Apostolic Faith Mission born out of the Azusa Street revival ended where it was birthed, as a home church of working-class African Americans.

While the Azusa Street revival played an important role in the dissemination of Pentecostalism throughout the United States and abroad, it is important not to grant the revival in Los Angeles a mythical status as the source of origination for other occurrences of Pentecostalism around the world (Creech 1996). The fact is that there were Pentecostal-like revivals containing similar phenomena occurring all over the world years before Seymour ever arrived in Los Angeles, and there were also many Pentecostal missions formed at the same time and even after Azusa Street that were not connected with what was happening in the United States (Anderson 2007, Stewart 2010). That being said, there is no denying the both tangible and symbolic influence that Seymour and the Azusa Street Mission and revival had in making Pentecostalism one of the world's largest and fastest-growing religious traditions in less than one hundred years.

REFERENCES AND SUGGESTIONS FOR FURTHER READING

Anderson, Allan. 2007. *Spreading Fires: The Missionary Nature of Early Pentecostalism.* Maryknoll, NY: Orbis.

Creech, Joe. 1996. "Visions of Glory: The Place of the Azusa Street Revival in Pentecostal History." *Church History* 65(3): 405–24.

Dayton, Donald W. 1987. *Theological Roots of Pentecostalism.* Peabody, MA: Hendrickson.

Jacobsen, Douglas. 2003. *Thinking in the Spirit: Theologies of the Early Pentecostal Movement.* Bloomington: Indiana University Press.

Robeck, Cecil M., Jr. 2006. *The Azusa Street Mission and Revival: The Birth of the Global Pentecostal Movement.* Nashville, TN: Nelson.

Stewart, Adam. 2010. "A Canadian Azusa? The Implications of the Hebden Mission for Pentecostal Historiography." In *Winds from the North: Canadian Contributions to the Pentecostal Movement,* ed. Michael Wilkinson and Peter Althouse, 17–37. Leiden and Boston: Brill.

Synan, Vinson. 1980. Introduction to *Azusa Street: The Modern Day Roots of Pentecost,* by Frank Bartleman, ix–xxvi. South Plainfield, NJ: Bridge.

Baptism of the Holy Spirit

ROGER J. STRONSTAD

The literature of the New Testament contains seven references to being baptized with/in the Holy Spirit. On the one hand, there is Paul's single reference, "For in the one Spirit we were all baptized into one body" (1 Cor 12:13). On the other hand, each of the four Evangelists—namely, Matthew, Mark, Luke, and John—report that earlier John the Baptist prophesied that his successor will "baptize you with the Holy Spirit and fire" (Mt 3:11–12; Mk 1:8; Lk 3:21–22; Jn 1:29–34). The Evangelist Luke, who wrote the only sequel to the Gospel, twice explicitly reports that Jesus baptizes his followers in the Holy Spirit (Acts 1:4–5, 11:15–17).

These alleged seven references to being baptized in the Holy Spirit actually only amount to three. Paul's unique reference is excluded because it is just that—unique. For Paul the Spirit (rather than the Christ) is the baptizer, and therefore, what Paul writes does not parallel John the Baptist's prophecy that his successor, the Messiah/Christ, will baptize his followers in the Holy Spirit. In addition, because each of the four Gospel references parallels the others, the four count as only one. Finally, Luke's reports about Jesus referring to John the Baptist's prophecy count in fact as two references. Therefore, in the final analysis, Luke-Acts contains all three references to being baptized in the Holy Spirit. No other writer has even one independent reference.

This brief survey of the relevant New Testament data shows that the phrase "baptized with the Holy Spirit" is distinctly Lukan. As reported by Luke, John the Baptist's thrice-reported prophecy that the Messiah will baptize in the Holy Spirit is about being commissioned and receiving power from the Holy Spirit. The following exposition of Luke's data explicates the New Testament doctrine of being baptized in the Holy Spirit.

The rich variety of terms that Luke uses to describe the presence and activity of the Holy Spirit in the lives of Jesus and his followers are, with but one exception, drawn from the earlier Greek translation of the Hebrew Bible, namely, the Septuagint (abbreviated LXX). The one exception is the phrase "baptized with the Holy Spirit." Apparently, John the Baptist introduced this concept when he prophesied that his successor (the Messiah/Christ) will baptize with the Holy Spirit and fire (Lk 3:16). In fact, all references to the phrase "baptized with the Holy Spirit" are directly related to John's prophecy (Lk 3:16; Acts 1:4–5, 11:15–17).

By the time that John the Baptist begins his ministry, many Jews believed that prophecy in Israel had ceased at the time of Malachi. Against this background, John the Baptist begins to minister in the Spirit and power of Elijah (Lk 1:17; Mal 3:1, 4:5). Thus, John the Baptist is the first prophet of the long-awaited restoration of prophecy among God's people, ministering as the Spirit-filled prophet of the Most High (Lk 1:15, 76). John's first and most important prophecy (in the popular sense of prediction) is that his successor will baptize in the Holy Spirit and fire (Lk 3:16).

John the Baptist's prophecy about his successor has no direct antecedents in the Hebrew or Greek Scriptures of his audiences. Therefore, they would have understood it in the immediate context of his own ministry. Using a commonplace harvest metaphor, John the Baptist explains that the Messianic Spirit-baptizing will have two dimensions: blessing (upon the penitent—he will gather the wheat harvest into his barn), and judgment (upon the impenitent—he will burn up the chaff with unquenchable fire). This chaff-destroying fire of judgment echoes his own preaching about the tree-destroying fire of judgment that he directed against impenitent Israel (Lk 3:9).

John the Baptist prophesied that his successor will baptize in the Holy Spirit and fire. But John the Baptist's successor is not qualified to do this until he, himself, is first anointed by the Holy Spirit. This happens through John the Baptist's ministry when his cousin, Jesus of Nazareth, comes to him to be baptized at the Jordan River. Luke identifies the essential elements of this episode, writing, "when Jesus also had been baptized and was praying, the heaven was opened, and the Holy Spirit descended upon him in bodily form like a dove. And a voice came from heaven, 'You are my Son, the Beloved; with you I am well pleased'" (Lk 3:21–22). Thus, in the context of Jesus' own baptism by John, God publicly approves of Jesus by two witnesses: (1) the visual witness of the Spirit's descent, and (2) the audible witness of God's voice. But what does this unprecedented episode mean?

The meaning of Jesus' baptismal experience—both for John the Baptist's audience and for Luke's readership—is not a matter for speculation. This is because Luke, alone among the Gospel quartet, reports Jesus' own Spiritful explanation. In the words of the prophet Isaiah, Jesus identifies his reception of the Spirit to be his anointing by the Spirit to preach the gospel about the favorable year of the Lord's favor for the poor, the captives, the blind, and the downtrodden (Is 61:1). Therefore, according to Jesus' own explanation (an example of "charismatic exegesis"), his experience at the Jordan is his commissioning-empowerment as the Lord's Christ (that is, anointed one). Indeed, from his Jordan experience onward, Jesus is now, and remains, the Spirit-anointed, Spiritful, Spirit-led, and Spirit-empowered prophet (Lk 3:22, 4:1, 14, 18). Finally, having been anointed by the Spirit, Jesus in turn will fulfill John the Baptist's prophecy that John's successor will baptize in the Holy Spirit.

Luke's first book narrates the story of Jesus—his birth, his commissioning, and his lifelong Spirit-anointed, Spiritful, Spirit-led, and Spirit-empowered ministry. Jesus is born to be a Savior (Lk 2:11), and the climax and the consummation of his ministry is to be found in his death, his resurrection, and his ascension (Lk 23–Acts 1). However, the climax and consummation of Jesus' ministry as anointed prophet happens on the first post-Easter day of Pentecost, when he begins to fulfill John the Baptist's prophecy that he will baptize in the Holy Spirit (Acts 1:4–5). On this day, at the Temple at the hour of morning prayer and accompanied by two typical signs of theophany (wind and fire), Jesus baptizes about 120 of his followers in the Holy Spirit (Acts 2:1–4). This commissions them to be his Spirit-empowered, Spirit-filled witnesses (Acts 1:8, 2:4). Luke will later report ongoing examples of Jesus' baptizing of new believers in the Holy Spirit (for example, Acts 8, 10, 19).

Luke reports four examples of Jesus' fulfilling John the Baptist's prophecy. Two of these four examples fulfill the prophecy explicitly—the Spirit baptism of the 120 on the day of Pentecost (Acts 2:1–21), and the Spirit baptism of the extended household of the centurion Cornelius (Acts 10:1–11:17). Two of Luke's examples are implicit Spirit baptisms: specifically, the new believers in Samaria (Acts 8) and the believers at Ephesus (Acts 19). As an interpretative principle, just as Jesus' Spirit-anointed commissioning is a paradigm for the Spirit baptism of the 120 disciples in the day of Pentecost, so also the Spirit baptism of these disciples is a paradigm for interpreting Luke's subsequent examples of Spirit baptism. Significantly, this principle is validated by the two examples of Peter's charismatic exegesis (Acts 2:14–21, 11:15–17).

The four examples of Jesus' baptizing of his followers and their converts will be examined by the following grid: (1) Luke identifies the antecedent spiritual state of those who will subsequently be Spirit baptized; (2) Luke reports their experience of receiving the Holy Spirit; (3) Luke identifies the sign of being baptized in the Holy Spirit; and (4) Luke explains each example of being baptized in the Holy Spirit.

After his resurrection, Jesus transfers the center of his ministry (now to be performed by his disciples) from Capernaum to Jerusalem. Thus, it is in Jerusalem, not in Galilee, that Jesus initially fulfills John the Baptist's prophecy that he will baptize his followers in the Holy Spirit (Acts 1:4–5).

Luke's post-Easter Pentecost narrative includes four essential elements. First, the Gospel record identified the antecedent Spirit state of the disciples. Simply put, they are believers before Jesus baptizes them in the Holy Spirit (Jn 2:11; Acts 11:17). Second, when Jesus pours out the Spirit upon them, they have a rich variety of complementary experiences—they are baptized in the Holy Spirit, they are empowered by the Spirit, and they are filled with the Spirit (Acts 1:5, 8, 2:4). Third, several signs attest to the outpouring of the Spirit. These include the two metaphorical signs of theophany (the wind and the fire; Acts 2:2–3), and the sign of being baptized in the Spirit—namely, inspired by the Spirit they speak unlearned foreign languages (Acts 2:4–8). Fourth, Peter explains what the outpouring of the Spirit means by applying the Joel text to their experience—namely, God has poured out the Spirit of prophecy upon them (Acts 2:14–21; Jl 2:28–32).

Clearly, what the 120 believers experienced on the Day of Pentecost is their commissioning-empowerment to be Jesus' witnesses. Therefore, their Spirit baptism echoes and is functionally equivalent to the earlier Spirit-anointing of Jesus. Further, because the disciples are believers long before the day of Pentecost dawns, and because their experience of the Spirit is functionally equivalent to Jesus' Spirit-anointing, the idea that Spirit baptism marked their conversion or initiation into the church is an arbitrary, presuppositionally driven misreading of Luke's Pentecost narrative.

Jesus modeled both a countercultural and a cross-cultural ministry. For example, he not only made a despised Samaritan the "hero" of one of his parables (Lk 10:25–37), but he also spent two days ministering in Samaria (Jn 4:1–42). As a result, many Samaritans believed that Jesus was the Savior (Jn 4:42). Therefore, it should not surprise Luke's readership that, when persecution against Hellenistic Jewish Christians erupts in Jerusalem, at least one of them—namely, Philip—flees to the more "gospel friendly" cities of Samaria.

Philip's ministry in Samaria proves to be as effective as Jesus' earlier ministry there had been. Luke reports that many of the Samaritans "believed" his witness about Jesus and were baptized (Acts 8:12). Thus, prior to their reception of the Spirit at the hands of Peter and John, they had the same antecedent spiritual state—they believed, as the disciples themselves had believed prior to the day of Pentecost. Luke describes their experiences of the Spirit by two terms, "receiving the Spirit" and having the Spirit "fall upon" them (Acts 8:15–17). Unlike his earlier Pentecost narrative, Luke's Samaritan narrative is silent about the sign(s) and the explanation of their reception of the Spirit. Nevertheless, a certain magician, Simon, saw an unidentified sign (Acts 8:18), and in the absence of any explanation from Luke his readership will interpret the Samaritan believers' reception of the Spirit according to his earlier Pentecost narrative. Therefore, Luke's readership may tentatively conclude that the Samaritan believers are baptized in the Holy Spirit when Peter and John pray, and that this experience of the Spirit is their commissioning-empowerment and not their conversion-initiation.

In New Testament times, the port city of Caesarea was the administrative center for the Roman province. Sometime after Philip evangelized Samaria, he settled in this city of coastal Judea (Acts 8:40), and sometime after Philip settled in Caesarea, Peter will visit the household of a Roman centurion named Cornelius in Caesarea (Acts 10:1–48). This Cornelius is a Gentile, but he is not an idolatrous pagan. Indeed, his spiritual state is astonishing. On the one hand, he has the same "righteous" antecedent spiritual state as did Zacharias, Elizabeth, and Simeon before they experienced the Holy Spirit (Acts 10:22; Lk 1:6, 2:25). On the other hand, Cornelius has the same "believing" antecedent spiritual state as did the disciples before they were baptized in the Holy Spirit on the Day of Pentecost (Acts 11:17). While Peter witnesses to him, Cornelius experiences the Holy Spirit fall upon him—that is, being poured out upon him (Acts 10:44–45). The sign that Cornelius has received the Holy Spirit (Acts 10:47) is that he begins "speaking in tongues and extolling God" (Acts 10:46; compare 2:4, 11). This data implies that, like the disciples on the Day of Pentecost, Cornelius and his household have just been baptized in the Holy Spirit. And Luke confirms what his narrative implies, by reporting Peter's explanation of this episode to the brethren in Jerusalem. When he heard Cornelius speaking in tongues, Peter connected this sign with John the Baptist's prophecy that Jesus will baptize in the Holy Spirit (Acts 11:15–16). From this Peter concludes that Cornelius has received the same gift as the disciples received on the day of Pentecost (Acts 11:17). Luke's readership is, therefore, justified in concluding that for Cornelius (as for the disciples, earlier) his Spirit baptism is about commissioning-empowerment and not about conversion-initiation.

The last city that the prophet and apostle Paul evangelizes before he is arrested in Jerusalem is Ephesus, the great city of Asia (Acts 18:18–21, 19:1–41). It is not surprising that, having reported examples where Jesus has baptized his believing disciples in Jerusalem and then in all Samaria and Judea, Luke concludes his examples by reporting that about twelve believers in Ephesus are baptized in the Holy Spirit (Acts 19:1–7). As always, Luke begins his narrative by reporting on the spiritual state of the disciples—here the Ephesian twelve. He identifies their antecedent spirit state as having become believers (Acts 19:2). Luke concludes this narrative by reporting that at the hands of Paul, who has just returned to Ephesus, they will receive the Holy Spirit. This experience results in the sign of "speaking in tongues and prophesying" (Acts 19:6). In contrast to the Pentecost and Caesarean narratives, where Luke reports explicitly that believers were baptized in the Holy Spirit, here the Spirit baptism is implied in the sign. And so, in this example, as well as in each of his earlier examples, the Spirit-baptizing work of Jesus is about commissioning-empowerment and not about conversion-initiation.

The doctrine of being baptized in the Holy Spirit enters biblical history through the ministry of the prophet John the Baptist. He prophesies that his successor will baptize in the Holy Spirit (and fire). Luke subsequently reports two explicit and two implicit episodes where John the Baptist's successor, Jesus, baptizes his followers in the Holy Spirit. But about three years before Jesus begins to baptize in the Holy Spirit he, himself, is anointed by God with the Holy Spirit (Lk 3:22, 4:18). Jesus' Spirit-anointing is functionally equivalent to the Spirit baptism of his followers and is a paradigm for all subsequent examples of Spirit baptism.

When Jesus is baptized by John the Baptist he is also anointed by the Spirit for prophetic ministry. Similarly, as Peter's explanation of the outpouring of the Spirit on the Day of Pentecost makes clear, Jesus has just baptized his disciples in the Spirit to empower them for a worldwide prophetic witness (Acts 1:1–2:21). Many years later, when Jesus pours out the Spirit in Caesarea, Peter concludes that the Gentile believers there have just received the identical experience that he and his companions had earlier received on the Day of Pentecost (Acts 11:17). This can only mean that Jesus has baptized them in the Spirit to be prophetic witnesses. What is explicitly true of the Jerusalem and Caesarea Spirit baptisms (Acts 2, 10) is implicitly true for the Samaria and Ephesus gifts of the Spirit (Acts 8, 19).

The Spirit baptisms that Jesus performs throughout the history of Acts are objectively imperceptible spiritual experiences. Jesus, however, makes these experiences tangible by giving an attesting sign for the experience. This sign is to speak in (other) tongues, as the Spirit gives utterance. Luke reports this sign in his Jerusalem, Caesarea, and Ephesus narratives (Acts 2, 10, 19). In both the Jerusalem and Ephesus narratives, Luke identifies this tongues-speech to be a kind of prophesying (Acts 2:17, 19:6). Also, in both the Jerusalem and Caesarea narratives, he identifies what is spoken to be prophetic praise (Acts 2:11, 10:46). Finally, the sign of tongues-speech is implicit in the Samaria narrative (Acts 8:18).

The complementary facts that being baptized in the Holy Spirit is for prophetic ministry and that the attesting sign of Spirit baptism is, itself, a form of prophesying means that being baptized in the Spirit is an experience of commissioning-empowerment for prophetic witness about Jesus. No other interpretation explains the data so well. Luke builds his doctrine of being baptized in the Holy Spirit on the firm foundation of John the Baptist's prophecy that his successor will baptize in the Holy Spirit. In addition, Jesus, whose own ministry is inaugurated when he is anointed by the Spirit at his baptism, is the chief cornerstone of the doctrine (Lk 3:21–22, 4:18–21). As the chief cornerstone, Jesus makes "true" the walls that will later be erected. These four walls, "trued" to Jesus' paradigmatic experience of the Holy Spirit, are the four examples of commissioning-empowerment when, in turn, Jesus baptizes in the Holy Spirit believers in Jerusalem, Samaria, Judea (Caesarea), and at the ends of the earth (Ephesus). The roof remains under construction, and throughout the ages Jesus continues to baptize, that is, commission-empower believers to be his Spirit-baptized, Spirit-empowered, Spirit-filled, and Spirit-led witnesses from their own Jerusalem and around about to the ends of the earth.

REFERENCES AND SUGGESTIONS FOR FURTHER READING

Brand, Chad Owen, ed. 2004. *Perspectives on Spirit Baptism: Five Views.* Nashville, TN: Broadman and Holman.

Dunn, James D. G. 1970. *Baptism in the Holy Spirit.* London: SCM Press.

Palma, Anthony D. 1999. *Baptism in the Holy Spirit.* Springfield, MO: Gospel Publishing House.

Stott, John R. W. 1964. *The Baptism and Fullness of the Holy Spirit.* London: Inter-Varsity Press.

Stronstad, Roger. 1984. *The Charismatic Theology of St. Luke.* Peabody, MA: Hendrickson.

Charismatic Movement

The designation "the Charismatic movement" has historically been used in a variety of ways. Nonetheless, in its most basic form, it constitutes a generic term denoting the spread, since the early 1950s, of Pentecostal-type phenomena associated with the charismata and accompanying theology, most notably the baptism in the Holy Spirit, outside the boundaries of the traditional Pentecostal denominations or "classical Pentecostalism."

The beginning of the Charismatic movement is frequently associated with the public congregational announcement made by the Episcopalian priest Dennis Bennett in 1960, that he had spoken in tongues. There had, however, been earlier recorded cases in the 1940s and 1950s of mainstream denominational clergy laying claim to such experiences (Hunt 2009, 156). Nonetheless, in the early 1960s the Charismatic movement took off in earnest in the United States, emerging initially in largely Episcopalian circles, followed by the slow diffusion of Pentecostal experiences throughout a vast range of Protestant denominations including Baptist, Methodist, Lutheran, and Presbyterian. The Pentecostal-type experiences of prominent individuals within the mainline denominations constituted a discernible feature of the Charismatic movement at its inception. These prominent figures, whom Quebedeaux refers to as "denominational entrepreneurs," were instrumental in advancing "renewal" within their respective denominations (Quebedeaux 1983, 91, 92). They included Dennis Bennett, Harold Bredesen, Tommy Tyson, Agnes Sandford, Jean Stone, and in Britain, Michael Harper.

Peter Hocken (2002, 477–89) identifies four major phases within the North American Charismatic movement. First, "the earliest stirrings" of the movement before 1960 included not only the beginning of the movement but also the rise of itinerant Pentecostal ministries that impacted it. Second, in "the emergence of the movement" (1960–1967), key events led to the Charismatic movement's early spread through the historic churches and its subsequent higher public profile. Third, "the movement takes shape" (1967–1977), whereby the Charismatic movement advances into Roman Catholic spheres while, in Protestant circles, theological debates arise, even among its advocates, regarding the role of speaking in tongues and the charismata in general, alongside the precise meaning of the term "baptism in the Holy Spirit." Fourth, during a period of "consolidation," the movement settles down with a greater degree of acceptance and respectability within many of the mainline denominations. This greater legitimacy, however, tended to dilute the impact of the more radical elements of the movement as it settled down to become an established part of congregational life. Nonetheless, from its beginnings, the Charismatic movement was met with opposition from both within and without the mainline denominations. In the United States in particular, the Charismatic movement has continued to experience difficulty in penetrating the realms of conservative evangelicalism and fundamentalism, most notably within the Southern Baptist Alliance, which, however, is not without its Charismatic enclave.

While the Charismatic movement remained rather muted in the Orthodox Church, it had a significant impact on the Roman Catholic Church beginning in the early 1970s, somewhat later than in the mainline Protestant denominations. The Catholic Charismatic Renewal, as it is sometimes called, had its early advocates including Kevin Ranaghan, Stephen Clark, and James Connelly, but perhaps most influential of all was the ecumenicist Cardinal Joseph Suenens, a key figure in the Second Vatican Council. The roots of the Catholic Charismatic Renewal are not found in Roman Catholic parishes but, rather, can be traced to the Pentecostal experiences of professors and students at two American Roman Catholic universities, namely, Duquesne University in Pittsburgh, Pennsylvania, and the University of Notre Dame in Notre Dame, Indiana.

There are perhaps three distinguishing features of the Catholic Charismatic Renewal. First, it could be considered a cultural revolution within the church (McGuire 1982). It is distinguished by expressive forms of worship and ecumenical tendencies. Second, the movement has not generated the same level of controversy as was evident within the mainline Protestant denominations and was more easily incorporated into Catholic ecclesiastical structures and theology. Third, the Catholic Charismatic Renewal spawned "intentional communities" of collective Christian living. This included the Word of God Community in Ann Arbor, Michigan, founded in 1967 and the People of Praise Community formed in South

Bend, Indiana. Graham Pulkinham's Church of the Redeemer in Houston, Texas, was probably the most significant Protestant counterpart to these types of ecclesial communities.

It is difficult to gauge the level of success reached by the Charismatic movement at its apogee. Certainly very few mainstream churches have not been impacted by renewal. Its large-scale ecumenical conferences were well attended, such as the one held in Kansas City in 1977, which attracted approximately fifty thousand people. Citing a 1967 source, Hollenweger (1972) estimated that over one thousand Presbyterian ministers, seven hundred Episcopalian priests (10 percent of the total), and ten thousand Roman Catholic lay people and clergy in the United States had received the Pentecostal experience. As recent as the late 1980s, Smidt (1988) reported that some 6.6 percent of Americans described themselves as "Charismatic." A good number of these, however, were members of independent Charismatic churches. More recently, a survey conducted by the Pew Forum on Religion and Public Life found that 18 percent of the adult American Christian population identified as Charismatic, comprising approximately 14 percent of the total adult American population (Lugo et al. 2006). There are also widely accepted failings of the Charismatic movement, perhaps above all the fact that the appeal of its expressive and informal style of worship, alongside other cultural attributes, is often limited to its white, middle-class cadres (Neitz 1987).

Despite its departures from traditional Pentecostalism, the Charismatic movement also features a certain measure of continuity with the earlier classical Pentecostal movement. There were the noteworthy ecumenical endeavors of men such as the South African (then American) David du Plessis and Donald Gee in Great Britain, who both sought reconciliation with the mainstream churches but, at the same time, wished to inculcate them with the Pentecostal message. David du Plessis, for instance, claimed to be fulfilling the prophecy of the British healing evangelist Smith Wigglesworth (1859–1947), who claimed there would be a Pentecostal-style revival in the established denominations.

Simultaneously, a common feature of both Protestant and Roman Catholic wings of the Charismatic movement during its infancy was the influence of independent itinerant ministries, many initially derived from the older Pentecostal churches, but which, in some instances at least, significantly departed from them by way of theology and praxis. Some noteworthy ministries included the Full Gospel Business Men's Fellowship International, founded by Demos Shakarian (1913–1993) in 1951, and those of William Branham (1909–1965), Gordon Lindsay (1906–1973), T. L. Osborn, and more directly impacting the Charismatic movement, that of Oral Roberts (1918–2009). Also influential in the early 1960s was David Wilkerson (1931–2011), particularly through his book *The Cross and the Switchblade* (1963).

The wider rubric of "the Charismatic movement" does not end there. Other Pentecostal-style developments have regularly been classified as additional components. This includes the youth-orientated Jesus People, which from the late 1960s spread from California across the United States; the Word of Faith movement, with its tenuous link with classical Pentecostalism (associated chiefly with the ministries of Kenneth Copeland and the late Kenneth Hagin, Sr.); and, in Britain, the "house church" movement (otherwise known as Restorationism). However, many of these movements largely occur within independent rather than denominational churches, so they can more rightly be designated Neo-Pentecostal rather than Charismatic. The fact that such movements are often classified under the broad heading of "the Charismatic movement" is evidence of how contested the term has now become.

REFERENCES AND SUGGESTIONS FOR FURTHER READING

Hamilton, Michael P., ed. 1975. *The Charismatic Movement.* Grand Rapids, MI: Eerdmans.

Hocken, Peter D. 2002. "Charismatic Movement." In *The New International Dictionary of Pentecostal and Charismatic Movements.* Revised and expanded edition, ed. Stanley M. Burgess and Eduard M. van der Maas, 477–519. Grand Rapids, MI: Zondervan.

Hollenweger, Walter J. 1972. *The Pentecostals: The Charismatic Movement in the Churches.* Minneapolis, MN: Augsburg.

Hunt, Stephen J. 2009. *A History of the Charismatic Movement in Britain and the United States of America: The Pentecostal Transformation of Christianity.* 2 vols. New York: Edwin Mellen.

Lugo, Luis, et al. 2006. *Spirit and Power: A Ten-Country Survey of Pentecostals.* Washington, DC: Pew Forum on Religion and Public Life.

McGuire, Meredith B. 1982. *Pentecostal Catholics: Power, Charisma, and Order in a Religious Movement.* Philadelphia, PA: Temple University Press.

Neitz, Mary Jo. 1987. *Charisma and Community: A Study of Religious Commitment within the Charismatic Renewal.* New Brunswick, NJ: Transaction Books.

Poloma, Margaret M. 1982. *The Charismatic Movement: Is There a New Pentecost?* Boston: Twayne.

Quebedeaux, Richard. 1983. *The New Charismatics II.* San Francisco: Harper and Row.

Ranagan, Kevin, and Dorothy Ranagan. 1969. *Catholic Pentecostals.* New York: Paulist Press.

Smidt, Corwin. 1988. "'Praise the Lord' Politics: A Comparative Analysis of the Social Characteristics and Political Views of American Evangelical and Charismatic Christians." *Sociological Analysis* 50(1): 53–72.

Wagner, C. Peter. 1988. *The Third Wave of the Holy Spirit: Encountering the Power of Signs and Wonders Today.* Ann Arbor, MI: Vine Books.

Wilkerson, David. 1963. *The Cross and the Switchblade.* Westwood, NJ: Fleming H. Revell.

Dispensationalism

STEPHEN J. HUNT

❧   The term "Dispensationalism" is generally associated with a distinctly Protestant, specifically fundamentalist, biblical hermeneutical tradition. Constituting a theological schemata, it refers to a number of chronological stages of history or "dispensations" marking God's dealing with humankind, divinely revealed. At its core is a distinctive "Last Days" scenario characterized by the rapture or the removal of the church from earth before God initiates a seven-year period of "tribulations" preceding the premillennial return of Christ, during which time he will establish a thousand-year reign of peace. Most renderings of dispensationalism commence with a progressive revelation—beginning with the Old Testament, subsequently unfolding in the New Testament, and culminating in Christ's second coming. Since the movement's emergence, ongoing academic scrutiny has rarely focused on Pentecostalism's subscription to dispensationalist doctrine. However, early Pentecostalism would certainly appear to have embraced selected components of preexisting nineteenth-century dispensationalist schemata because of several influences, not least of all that of premillenarian dogma.

Contributing to the melting pot of religious fervor and theological strands that fed into the emergence of Pentecostalism were earlier movements in the form of Protestant sectarianism in Europe and North America. A sizeable number embraced one variety or another of dispensationalist theology, while simultaneously anticipating Pentecostalism in their additional doctrines. One of the commonly attributed origins of both dispensationalism and Pentecostalism emerging from Britain were the writings of John Nelson Darby (1800–1882), the founder of Brethrenism, who derived many of his ideas from the Adventist speculations of Charles Irving (1792–1834). In particular, in the early Pentecostals' embrace of dispensationalism, largely inspired through the diffusion of the works of Darby, there was an obvious overlap with the Catholic Apostolic Church established by followers of Irving in 1830 (Patterson and Walker 2001). Irving, unlike Darby, had made a compelling biblical argument in favor of the legitimacy of the charisma (even if concerns with the restored charismata divided early factions of Darby's movement), insisting that spiritual "power" would return to the "true" church in the Last Days—a belief that was also to have resonance in early twentieth-century Pentecostalism (Allen 1994).

Dispensationalism first emerged in America with the writings of John Inglis (1813–1879), who introduced his teaching to a small but influential cadre of evangelicals, and following his death James H. Brookes (1830–1898), a pastor in St. Louis, who further disseminated dispensationalist tenets. The core theology was then popularized by the revivalism of Dwight L. Moody (1837–1898), who attempted to construct a combination of biblical inerrancy and a rudimentary premillenarian dispensationalism, alongside the enthusiastic religion that was to become the hallmark of Pentecostalism. In the United States, further antecedents included the teachings of John Alexander Dowie (1847–1904), who impacted Pentecostalism not only by his emphasis on divine healing but also by advancing eschatological teaching with a strong stress on evangelism, consequently establishing a link between the Pentecostal movement and Irvingism (Faupel 1993).

Despite the theological divergences within the movement, from its very inception Pentecostalism was also infused by prevailing early twentieth-century doctrines of fundamentalist dispensationalism, along with its pessimistic and apocalyptic premillenarian tendencies. By then, the Western world was becoming increasingly modern, industrial, and secular, marked by disbelief and religious decline rather than revival. The marginalization of evangelical constituencies and the resultant pessimism increasingly fed off a wider culture of despair that was wrought by the global conflicts, revolutionary upheavals, and economic disasters of the period. Premillenarianism thus gained greater credence among fundamentalists and evangelicals, forging a way of understanding their place in chaotic times. In the words of Randall Stephens, "Evangelicals, now prone to see history spiraling into chaos and destruction before Jesus' return, widely accepted the theology of pre-millenarianism" (2001, 4).

The Pentecostal faith was seemingly drawn from similar premillenarian aspirations, which arguably came to underscore the movement's fundamentalist credentials. Two substantive issues provided the impetus for this endorsement. First was the spiritual condition of the mainstream churches. In this respect, Darby's writings were influential for the emerging Pentecostal movement since he called conservative Christians to leave the mainline denominations, which he viewed as apostate. Second was persecution from other Christians including, ironically, the fundamentalist camp. For instance, the staunch Presbyterian and uncompromising dispensationalist Benjamin B. Warfield condemned the Pentecostals for believing that miracles still took place in the post-apostolic age. Such persecution only enhanced Pentecostal apocalyptic tendencies that, again ironically, brought them closer to dispensationalist dogma concerning the "rapture"—the premillenarian teaching which asserted that persecuted "true" believers would be miraculously removed from earth before the foretold "time of tribulation."

Thus, although fundamentalist-dispensationalist teachers rejected the Pentecostals' modification of dispensationalism, this did not change the latters' system of interpreting biblical history, which played a major role in their eschatological thought. Pentecostals remained enmeshed in prevailing dispensationalism. Many of the early Pentecostals boasted of their fundamentalist credentials, being at home with terms such as biblical "infallibility" and "inerrancy," while the term "fundamentalist" appeared in many a Pentecostal confession of faith. Official Pentecostal support was widespread for *The Fundamentals* published between 1910 and 1915 by leading conservatives from the Princeton School of Theology, and many Pentecostals were dedicated readers of the very popular Scofield Reference Bible, which was published in 1909 and produced by C. I. Scofield (1843–1921), who added to dispensationalism's academic respectability within the fundamentalist world.

From the evidence it might be concluded that the early Pentecostals were only incidentally fundamentalists and dispensationalists, despite Pentecostalism's Pietist and Holiness roots. This is speculated in Dayton's (1987) revisionist history of American Pentecostalism, where he contends that Pentecostalism followed the lead of other Christian groups of the time—for whom being able to claim evangelical credentials meant it was also necessary to be fundamentalist. However, while both Pentecostalism and dispensationalist fundamentalism appeared to be sibling branches of conservative Protestantism, it was the teaching of the "Latter Rain" revival, or the return of the gifts of the Holy Spirit within the church, that separated the majority of Pentecostals from the fundamentalists. Rejecting the Latter Rain doctrines by which Pentecostals legitimated their place in God's plan, dispensationalists effectively eliminated the biblical basis for Pentecostal theology. For their part, Pentecostals remained irrevocably distanced from fundamentalists because of Pentecostalism's teaching on the place of spiritual gifts in the church. Hence, Pentecostals were forced to modify their dispensationalism to fit their Pentecostal faith and experience. As Blumhofer (1989) explores, the Pentecostals introduced into Darby's system their own dispensational setting where the charismata could again operate in the church.

The Pentecostals, however, went further. They not only defended the faith against modernism and secularism but sought to restore the first-century church by way of rediscovering its lost spirituality and millenarian hope, if not its ecclesiology. Thus, Steven Land suggests that early Pentecostalism was simultaneously restorationist and eschatological (Land 1993, 8–18). The early participants believed that God was restoring the apostolic faith and power for the End Times through signs and wonders. There were also other analogies to the New Testament church including an aversion to creeds, which divided and thus hindered the mission of the faith. There was a suspicion of embellished doctrinal schemes including a detailed dispensationalism.

While many classical Pentecostal groupings are firmly premillennial in orientation, the relationship with dispensationalism has remained a complicated one (Sheppard 1984). The Pentecostals, nevertheless, continued to subscribe to the dominance of premillenarianism and its accompanying "sign watching" in the Last Days. They have tended to espouse aspects of what Mark Sweetnam (2006) refers to as "mutating dispensationalism." There is more to this picture, however.

The complexity of Pentecostal dispensationalism has in recent years been subject to further complication, given that Pentecostalism has borne new protégés. Many of these are found in the Global South, where Pentecostals have been less concerned with the schemas of dispensationalism that have helped bolster Western fundamentalist dogma for well over a century. Pentecostals have been enveloped in the new wave of revivals since the 1960s, in which they appeared to lose many of their distinctive teachings. In particular, the early movement's dispensationalism was challenged by the more optimistic postmillenarianism of the Charismatics with their hope of a Last Days revival, leaving classical Pentecostalism now faced with the prospect of drowning in a sea of the various "Pentecostalisms" that it had initially inspired.

References and Suggestions for Further Reading

Allen, David. 1994. *The Unfailing Stream: A Charismatic Church History in Outline*. Tonbridge, UK: Sovereign World.

Blumhofer, Edith L. 1989. *The Assemblies of God: A Chapter in the Story of American Pentecostalism*. Vol. 1. Springfield, MO: Gospel Publishing House.

Dayton, Donald W. 1987. *Theological Roots of Pentecostalism*. Peabody, MA: Hendrickson.

Faupel, D. William. 1993. "Whither Pentecostalism?" *Pneuma* 15(1): 9–27.

Land, Steven J. 1993. *Pentecostal Spirituality: A Passion for the Kingdom*. Sheffield: Sheffield Academic Press.

Patterson, Mark, and Andrew Walker. 2001. "'Our Unspeakable Comfort': Irving, Albury, and the Origins of the Pre-tribulation Rapture." In *Christian Millenarianism: From the Early Church to Waco*, ed. Stephen Hunt, 98–115. Bloomington: Indiana University Press.

Sheppard, Gerald T. 1984. "Pentecostalism and the Hermeneutics of Dispensationalism: The Anatomy of an Uneasy Relationship." *Pneuma* 6(2): 5–34.

Stephens, Randall. 2001. "More Recovered: A Review of Recent Historical Literature on Evangelicalism in the Late Victorian Era." *Quodlibet Journal* 3(1) http://www.quodlibet.net/articles/stephens-victorian.shtml.

Sweetnam, Mark K. 2006. "Tensions in Dispensational Eschatology." In *Expecting the End: Millennialism in Social and Historical Context*, ed. Kenneth G. C. Newport and Crawford Gribben, 173–92. Waco, TX: Baylor University Press.

William Howard Durham

ANDREW K. GABRIEL

✂   William Howard Durham was one of the most well-known Pentecostal preachers in the early Pentecostal movement in North America,
and the first major proponent within the movement of the doctrine of the
"finished work of Calvary." Durham was born in central Kentucky on 10
January 1873, to a Baptist family of English descent. At the age of seven-
teen, he left his family in Kentucky and set off for Chicago. Soon after, he
settled in Tracy, Minnesota. Durham's faith came alive in 1898 at a revival
service sponsored by the World's Faith Missionary Association (WFMA).
Durham's colleagues from the Holiness tradition taught him to seek the
blessing of sanctification, and in 1901 he had an experience of entire sanctification. On 18 February 1902, he was ordained by the WFMA, a nondenominational association that credentialed people working in evangelism
and urban missions. At this time, Durham began preaching throughout the
upper Midwest of the United States, and this marked the beginning of a life
of itinerant preaching. In 1904 Durham moved to Chicago, and in June the
following year he married Bessie Mae (Whitmore) of Tracy, Minnesota. In
their first year of marriage, the Durhams spent only seven weeks at home
in Chicago because of Durham's preaching schedule. He preached the standard Holiness message of salvation and sanctification. Even in these early
ministry days, Durham reported how people would shout in his meetings
and how others would fall "under the power" of God.

The commencement of the Azusa Street revival in April 1906 coincided
with the birth of the Durhams' first child. Very soon people arrived in
Chicago who had received the Pentecostal experience and who advocated
tongues speech, including some he knew through the WFMA. At first
Durham was hesitant to endorse the revival. However, at the urging of
friends who lived in Los Angeles, Durham left his young son and wife
and headed west to see the event firsthand. He arrived in Los Angeles in
February 1907. Durham sought after the Pentecostal experience for three
weeks before he received it. He reported:

He worked my whole body, one section at a time, first my arms, then my limbs, then my body, then my head, then my face, then my chin, and finally at 1 A.M. Saturday, March 2, after being under the power for three hours, He finished the work on my vocal organs, and spoke through me in unknown tongues. I arose, perfectly conscious outwardly and inwardly that I was fully baptized in the Holy Ghost. (Blumhofer 2002, 130–31)

While at the Azusa Street Mission, William J. Seymour prophesied that the Holy Spirit would come upon people whenever Durham preached.

Durham arrived back in Chicago just before Easter 1907. He held ten services a week at the Gospel Mission Church (better known as the North Avenue Mission) where he taught about the baptism in the Holy Spirit manifested by speaking in tongues. As a result, the North Avenue Mission became a new center for Pentecostal revival. Chicago eventually surpassed Los Angeles as the center of the Pentecostal movement in North America. Thousands of people traveled long distances to attend the crowded meetings. Although the leadership of the North Avenue Mission seems to have been primarily people of Scandinavian descent, the meetings attracted ethnically diverse crowds, like they did at Azusa Street. Many people who became leaders in the early Pentecostal movement attended Durham's meetings in Chicago, including Andrew H. Argue, a pioneer in the Pentecostal Assemblies of Canada; Eudorus N. Bell, the first general superintendent of the Assemblies of God; Daniel Berg, a Swedish missionary and the founder of the Brazilian Assemblies of God; Aimee Semple McPherson, the founder of the International Church of the Foursquare Gospel; and G. Smidt, a founder of the Pentecostal movement in Finland.

In 1908 Durham's wife, Bessie Mae, gave birth to their second child. Later that year, Bessie Mae experienced complications during the delivery of her third child. She did not recover and passed away in August 1909 at the age of twenty-seven. The following February in Chicago, Durham's youngest child died of pneumonia. In the midst of all of this, Durham continued preaching. He spent a couple of months in Ontario, Canada, from January to February 1910. Durham believed that the church was too worldly and full of unbelief. He preached against the growing liberal theology that was found in the mainstream churches. He also preached against preachers (who later became known as fundamentalists) who rejected contemporary miracles and the restoration of the Pentecostal experience. Besides preaching, Durham circulated his teaching on many issues through his publication the *Pentecostal Testimony*, which he distributed free of charge. By mid-1912, 367,000 copies of the publication were circulating. Durham also published prophecies given in the form of tongues and interpretation in *Heavenly Messages*. Although Durham wrote and preached about many issues, he is best-known for starting the "finished work" controversy within the North American Pentecostal movement.

By 1910 Durham had become convinced that the Holiness doctrine that sanctification was a "second work of grace" was an error. This doctrine presented sanctification as something that happened at a specific moment subsequent to conversion. Holiness preachers often described this as an instantaneous experience of "entire sanctification" or "Christian perfection." Durham's strenuous opposition to the doctrine was controversial because it was a common doctrine among Pentecostals in his day; indeed, it was a doctrine that Durham himself had previously preached. Although there were numerous sources that probably influenced his theological shift, based on his own testimony it seems it was primarily his experience of being baptized in the Holy Spirit that caused him to shift his views regarding the doctrine of sanctification. Regarding his experience of Spirit baptism, Durham reported, "From that day to this, I could never preach another sermon on the second work of grace theory. I had held it for years, and continued to do so for some time, but could not preach on the subject again. I could preach Christ . . . holiness, as never before, but not as a second work of grace" (Faupel 1992, 92).

Durham first widely presented his views on the doctrine of sanctification in May 1910 in a sermon entitled "The Finished Work of Calvary" at a midwestern Pentecostal convention in Chicago, and later the same year at camp meetings in Arkansas. Durham argued that the work of the cross not only resulted in the forgiveness of sins but also included the provision for sanctification. Most significant, he argued that a person received the benefits of this work at the point of conversion. He reasoned that if Christ provided all that is needed for sanctification there is no need for a second work of grace (sanctification) subsequent to regeneration. Durham wrote, "In conversion we come into Christ, our Sanctifier, and are made holy as well as righteous. When one really comes into Christ, he is as much in Christ as he will ever be. He is in a state of holiness and righteousness" (Jacobsen 2003, 155). At the same time, although the finished work of Christ was available to believers at the time of regeneration, Durham believed that believers continued to be sanctified over the course of their entire life. Durham's break with the Holiness tradition was not so much that he believed sanctification was provided through the cross of Christ but, rather, because of the implications that he made from this; namely, he taught a two-stage Pentecostal experience of conversion and then baptism in the Holy Spirit, rather than the three-stage Pentecostal experience his Pentecostal-Holiness counterparts were teaching (conversion, sanctification, and then baptism in the Holy Spirit).

While Durham had previously spent much time defending speaking in tongues as the initial evidence of Spirit baptism, he now focused his efforts on arguing for "the finished work of Calvary" (sometimes rather harshly). He believed he was in the end of the age before Christ returned to earth and that God was calling Pentecostals to rid themselves of theological error as God prepared the church to receive more of his power. Durham viewed his efforts as a battle against heresy that came from the devil. His opponents, on the other hand, declared that Durham's teaching was from the devil.

In February 1911, Durham headed back to Los Angeles (eventually making it his permanent residence), this time to instruct others regarding the finished work of Christ. During this time he continued traveling, often, throughout the United States, including back to Chicago. He also preached to Pentecostal conventions in Canada: at Ottawa, Ontario, in June 1911, and Winnipeg, Manitoba, in November 1911.

When Durham first arrived in Los Angeles he did not receive access to key Pentecostal congregations because their leaders rejected his doctrine. At first Durham found a welcome hearing at the Azusa Street Mission, and the meetings became known as a second Azusa outpouring. However, when William J. Seymour returned to the mission from a preaching tour, he would not let Durham preach there any longer. So Durham set up a new mission, and many people followed him from the Azusa Street Mission. As in Chicago, hundreds of people flocked to attend the meetings where Durham preached.

Around the beginning of 1912, Durham married Gertrude Taylor, who had served with him as his housekeeper since the death of Bessie Mae. Unfortunately, Durham then became ill with tuberculosis. Although exhausted he continued preaching, and on 7 July 1912, at the age of thirty-nine he died, leaving behind two young children from his first marriage and a pregnant twenty-nine-year-old widow. The theology that Durham produced in just two short years (1910–1912) continued in its influence as the finished work controversy raged on.

REFERENCES AND SUGGESTIONS FOR FURTHER READING

Blumhofer, Edith L. 2002. "William H. Durham: Years of Creativity, Years of Dissent." In *Portraits of a Generation: Early Pentecostal Leaders*, ed. James R. Goff, Jr., and Grant Wacker, 123–42. Fayetteville: University of Arkansas Press.

Clayton, Allen L. 1979. "The Significance of William H. Durham for Pentecostal Historiography." *Pneuma* 1(2): 27–42.

Faupel, D. William. 1992. "William H. Durham and the Finished Work of Calvary." In *Pentecost, Mission, and Ecumenism: Essays on Intercultural Theology: Festschrift in Honour of Professor Walter J. Hollenweger*, ed. Jan A. B. Jongeneel, 85–95. Studien zur interkulturellen Geschichte des Christentums, 75. New York: Peter Lang.

Jacobsen, Douglas. 2003. *Thinking in the Spirit: Theologies of the Early Pentecostal Movement*. Bloomington: Indiana University Press.

Macchia, Frank D. 2008. "Pentecost as the Power of the Cross: The Witness of Seymour and Durham." *Pneuma* 30(1): 1–3.

Ecclesiology

PETER ALTHOUSE

The doctrine of the church is an area in theology that is underdeveloped in Pentecostalism. Pentecostals place more emphasis on a low-church ecclesiology, the autonomy of the local church, and pragmatic ministry techniques. They have not been concerned with the catholic or universal church generally, except to affirm the invisibility of the church universal. Historically, Pentecostals have been suspicious of formal institutional structures of the church, believing that these are impediments to charismatic experiences of the Spirit. On the whole, Pentecostals prefer to speak of the church as an organism rather than as an organization. Despite their suspicion of institutional, denominational structures, over time Pentecostals organized and developed their own denominational institutions and have shifted from an egalitarian practice of ministry (common in the first few decades of the movement) to the current professionalization of the clergy.

The Reformed wing of the Pentecostal movement with such churches as the Assemblies of God (AG) and the Pentecostal Assemblies of Canada (PAOC) have organized congregationally, placing the authority of the local church in the democratic practices of the congregation. With the rise of the megachurch, however, this structure appears to be shifting to a hierarchical structure with authority residing in a charismatic leader, who exerts institutional authority over the church, and a clergy that is becoming more professionalized. Nevertheless, each AG or PAOC church is organized so that the local church is self-governing, with an elected board of elders or deacons and the pastor acting as chair of the board. National governance has been organized according to presbyterial structures, in which regional districts elect superintendents who function as overseers for the various local churches. There is a national superintendent who oversees the interests of the denomination. Margaret Poloma suggests that the dual presbyterian/congregational structure has allowed the AG to navigate its institutional dilemmas of organization while allowing charisma at the local level of the church. However, the activity of charisma within the church reflects the charisma demonstrated by the pastor (Poloma 1989).

The Wesleyan Holiness wing of Pentecostal ecclesiology—including, for example, the Church of God (Cleveland, Tennessee) (COG), and the Church of God in Christ (COGIC)—has developed along modified episcopal structures following the various polities within the Wesleyan traditions. More authority is placed in the positions of elders and/or bishops, and greater emphasis is given to the sacramental nature of the church. The COG organizes itself so that there is an executive and administrative council of bishops, who are elected with term limits. The council then appoints administrative bishops to the various states and regions. The local church elects a council from the congregation who acts as an advisory board to the pastor, who is appointed to each church by the regional or state bishop. However, congregations usually have a fair amount of input in the pastoral appointment. COGIC is organized along episcopal structures as well, with regional jurisdictions under the authority of bishops. The general assembly is the administrative and legislative body composed of ordained and licensed ministers. The general assembly elects a presidium, consisting of twelve people who function as apostles and oversee the international operation of the church. In current Pentecostal churches generally, charismatic authority resides in the senior pastor who holds authority within the context of structured bureaucracies, yet without the rationalization of the position one would expect to see in other socioeconomic institutions (Weber 1947).

With the outbreak of the Charismatic movement in the 1960s and greater acceptance of charismatic activity in the liturgical and historic Protestant and Roman Catholic traditions, Pentecostal-like spirituality created tensions within formal ecclesial structures. Unlike Pentecostals of the early twentieth century, Charismatics were accepted within their own denominations and afforded a place in the ongoing renewal of the church in the building up of the church through the charismatic gifts. The work of the Spirit, the healthy life of the church, and the recovery of mystical theology are the immediate results of the Charismatic movement.

Conversely the Neo-Pentecostal movement has eschewed the older type of denominational structures and institutional organizations in favor of loose networks of diverse churches. These loose networks of churches, nonetheless, share a family resemblance in regards to their emphasis on the restoration of New Testament spirituality, charismatic praise, practices, and gifts. Because of tax laws and government regulations, these groups have also been forced to institutionalize to a certain degree. Neo-Pentecostal churches include a broad spectrum, such as the House Church, the Shepherding movement, the Vineyard Christian Fellowship, and the newly named Catch the Fire Ministries (CTF; formerly Toronto Airport Christian Fellowship).

John Wimber emphasized relationships among Vineyard pastors and organized a consortium of national leaders, who now oversee about thirty Vineyard churches in various regions or countries. The consortium functions without the controlling power of bureaucratic apparati. As an organization, the Vineyard defines itself around a set of core values rather than beliefs and practices, which gives Vineyard pastors a fair amount of liberty on non-core beliefs and practices (Kay 2007). CTF is undergoing rapid organizational changes but currently has structured itself apostolically so that charismatic leaders function as apostles, while the pastors of CTF churches oversee the ministry of the local church. CTF Toronto functions as the mother church, while other CTF churches link to Toronto via its apostolic network. The apostolic leaders also relate across institutional boundaries so that the legitimacy of apostolic leaders of other organizations such as Randy Clark's Global Awakening or Heidi Baker's Iris Ministries is recognized.

In recent years a shift has occurred to what can be termed an apostolic model of the church, in which authority is placed in the office of apostle personified in a charismatic leader who has authority to govern the church. Although this apostolic model first emerged in the Latter Rain revival of the 1940s, it has taken root among newer Neo-Pentecostal churches. There is evidence that some classical Pentecostal churches are starting to move away from congregational models and are organizing apostolically. The apostolic model is more conducive to the current megachurch movement with its "anointed apostolic leadership," but with the risk of disempowering smaller local churches and the egalitarian authority of their congregations. One cannot help but notice that the apostolic authority that underwrites the megachurch phenomenon reflects an accommodation to current socioeconomic structures of transnational corporations and businesses.

Historically, Pentecostals have been more concerned with the pragmatics of practical ministry than to reflect on a theology of the church. However, there is emerging a new body of Pentecostal and Charismatic scholars who are attempting to think critically about the church. Scholars such as Miroslav Volf, Shane Clifton, Frank Macchia, Simon Chan, and Amos Yong have made nascent attempts at constructing a Pentecostal ecclesiology coherent with theological tradition and Pentecostal identity (more work is needed in this enterprise). Perhaps, however, this suggests another shift in Pentecostal and Charismatic ecclesiology that moves away from the anti-intellectualism that defines much of the early rhetoric to a more sustained reflection as the ongoing ministry and teaching of the church.

References and Suggestions for Further Reading

Chan, Simon. 1998. *Spiritual Theology: A Systematic Study of the Christian Life.* Downers Grove, IL: InterVarsity Press.

———. 2006. *Liturgical Theology: The Church as Worshiping Community.* Downers Grove, IL: IVP Academic.

Clifton, Shane. 2009. *Pentecostal Churches in Transition: Analysing the Developing Ecclesiology of the Assemblies of God in Australia.* Leiden: Brill.

Hocken, Peter D. 2002. "Church, Theology of the." In *The New International Dictionary of Pentecostal and Charismatic Movements.* Revised and expanded edition, ed. Stanley M. Burgess and Eduard M. van der Mass, 544–51. Grand Rapids, MI: Zondervan.

Kay, William K. 2007. *Apostolic Networks of Britain: New Ways of Being Church.* Milton Keynes, UK: Paternoster.

Poloma, Margaret M. 1989. *The Assemblies of God at the Crossroads: Charisma and Institutional Dilemmas.* Knoxville: University of Tennessee Press.

Volf, Miroslav. 1998. *After Our Likeness: The Church as the Image of the Trinity.* Grand Rapids, MI: Eerdmans.

Weber, Max. 1947. *The Theory of Social and Economic Organization.* Translated by A. M. Henderson and Talcott Parsons. Glencoe, IL: Free Press.

Wilson, Dwight J. 2002. "Ecclesial Polity." In *The New International Dictionary of Pentecostal and Charismatic Movements.* Revised and expanded edition, ed. Stanley M. Burgess and Eduard M. van der Mass, 596–97. Grand Rapids, MI: Zondervan.

Eschatology

PETER ALTHOUSE

Eschatology is the doctrine of the last things, the final events at the end of history immediately preceding the coming of Jesus Christ to fulfill his kingdom reign. Pentecostal eschatology has been influenced by popular forms of dispensational premillennialism, a theological schemata which argues that salvation history is divided into different historical periods: at the end of the age of the church, a secret rapture, a seven-year period of tribulation, and the second coming of Christ will all occur, commencing the final millennial reign of Christ on earth. However, Pentecostals have exhibited distinct differences from dispensational premillennialism as well. Historically, Pentecostal eschatology has passed through three different stages. Early Pentecostals articulated a theology of the latter rain, which validated their charismatic experiences of the Spirit's outpouring. Based in the agricultural climate of the Near East, an early rain falls for the planting of crops, and a latter rain falls to mature the crops preceding harvest. Based on this metaphor, early Pentecostals believed that the outpouring of the Spirit and subsequent charismatic activity in the early church was the early rain, and the outpouring of the Spirit and restoration of charismatic activity at the dawn of the twentieth century was the latter rain, preparing the world for a great harvest of souls immediately preceding the return of Christ in glory to establish his kingdom reign. Pentecostals were able to make sense of their spiritual experiences through the theology of the latter rain, explaining charismatic phenomena as a foretaste of the imminent return of Christ.

As Pentecostals moved into the middle of the twentieth century, their eschatological understanding changed. As Gerald T. Sheppard noted (1984), early Pentecostals did not hold to a fundamentalist-dispensational eschatology, and its adoption created problems for ecclesiology. According to fundamentalist theology, the charismatic gifts ceased with the close of the apostolic church. The use of latter rain imagery by early Pentecostals was a way to authenticate their experiences of and belief in the restoration of the charismatic gifts as valid for the contemporary church. Nevertheless, mid-twentieth-century Pentecostals shifted their eschatology, partly because of a new Latter Rain revival (also known as the New Order of the Latter Rain) and partly because of greater acceptance by evangelicals. In 1947, this new charismatic revival emerged out of North Battleford, Saskatchewan, under the leadership of Herrick Holt and George Hawtin in reaction to what appeared to be the waning of Pentecostal spirituality. Using the logic of the latter rain, the New Order claimed that older denominational Pentecostals had lapsed into spiritual drought, and that the former rain at the dawn of the twentieth century was now being poured out in a new latter rain. Classical Pentecostals were also being asked to join the National Association of Evangelicals, a new alliance of ecumenically minded evangelicals. Consequently, these Pentecostal groups were now expected to adopt all evangelical doctrine, including dispensational premillennialism. However, Pentecostals also became embroiled in debates over pre-, mid-, and post-tribulation doctrine.

Currently, a new wave of theological inquiry has called into question the role of dispensational premillennialism in Pentecostal theology and has suggested a proleptic or inaugural eschatology that sees the eschatological kingdom as already being manifest in history—through the death and resurrection of Christ and the outpouring of the Spirit at Pentecost—but not yet here in its fullness. The already-but-not-yet tension of the coming consummation of the eschatological kingdom is more in keeping with the charismatic center of Pentecostalism, in that it sees the baptism in the Spirit, glossolalic utterance, healing, and charismatic gifting as foretastes of the eschatological kingdom, already here through Christ's pouring out of the Spirit as depicted in Acts, but as anticipatory signs of the fullness of the kingdom that is coming. Yet at the same time, the kingdom has not yet come, and charismatic gifting enables Pentecostals to work in service to the kingdom in preparation for its final manifestation, as a sovereign act of God.

Pentecostalism is a movement of diverse entities, however, with diverse theological positions. The Charismatic movement, which emerged in the 1960s among liturgical Protestant and Roman Catholic churches, and the emergence of Independent Charismatics or Neo-Pentecostals since the late 1970s have taken up the theology of the latter rain and used it to support the continuing manifestation of charismatic phenomena and intense religious experiences. These groups are not committed to the premillennial-dispensational eschatologies of mid-twentieth-century Pentecostal and evangelical groups but, instead, opt for other forms such as postmillennial social reconstruction (Kingdom Now Theology or Pat Robertson's American conservatism, for example) or variations of realized eschatology as seen in the practice of charismatic presence, praise, and worship.

REFERENCES AND SUGGESTIONS FOR FURTHER READING

Althouse, Peter. 2003. *Spirit of the Last Days: Pentecostal Eschatology in Conversation with Jürgen Moltmann.* London: T&T Clark International.

Althouse, Peter, and Robby Waddell, eds. 2010. *Perspectives in Pentecostal Eschatologies: World without End.* Eugene, OR: Pickwick.

Anderson, Robert Mapes. 1979. *Vision of the Disinherited: The Making of American Pentecostalism.* New York: Oxford University Press.

Faupel, D. William. 1996. *The Everlasting Gospel: The Significance of Eschatology in the Development of Pentecostal Thought.* Sheffield: Sheffield Academic Press.

Land, Steven J. 1993. *Pentecostal Spirituality: A Passion for the Kingdom.* Sheffield: Sheffield Academic Press.

Macchia, Frank D. 1993. *Spirituality and Social Liberation: The Message of the Blumhardts in Light of Wuerttemberg Pietism.* Metuchen, NJ: Scarecrow Press.

Riss, Richard M. 1987. *Latter Rain: The Latter Rain Movement of 1948 and the Mid-twentieth-century Evangelical Awakening.* Mississauga, ON: Honeycomb Visual Productions.

Sheppard, Gerald T. 1984. "Pentecostalism and the Hermeneutics of Dispensationalism: The Anatomy of an Uneasy Relationship." *Pneuma* 6(2): 5–34.

European Pentecostalism

ALLAN HEATON ANDERSON

✂ European Pentecostalism differs from the American movement in several important aspects. Although it also had roots in the Holiness movement, there were stronger influences from the Keswick movement and its position on sanctification, Pietism in the state churches, and the Welsh revival (1904–1905). There were several revivals with sporadic outbursts of charismata in the nineteenth and early twentieth centuries that preceded the events in Los Angeles in 1906. Examples of these were the ministry of Scottish Presbyterian minister Edward Irving (1792–1834), when prophecy and speaking in tongues broke out in Glasgow in 1830 and in Irving's church in London and were practiced and recorded in the subsequently formed Catholic Apostolic Church until about 1879. The Irvingite movement is an important precedent for Pentecostalism. In Sweden in 1841, a revival with frequent speaking in tongues was reported. Finland had a long tradition of charismatic manifestations in the Lutheran church, including speaking in tongues in the "Awakened" movement since 1796 and in the Laestadians since 1889. Lutheran Johann Christoph Blumhardt (1805–1880), from a Pietist background, operated a healing center in Bad Boll, Germany, for thirty years. His reputation as a healer and exorcist was known internationally, and he linked the healing ministry of Christ with the power of the Spirit. In Männedorf, Switzerland, Dorothea Trudel (1813–1862) and her successor Samuel Zeller (1834–1912) operated a similar center for healing through prayer called Elim. These healing centers were an important precedent for the American healing movement.

A revival began in Russia and Armenia in 1855, with people speaking in tongues, but it was limited to a group in the Black Sea area who called themselves Pentecostal Christians. In 1880, an experience of Spirit baptism was received by a group of Armenian Presbyterians who began in fellowship with the Russian Pentecostals. A Russian boy prophesied about coming Turkish invasions, and the Pentecostals started leaving for North America between 1900 and 1912. They formed Pentecostal congregations there that predated the classical Pentecostal denominations in origin by fifty years. In the Welsh revival, the Pentecostal presence and power of the Holy Spirit was emphasized; meetings lasted for hours and were spontaneous, seemingly chaotic, and emotional; "singing in the Spirit," simultaneous and loud prayer, revelatory visions, and prophecy occurred frequently. Revival leader Evan Roberts (1878–1951) taught a personal experience of Holy Spirit baptism to precede the end-time Pentecost of Acts 2, the worldwide revival promised by biblical prophets. Several early British Pentecostal leaders were converted in the Welsh revival, and the first leader of Pentecostalism in Britain, Anglican vicar Alexander Boddy, visited it. Early European Pentecostal leaders drew inspiration from this revival and saw their movement as springing from it.

Most western European Pentecostal churches have their immediate origins in the revival associated with Thomas Ball Barratt (1862–1940) in Oslo (then Kristiania), Norway. Barratt was a minister in the Methodist Episcopal Church of Norway who visited the United States in 1906 to raise funds (unsuccessfully) for his City Mission. In New York he was baptized in the Spirit before sailing back to Norway via Liverpool with a party of Azusa Street missionaries. Barratt was destined to become the founder and prime motivator of classical Pentecostalism in Europe. He was eventually forced to leave the Methodist Church, and he founded what is now the largest non-Lutheran denomination in Norway, a fellowship of independent churches known as Pinsebevegelsen (Pentecostal revival). The revival in Barratt's independent Filadelfia Church in Oslo was a place of pilgrimage for people from all over Europe, and large crowds attended Barratt's meetings. Barratt sent missionaries to Sweden and Germany and went himself all over Europe and to the Middle East and India. He wrote to Willis Collins Hoover (1858–1936) in Chile, encouraging him and others wherever he went to establish self-governing, self-supporting, and self-propagating churches. Unlike the hierarchical Pentecostalism that was to develop in North America, Barratt's churches were strictly independent and congregational. By 1910, Norwegian Pentecostal missionaries had already gone to India, China, South Africa, and South America. From Oslo, the Pentecostal movement spread to other parts of Europe. Pentecostals in Sweden, Norway, and Finland soon became the biggest churches outside the Lutheran state churches.

Lewi Pethrus's Filadelfia Church in Stockholm, Sweden, was the largest Pentecostal congregation in the world with over six thousand adult members until the 1960s. Pethrus (1884–1974) was a Baptist pastor who became a Pentecostal after visiting Barratt in Oslo in 1907. He became pastor of the Filadelfia Church in Stockholm in 1911, and he and his congregation were expelled from the Baptist denomination in 1913. Pethrus remained Baptist in ecclesiology, a strong advocate of the independence of the local church with no outside interference or denominational organization. This principle has influenced Scandinavian Pentecostal churches and missions all over the world. Pethrus was probably the most influential Pentecostal in Europe during his lifetime. One of the largest Charismatic congregations in northern Europe today is the Word of Life (Livets Ord) church in Uppsala, a Charismatic church founded in 1983 by Ulf Ekman, a former Swedish Lutheran minister. This church's influence extends to a network of some ninety congregations in Sweden and, through its Bible school, much further in Europe.

Alexander A. Boddy (1854–1930), Anglican vicar at All Saints in Sunderland since 1886, visited Barratt's church in Oslo in March 1907 and invited Barratt to preach in his parish in September that year, when many of the people in attendance received Spirit baptism. Boddy's Anglican church became the most significant early Pentecostal center in Britain, and Boddy provided leadership and direction that shaped its future. Annual Whitsun (Pentecost) conventions from 1908 to 1914 drew Pentecostals from all over Britain and continental Europe. Boddy edited the widely influential periodical *Confidence* (1908–1926), which reported on Pentecostal revivals all over the world and expounded the doctrine of Spirit baptism and spiritual gifts. The fastest-growing churches in Britain today are the mostly independent Charismatic churches in some thirty associations including Ichthus, Pioneers, New Frontiers, and the Vineyard Association. Pentecostalism has also profoundly affected older churches in Britain, particularly Anglican and Baptist churches, which include a significant proportion of Charismatic churches.

From Britain, Pentecostalism spread to France, and from Brazil to Portugal. Pentecostalism began among the Roma (Gypsy) people in 1952 when Clément le Cossec began ministry to about thirty Roma people in Brest, Brittany. A revival broke out among Roma people worldwide, and in France and Spain about a quarter of the Roma population belongs to a Pentecostal church. Italy has the second-largest population of Pentecostals in western Europe, after Britain. Largely drawn from the exploited poor classes, they number twice as many as all other Italian Protestants combined. They were only officially recognized in 1960 after great persecution and harassment, especially under Mussolini's fascist government and with the support of the Catholic Church between 1935 and 1945. Italian Pentecostals were only given government permission to evangelize in 1987.

Pentecostalism spread from Scandinavia to other parts of Protestant Europe, including Finland, Denmark, Iceland, the Netherlands, Germany, and Switzerland. Opposition to Pentecostalism was mounting, and in September 1909 the German evangelicals' Berlin Declaration set itself firmly against the Pentecostal movement. Pentecostalism was condemned as "demonic spiritualism" and speaking in tongues as "not from above, but from below." The Berlin Declaration isolated the Charismatic Lutheran and Reformed ministers in the German state churches and greatly hindered the expansion of the movement. One Pentecostal association in Germany, the Bund Freier Pfingstmeinden (Federation of Free Pentecostal Churches), was formed after the Second World War, and its international evangelist Reinhard Bonnke's Christ for All Nations crusades in Africa since the 1980s have attracted enormous crowds and had a significant effect on the popularizing of Pentecostalism in Africa.

The Pentecostal movement has been relatively more successful in eastern Europe, where it has grown in the face of severe restrictions and persecution from state or dominant churches and from communist regimes. There are over three hundred thousand Pentecostals in Romania, where the Pentecostal Apostolic Church of God is the largest denomination. This was founded in 1922 by George Bradin and later united with other groups, in 1929 and 1950, the last occasion at the behest of the Communist government. This church was largely a rural phenomenon until the 1950s, when it began to work in urban areas, and it now has flourishing city churches. Since 1996 the church has been known simply as the Pentecostal Union.

In the Baltic states and in Russia, Pentecostal influence came from neighboring Scandinavia and from an Englishwoman, Eleanor Patrick, and a Latvian, William Fetler (1883–1957), who is known also by his pen name, Basil Malof. Swedish Pentecostals established the movement in Estonia, and three Russian Pentecostal women missionaries began a Pentecostal movement in Lithuania. Fetler had established a Russian missionary society and traveled extensively throughout Russia. T. B. Barratt had a successful evangelistic campaign in St. Petersburg in 1911, leaving behind a sizeable Pentecostal congregation. Ivan Voronaev (1886–c.1940) established eighteen Pentecostal congregations in Bulgaria in 1920 and traveled to Odessa and St. Petersburg, preaching and establishing churches. His church in Odessa soon had a thousand members. In 1927 the first Pentecostal Congress for the Soviet Union took place in Odessa, and Voronaev was appointed president of the Union of Christians of Evangelical Faith. An estimated eighty thousand Pentecostal members enjoyed the favor of the Communist state that had liberated them from Orthodox persecution. But after the passing of the antireligious laws, in 1930 Voronaev and eight hundred pastors were arrested and sent to Siberian concentration camps, where, after a brief release in 1935, Voronaev disappeared and was later presumed dead. The Pentecostal churches continued to grow.

Since the disintegration of European Communism in the 1980s, there has been more freedom for Pentecostals, but this has not been without problems. In particular, new Pentecostal groups from the West have flooded into former Communist countries with aggressive evangelistic techniques, and this has led to opposition from dominant Orthodox churches and even from national governments. Some of the new churches resulting have succeeded in attracting large crowds to their services. The institutionalizing of Pentecostal denominations forced to share their identity with evangelicals and Baptists and the creation and expansion of Pentecostal theological colleges have resulted in a more inward-looking Pentecostal movement in some countries. In Ukraine, the Evangelical Pentecostal Union is the largest Pentecostal denomination in Europe, with some 370,000 members in 2000. By 2000 there were an estimated 400,000 Russian and 780,000 Ukrainian Pentecostals in total, the highest number of Pentecostals in any European nation. The largest congregation in Europe is the Embassy of the Blessed Kingdom of God for All Nations, in Kiev, led by a Nigerian, Sunday Adelaja, with over 20,000 members—and five times that number throughout Ukraine, with congregations elsewhere in eastern Europe also. In contrast to most other parts of the world, the Pentecostal movement in Europe is quite small, but it has been an essentially European phenomenon, which in some countries has shown evidence of growth that contradicts the general decline of European Christianity in the twentieth century.

REFERENCES AND SUGGESTIONS FOR FURTHER READING

Anderson, Allan. 2004. *An Introduction to Pentecostalism: Global Charismatic Christianity.* Cambridge: Cambridge University Press.

Cox, Harvey. 1995. *Fire from Heaven: The Rise of Pentecostal Spirituality and the Reshaping of Religion in the Twenty-First Century.* Cambridge, MA: De Capo Press.

Hollenweger, Walter J. 1972. *The Pentecostals.* London: SCM Press.

————. 1997. *Pentecostalism: Origins and Developments Worldwide.* Peabody, MA: Hendrickson.

Martin, David. 2002. *Pentecostalism: The World Their Parish.* Oxford: Blackwell.

Exorcism

KEITH WARRINGTON

✹ Pentecostals accept the existence of a devil and of influential demons. Although they hold diverse views concerning the demonic and exorcism, most have preferred to maintain a sanguine stance with regard to these issues and have generally sought to be guided by the biblical narrative for their beliefs and praxis. This has often resulted in cautious assessments and assertions concerning exorcistic practices.

The New Testament provides more information than does the Old Testament concerning demons, possibly because, in the time of Jesus, the Jews had an inadequate, largely mythical demonology. Within Judaism demons were often viewed as mischievous, but rarely as a spiritual threat. The New Testament data indicates that they are ruled by (the) Satan (Rv 12:9–10) and are antagonistic to God (1 Cor 8:4–6, 10:20). They often harm those they inhabit, either with an illness (Mk 9:17) or by impelling the victim to self-harm (Mk 5:5), and they are described as dirty or unclean (Mk 5:2), and evil (Lk 11:26). Since the devil is characterized as being involved in temptation (Gn 3:14; 2 Cor 11:3), Pentecostals assume that demons have a similar role, oppressing Christians and initiating negative behavior. Consequently, they subscribe to the view that such malevolent forces need to be excised wherever possible.

Pentecostals believe that casting out demons, or exorcism, is part of the Gospel commission, the authority contained therein being available to all Christians (Mt 10:8; Mk 16:15–20; Lk 9:1). In general, the impact of the devil (also known as [the] Satan) upon Christians and non-Christians has been subsumed under two categories, possession and oppression, though in recent years such terms have been identified as rather simplistic, and a desire has grown to offer a more sophisticated diagnosis for demonic influence. Some argue it is helpful to think of demonic activity directed toward the Christian as on a sliding scale of intensity from temptation, through persistent oppression of the mind, to total control of a specific area of one's life. However, demonic influence in the lives of Christians should be differentiated from the dominating influence a demon may have over a non-Christian, given that Christians are believed to have considerable supernatural resources available to combat demonic influence, as delegated to them by God.

Pentecostals believe that Jesus has gained victory over the devil, a victory that will be consummated at the end of time though it may be experienced in the present, both personally and globally, by resisting him through prayer and self-discipline and by maintaining a close relationship with God. Most Pentecostals would accept that, on some occasions, sickness or suffering may be caused by the presence of demons that need to be exorcised (Mt 9:32–34, 12:22–29, 17:14–21). However, it is not to be assumed that, because an illness was associated with demonic activity in the Gospels (Mt 12:22–29), such an illness always results from demonic activity (Mk 7:31–37).

Pentecostals accept that the devil and demons are antagonistic foes of the church and still affect individuals malevolently (2 Cor 4:4; Eph 6:12). It is also believed, however, that these forces have been eternally vanquished by Jesus, who is presented as the conqueror of the evil age and the redeemer of people from it (Gal 1:4; Eph 2:2; Col 1:13). Consequently, the devil and demons can be resisted and overcome with God's help (Eph 6:10–11).

Although forms of exorcism vary, a number of features remain constant. These include the need for preparation by those engaged in the exorcism, including prayer and possibly fasting, and the recognition of the importance of the gift of discernment to diagnose the situation and offer a prognosis. Although a methodology is not prescribed, nor may one be identified in the Bible, the use of the name of Jesus (Mk 16:17; Acts 16:18) and the incorporation of a command that the demon leave its victim (Mk 1:25) are of importance. Finally, recognition of the authority that God has invested in the Christian is viewed as an important premise in relating combatively with demons. Post-exorcistic support and counseling are also affirmed as very important, especially with reference to developing a close relationship with God.

Although Pentecostals do not distinguish between leaders or clergy and laity functioning in exorcism, they have generally expressed caution in areas relating to the demonic, a caution driven partly by awareness of the dangers associated with getting this ministry wrong. Few would claim to have a gift of exorcism, and the role of exorcist has not been adopted within Pentecostalism.

Although exorcisms are included in the Synoptic Gospels, it is significant to note that John's Gospel does not record any. The paucity of exorcisms in the Acts of the Apostles and the absence of exorcisms in the rest of the New Testament are also of interest. Some Pentecostals believe that exorcisms were more prominent in the ministry of Jesus because of the dynamic nature of his person and his radical message concerning the new kingdom, which resulted in a violent backlash from his demonic foes. Jesus' exorcisms were clear proof of his initiation of the kingdom and demonstrated his ability to control its development. Thus, although the biblical text provides information relating to the combat between believers and demonic forces, it offers little by way of guidance for the implementation of a normative exorcistic procedure. It does not provide answers to many of the questions that have been asked in recent years concerning the demonic. Indeed, outside the ministry of Jesus in the Synoptics, there is only one successful exorcism recorded in the rest of the New Testament, which is carried out by anyone other than Jesus (Acts 16:18).

Outside the Synoptics, the guidance offered by other New Testament writers concerning the demonic is that the most appropriate way of responding to such forces is resistance (1 Pt 5:8), and to take advantage of the resources God makes available to believers (Eph 6:10–18). In Romans 16:20, Paul encourages Christian behavior, as a result of which God will diminish the power the devil can wield in an individual's life. Similarly, self-control (1 Cor 7:5; Eph 4:26–27) and forgiveness (2 Cor 2:11) are viewed as antidotes to Satan's measures against the believer. Indeed, Paul deduces that all supernatural forces are subservient to Christ (Col 2:10), were originally created for him (Col 1:16), and were disarmed at the cross (Col 2:15; cf. Rom 8:38–39). At the same time, Paul is aware of demonic malevolence (Eph 2:2, 6:12), and he calls believers to resist demonic influences. Thus, Paul asserts that his readers are supported by the powerful Spirit in their battle with evil. Rather than explore secondary questions related to demons, he identifies the resources of believers to undermine the role of evil in their lives and contexts.

Some Pentecostals also believe that the role of the demonic in many Western contexts is more subtle and disguised than elsewhere. Rather than assume that the limited number of exorcisms in the West indicates an absence of the demonic, they argue that the paucity of such phenomena may actually point to the ubiquity of the demonic in the Western world. It is probable, they assert, that demonic activity in the West is even more dangerous by its devious nature; believers must be aware that the battle is not always overt but subliminal and no less undermining. The Bible, the Spirit, as well as other believers are all recognized as potentially playing a significant part in combating demonic activity.

References and Suggestions for Further Reading

Macchia, Frank D. 1994. "Repudiating the Enemy: Satan and Demons." In *Systematic Theology: A Pentecostal Perspective*, ed. Stanley M. Horton, 194–212. Revised edition. Springfield, MO: Logion Press.

McClung, L. Grant, Jr. 2002. "Exorcism." In *The New International Dictionary of Pentecostal and Charismatic Movements.* Revised and expanded edition, ed. Stanley M. Burgess and Eduard M. van der Maas, 624–28. Grand Rapids, MI: Zondervan.

Moreau, A. Scott, Bryant L. Myers, David G. Burnett, Hwa Yung, and Tokunboh Adeyemo, eds. 2002. *Deliver Us from Evil. An Uneasy Frontier in Christian Mission.* Monrovia, CA: World Vision International.

Thomas, John Christopher. 1998. *The Devil, Disease, and Deliverance: Origins of Illness in New Testament Thought.* Sheffield: Sheffield Academic Press.

Warrington, Keith. 2008. *Pentecostal Theology: A Theology of Encounter.* New York: T&T Clark.

Finished Work Controversy

DAVID A. REED

The Finished Work Controversy sparked the first schism in the early Pentecostal revival. It was a direct challenge to the doctrine of entire sanctification commonly held by Pentecostals since their inception in 1901 and taught by their founding patriarchs, Charles Parham (1873–1929) and William Seymour (1870–1922). Inherited from Wesleyan Holiness roots, entire sanctification is the belief that a second act of grace by the Holy Spirit eradicates all sin in the believer's life, including the "inbred root" or inclination to sin. The Finished Work Controversy challenged the two fundamental premises of this doctrine—that there is a second act of grace and that it eradicates the very desire to sin, which thereby renders the believer sinless.

It is impossible to separate the controversy, and the schism that followed in its wake, from the person who single-handedly led the attack. William Durham (1873–1912) was born in Kentucky and reared in a Baptist home, but he did not claim his real conversion until 1898 after he moved to Tracy, Minnesota. It was there that he came in contact with the World's Faith Missionary Association (WFMA), a Scandinavian Pietist evangelistic ministry. Through the WFMA, Durham's faith was awakened and his own call to ministry confirmed.

Durham was soon engaged in itinerant ministry. By 1903 he was ministering among Scandinavian immigrants in Chicago. But his life took a critical turn in August 1906 when he encountered a band of Pentecostal evangelists from the Azusa Street Mission in Los Angeles. Spiritually hungry for the experience called baptism of the Holy Spirit, in February 1907 Durham made his pilgrimage to the Azusa Street Mission. After five days of intense spiritual seeking, he was overcome with a dramatic experience of the Holy Spirit. On returning to Chicago, he immediately began holding nightly meetings that launched a revival which continued unabated from 1907 to 1910. During this period, Durham's North Avenue Mission rivaled the Azusa Street Mission as the epicenter of the Pentecostal revival. Many who visited the Chicago mission were to become the next generation of Pentecostal leaders.

The second major shift in Durham's ministry came in 1910. He had been struggling for some time over the doctrine of entire sanctification as a second work of grace and finally became convinced it was an erroneous teaching. His frontal attack came on 10 May 1910, at the well-attended annual Pentecostal convention in Chicago's prominent Stone Church. His address was entitled "The Finished Work of Calvary." The title soon became identified with a doctrine, then a controversy, a movement, and eventually the dominant stream within Pentecostalism.

Durham was so convinced of the urgency of the message that he immediately set out to convince the entire Pentecostal movement. Within two years, his Finished Work teaching had made inroads in three major constituencies: Azusa's Apostolic Faith movement, the Christian and Missionary Alliance, and remnants of Alexander Dowie's Christian Catholic Apostolic Church in Zion City, Illinois. His doctrine swept through the Midwest to Texas, into eastern and western Canada, and southwest to California. In February 1911 he set up headquarters in Los Angeles as his new base of operation. But before he could reach the Deep South, he died suddenly in July 1912 at age thirty-nine of pulmonary tuberculosis. Within two years, a new organization, the Assemblies of God, was formed by many of the leaders who had followed Durham and his teaching. By 1930, three out of five Pentecostals were Finished Work adherents.

Durham's new Finished Work doctrine was fundamentally a shift in focus from the work of the Spirit in sanctification to the atoning work of Christ on the cross. Durham's logic was that if entire sanctification is a second and subsequent work of grace, then one can be converted but only partially saved, since a fundamental act of grace contributes in some way to one's salvation. For Durham, this struck at the heart of the gospel, which for him was the complete and final work of Christ on the cross. In Finished Work theology, the work of sanctification shifted from the Holy Spirit to Christ.

Durham continued to use, but redefined, the language of "entire" sanctification. The Holiness doctrine taught that entire sanctification removes the three fundamental sources of sin: original sin inherited from Adam; sins committed by the person; and the "inbred root" of sin, whereby the believer is capable of attaining a state of perfection. Durham understood "entire" sanctification to mean that all vestiges of inherited and committed sins have been removed. The inbred capacity to sin, however, remains, so that when the believer sins, the remedy for removal is repentance and forgiveness based solely on the Finished Work of Calvary. Believers are not to strive for a perfected state that will render them immune to temptation but, rather, to seek God's appropriate provision for reconciliation through forgiveness.

Durham replaced the Holiness two-stage, sequential process of justification and sanctification with one initial act of grace, in which sanctification occurs simultaneously with justification. In the moment of conversion, the believer receives both "imputed" and "internal" righteousness, an external change in status and an internal change within the believer. Durham's favorite image was that of an infant, who is whole as a person at the moment of birth. There is nothing that must be added in order to complete the baby's full humanity. The only change is growth and development of what is already present at birth.

Consistent with Durham's christocentric shift, the life of the believer is summed up in the phrase "Identification with Christ." The believer's relationship with Christ is established by identifying through faith and baptism with his death, burial, and resurrection. Durham's initial paradigmatic text was Romans 6:4. His alternative to the Pentecostal-Holiness doctrine of two acts of grace and three experiences (conversion, sanctification, and Spirit baptism) was one act of grace and two experiences—conversion and baptism of the Holy Spirit. The believer receives Christ in conversion, but the promised Holy Spirit comes to abide only at the moment of Spirit baptism.

Water baptism was so integral to being identified with Christ, and the Pentecostal experience so fundamental, that Durham regarded Romans 6:4 and Acts 2:38 as complementary. Having shifted his Finished Work doctrine in a christocentric direction, he needed to account more directly for the work of the Holy Spirit. So the threefold action in Acts 2:38—repentance, water baptism, gift of the Holy Spirit—provided for Durham the "Pentecostalization" that the otherwise evangelical Finished Work doctrine needed. By 1912 he was posting Acts 2:38 on the masthead of his magazine, *Pentecostal Testimony.* This choice of a paradigmatic text was soon to be picked up by the Oneness movement, which appeared within two years of Durham's death and by 1916 was excommunicated from the Assemblies of God.

Durham's Finished Work doctrine was not entirely original with him. The "Finished Work of Calvary" was a familiar phrase in the more Reformed Keswick Higher Life movement, which viewed sanctification as progressive but never complete in this life. The source of Durham's exposure was probably the WFMA in Minnesota during his early years, since it was a blend of American Holiness and traditional evangelical Finished Work teaching. Another possible, though tenuous, influence could have been the evangelical radio preacher Essek W. Kenyon (1867–1948). Durham and Kenyon knew each other, and Kenyon held campaigns in Chicago in 1907 and 1908. They both promoted common themes such as the "Finished Work of Christ" and "Identification with Christ."

The impact of Durham on the early Pentecostal movement was immense, in part because the conditions were conducive to his Finished Work teaching. There was a growing vacuum of direction and leadership. The fires of Azusa were burning low. Issues of race, doctrine, and organization were beginning to surface without resolution. Both Parham and Seymour had lost much of their influence as spiritual patriarchs. Durham's success lay partly in his presenting the Finished Work as a fresh move of the Spirit, not just a doctrine. In two brief years he caused strife and division, but he also transformed a controversy into a catalyst for a new direction.

The Finished Work teaching as Durham presented it was left underdeveloped, however, because of his untimely death. Few of his followers either understood or held to the specifics of his doctrine. The one exception was Franklin Small, an early Oneness leader from Winnipeg, Canada. Three decades after Durham's death, Small devoted one whole issue of his magazine, *Living Waters*, to the Finished Work doctrine. He understood Durham's teaching and had embraced it as his own. For Durham's other followers, his legacy was to have successfully separated the Pentecostal experience from its Holiness roots and reconstituted it on the christocentric foundation of the atoning work of Christ.

REFERENCES AND SUGGESTIONS FOR FURTHER READING

Blumhofer, Edith. 2002. "William H. Durham: Years of Creativity, Years of Dissent." In *Portraits of a Generation: Early Pentecostal Leaders*, ed. James R. Goff, Jr., and Grant Wacker, 123–42. Fayetteville: University of Arkansas Press.

Farkas, Thomas. 1993. "Durham's 'Finished Work of Calvary' Teaching and Traditional Doctrines of Sanctification." PhD dissertation, Southern Baptist Theological Seminary.

Faupel, D. William. 1996. *The Everlasting Gospel: The Significance of Eschatology in the Development of Pentecostal Thought*. Sheffield: Sheffield Academic Press.

Reed, David A. 2008. *"In Jesus' Name": The History and Beliefs of Oneness Pentecostals*. Blandford, UK: Deo.

Full Gospel

KENNETH J. ARCHER

✖   The historical importance of the full gospel and its ongoing significance in shaping Pentecostal spirituality and ministry is undeniable.
The full gospel was understood to be a restoration of the New Testament
presentation of the gospel of Jesus Christ. It was a complete gospel that
emphasized the importance of Jesus Christ's redemptive ministry for humanity. The various theological motifs of Jesus as the Savior, Sanctifier,
Spirit Baptizer, Healer, and King soon returning, all created a dynamic
christocentric spirituality of hope and healing. The full gospel message
was spread wherever Pentecostals traveled. Missionaries and evangelists
proclaimed the full gospel to anyone who would listen. Pastors and teachers preached upon these theological truths regularly. The full gospel was
the heart and identifying characteristic of early Pentecostalism.

Donald Dayton's seminal work, *Theological Roots of Pentecostalism*
(1987), has shown that Pentecostalism is deeply rooted in the more radical
wing of the American Wesleyan Holiness movement of the late nineteenth
century. Pentecostalism is a creative reconfiguration of the motifs of Jesus
as Savior, Sanctifier, Healer, and soon-coming King. To these motifs Pentecostals added the newly recovered biblical doctrine of the baptism of the
Holy Spirit with the sign of speaking in other tongues. The Pentecostals
fused together a unique understanding of the full gospel of Jesus Christ.
The full gospel was the theological DNA that formed a new theological
tradition called Pentecostalism.

The full gospel was originally articulated through a fivefold pattern. The
fivefold gospel consisted of the following redemptive experiences achieved
through the atoning work of Christ: (1) justification was by faith through
grace for the forgiveness of sins, (2) sanctification was a second definite
work of grace enabling one to live a holy life in perfecting love, (3) the baptism in the Holy Spirit evidenced in other tongues was necessary for the
empowerment of mission, (4) physical healing of the body from sickness
was provided for in the atonement, (5) the premillennial return of Jesus

Christ was drawing near. Prior to 1910, all early Pentecostal movements embraced the fivefold gospel. The doctrine of sanctification as a second work of grace, however, was suppressed by the influential ministry of William H. Durham, who rejected the Wesleyan Holiness view. He argued that sanctification was positional and conditional and based this upon the Finished Work of Christ on Calvary. After 1910, the formation of most Pentecostal denominations would be based upon the fourfold gospel. Jesus is the Savior, Spirit baptizer, Healer, and soon-coming King. Sanctification dropped out of the gospel, but holiness remained a significant emphasis. The lynchpin that holds the full gospel together is Spirit baptism. It served as the catalyst forming a new tradition, which has a clear lineage from the Wesleyan and Holiness traditions.

Definitions of Pentecostalism always include as its distinctive characteristic the doctrine of the baptism with the Holy Spirit evidenced in speaking in other tongues. What is missing is the importance of understanding Spirit baptism as a necessary aspect of the full gospel. What is essential to Pentecostal spirituality and identity is the full gospel, which includes the experience of Spirit baptism. If Spirit baptism as a subsequent experience to justification-regeneration drops out of the gospel, then Pentecostalism ceases to be Pentecostal. Furthermore, if sanctification-deliverance and healing are no longer possibilities, then the gospel is no longer whole and complete. Without the imminence of the second coming, a passion for God's kingdom wanes and the importance of Spirit baptism as an essential part of the Pentecostal life diminishes. The full gospel is what distinguishes Pentecostalism from other theological traditions.

Pentecostals have a passionate desire to encounter Jesus, the bearer of the full gospel. The statements associated with the full gospel are confessional-doxological in character. Pentecostals praise the Lord Jesus for saving them, sanctifying them from the power of sin, healing their mind and body, baptizing them in the Holy Spirit, and they anticipate his soon return. The statements are shorthand testimonials of a person's redemptive experiences mediated by Jesus Christ. The full gospel is not a set of quaint platitudes but are deep-seated affectionate affirmations flowing from Pentecostals' worship of the Living God who has transformed their lives. The full gospel shapes their identity and guides their ministry activities. It reflects their understanding of holistic salvation for all who will call upon the name of Jesus Christ.

The full gospel is a holistic view of salvation in the sense that it affirms that God is concerned about the whole person and all of creation.

The same God who created is the same God who redeems and the same God who will restore all of creation. Pentecostals are concerned about the poor, the sick, and marginalized because God is concerned about them. The full gospel brings hope because it affirms that the mission of Jesus Christ has not stopped with his ascension. The Holy Spirit enables the churches to carry on the mission of Jesus Christ. Signs, miracles, and wonders continue to testify to the power of the gospel of Jesus Christ. For this reason, a Pentecostal theology grounded in the gospel will always emphasize the importance of worshiping God experientially and witnessing to the world holistically.

REFERENCES AND SUGGESTIONS FOR FURTHER READING

Archer, Kenneth J. 2007. "A Pentecostal Way of Doing Theology: Manner and Method." *International Journal of Systematic Theology* 9(3): 301–14.

Dayton, Donald W. 1987. *Theological Roots of Pentecostalism*. Peabody, MA: Hendrickson.

Kärkkäinen, Veli-Matti. 2007. "Encountering Christ in the Full Gospel Way: An Incarnational Pentecostal Spirituality." *Journal of the European Pentecostal Theological Association* 27(1): 9–23.

Land, Steven J. 1993. *Pentecostal Spirituality: A Passion for the Kingdom*. Sheffield: Sheffield Academic Press.

Globalization

MICHAEL WILKINSON

✳ "Globalization" is a highly contested term; it means many things to many people. For some, it means universalization and the homogenization of the world's cultures. For others, it means Westernization, which is a specific type of universalization and specifically American imperialism. For some it means liberalization, which is the idea that economic borders are easily transcended, leading to a global form of capitalism as the key characteristic of the world's economic system. Finally, some use "globalization" interchangeably with "internationalization," which refers to an increase in state-to-state relations. All of these views have some relationship with the term, yet "globalization" needs to be defined in such a way that it captures both continuity and discontinuity with these terms (Scholte 2005). "Globalization" refers to a process of worldwide social change and the transformation of social institutions and cultures over time, including an increased awareness of the world as a single place. What, therefore, are the implications of globalization for Pentecostal studies?

Scholars of Pentecostalism have employed the term "globalization" in some important ways, yet it appears that many have used the word with some inconsistency, often linking it to universalization or modernization. One tendency is to argue that Pentecostalism is evidence that modernization, and hence secularization, are incorrect interpretations of contemporary religion. Another tendency is the view that Pentecostalism has a single origin, which is then diffused throughout the world, leading to a focus on what Pentecostals share in common; a global Pentecostal culture. Some scholars of Pentecostalism have pushed back, arguing that this common origin theme is an example of American imperialism and that Pentecostalism does not have any one single origin. Rather, there are multiple streams contributing to the Pentecostal movement—most notably in Europe, India, and Africa. Scholars must account for historical continuity and discontinuity with the origins of American Pentecostalism, especially through the developments of Charles Parham's initial evidence doctrine and William Seymour's Azusa Street revival meetings. Pentecostal scholars also need to account for sameness and difference among the many groups of Pentecostal and Charismatic Christians throughout all regions of the world. In this sense we can speak about Pentecostalism as a movement. Scholars can also examine the varieties of Pentecostalism, including the ways in which the movement has multiplied and changed across cultures and history (Wilkinson 2008).

Different aspects of the Pentecostal movement can be viewed as having a family resemblance (Anderson 2004). This means they share something in common, but the many members of the family are not identical. This metaphor of family is one way to capture the diversity within the Pentecostal movement. Globalization, paradoxically, points to sameness and difference, which is an important optic for examining the Pentecostal movement (Robertson 1992). Some implications for Pentecostal studies include the recognition of similar and different origin stories; the role of missionary networks in spreading a Pentecostal ethos; indigenous and grassroots movements, and the role they played in establishing churches; migration, and the flow of Pentecostals from Europe to North America, Africa to Europe, Asia to Australia, and other points throughout the world; the mixing and merging of Pentecostalism with other forms of Christianity including historical churches such as the Roman Catholic Church and the Anglican churches worldwide.

Globalization taken to mean a process of social change highlights important questions to be explored around the relationship between religion and culture, the role of religion in global society, the relationship between Pentecostals and other religions, and relationships between Pentecostals, Charismatics, Neo-Pentecostals, and evangelicals. Each relationship demonstrates points of commonality but also areas of tension over orthodoxy, orthopraxy, and questions concerning authority, that is, whose Pentecostalism is the correct version (Beyer 2006). Various movements of Pentecostalism can be referred to as sacred flows between numerous points, movements across a range of borders through time and space that contribute to the construction of new forms of Pentecostalism as they mix and merge or recombine for the development of new patterns of experience, belief, and practice (Wilkinson 2007).

Pentecostal studies must also focus on the implications of globalization for North America. There is often an assumption among North American scholars that globalization is something that happens elsewhere. However, globalization is a worldwide phenomenon, and attention must be given to the way in which Pentecostalism is transformed through transnational networks, like networks among new immigrants who have arrived since the 1970s from Africa, Asia, and Latin America. In other words, Pentecostal studies in North America need to address the ways in which the movement is pluralized, and the implications of this for older forms such as the Assemblies of God and the Pentecostal Assemblies of Canada (Wilkinson 2008).

REFERENCES AND SUGGESTIONS FOR FURTHER READING

Anderson, Allan. 2004. *An Introduction to Pentecostalism: Global Charismatic Christianity.* Cambridge: Cambridge University Press.
Beyer, Peter. 2006. *Religions in Global Society.* New York: Routledge.
Robertson, Roland. 1992. *Globalization: Social Theory and Global Culture.* London: Sage.

Scholte, Jan Aart. 2005. *Globalization: A Critical Introduction*. New York: Palgrave Macmillan.

Wilkinson, Michael. 2007. "Religion and Global Flows." In *Religion, Globalization, and Culture*, ed. Peter Beyer and Lori Beaman, 375–89. Leiden: Brill.

———. 2008. "What's 'Global' about Global Pentecostalism?" *Journal of Pentecostal Theology* 17(1): 96–109.

Glossolalia

MARK J. CARTLEDGE

✖   "Glossolalia," or speaking in tongues, is one of those terms often associated with Pentecostalism. Indeed, in the public imagination, Pentecostalism has often been referred to as a "tongues movement," because "glossolalia" is a technical term (literally from the Greek, "tongues to speak") for the phenomenon of "speaking in tongues." Glossolalia is a key spiritual practice of Pentecostals, and to some extent of Charismatic Christians—although, since the 1980s, many Charismatic Christians have downplayed the importance of tongues speech as a spiritual practice in favor of other kinds of inspired speech, such as words of knowledge and personal prophecy. So, what exactly is glossolalia in the context of Pentecostalism? In order to answer this basic question we need to go back to the biblical texts that inform both the Pentecostal understanding and its practice.

Pentecostal Christians derive their identity from the account of the day of Pentecost in the Acts of the Apostles (2:1–4). Luke describes how the 120 were gathered together waiting for the promise of the Holy Spirit, who came upon them like a mighty wind, with tongues of fire resting upon each of them. As a result of this immersion into the presence of the Holy Spirit, the disciples began to declare the praise of God in foreign human languages other than their own (often referred to as xenolalia, or sometimes referred to as xenoglossa). Other accounts of tongues appear in Acts 10:46 and 19:6. In Acts 10:46, Peter is preaching the message of Jesus Christ to the Gentile household of Cornelius when, quite suddenly, the Holy Spirit came upon those listening to him. They spoke in tongues and praised God, just as the 120 had done on the day of Pentecost. This event is, therefore, often referred to as the Gentile Pentecost. In Acts 19:2, Paul is speaking to the disciples of John the Baptist at Ephesus. Paul places his hands upon them and prays for them to receive the Holy Spirit. Subsequently they speak in tongues and prophesy. Pentecostals have used these three accounts to construct a theology of baptism in the Spirit as a distinct post-conversion experience, which is symbolized by speaking in tongues as the Spirit gives utterance. Indeed, glossolalia is regarded as a consequence of the overwhelming experience of the Holy Spirit. Even today there are many classical Pentecostal denominations still maintaining that the "initial evidence" of having been baptized in the Holy Spirit is glossolalia. In this sense, glossolalia is still regarded as a sign of one's "personal" Pentecost.

Paul also refers to glossolalia in his Corinthian correspondence, but he does not locate the phenomenon in the church's missionary expansion as Luke does. Rather, he addresses glossolalia as it was being used in a settled Christian community at Corinth. And it is here that we encounter a problem, because at Corinth the practice of speaking in tongues has been hijacked by powerful leaders in the church, and it has become a badge of super-spirituality. Therefore, when we read Paul's comments we need to understand that he is addressing a situation of spiritual abuse. Paul identifies glossolalia as a gift (*charisma*), which should be used either publicly, with an interpretation to edify the congregation, or personally, to edify the individual. It is a gift for prayer and praise, as the human spirit joins with the Holy Spirit to express mysteries to God (1 Cor 14:2; cf. Rom 8:26). In the congregation, order must prevail; therefore, he recommends guidelines for its usage by stating that only two or three should speak publicly, and if there is no one to interpret the message in tongues, then the speaker should keep quiet (1 Cor 14:27–28). Pentecostals have understood this account to refer to the gift of glossolalia for prayer, praise, and prophecy (if interpreted). It is also used in spiritual warfare (Eph 6:18: "all kinds of prayer"). Thus, it forms part of the overall spirituality of Pentecostalism as members "pray in the s/Spirit," that is, in the human spirit with the aid of the Holy Spirit.

The early Pentecostals believed that tongues speech was the ability to speak a language for the sake of preaching the gospel in foreign lands, the so-called missionary tongues. Unfortunately, once they arrived in these foreign lands, they discovered that they had insufficient ability to do this and began to learn the language in a more conventional way. From the 1960s, when tongues speech as a key feature of Pentecostal spirituality began to infiltrate the mainline denominations through the Charismatic movement, social scientists began to give it serious attention. One of the key questions addressed at this time was whether the "tongues" spoken by Pentecostals were in fact real, unlearned, human languages (xenolalia) or not. Research in the 1970s suggested that most tongues speech did not communicate meaning semantically but, rather, affectively, via mood, and as a result they were therefore pseudo-languages. In the 1980s, it was suggested, however, that current linguistic theory at the time was unable to classify the unique features of tongues speech and a more cautious approach was required. The most recent research has moved away from semantics to pragmatics, which is concerned with what language does, that is, its performance in a given social context—for example, in a corporate worship setting (Cartledge 2006).

Theologians have matched these recent developments by considering glossolalia in a number of different ways. For example, it has been interpreted as a language game expressing intimacy between lovers or between parents and their child. It has also been understood as a sacramental sign of God's presence. It has been suggested that C. S. Lewis's notion of transposition can be applied to glossolalia: the higher (divine) supernatural experience is adapted and expressed in the lower (human) medium of glossolalia. Finally, glossolalia has been explored in terms of apophatic theology and postmodernism, that is, it is considered through the categories of mystery and aesthetics. These different perspectives suggest that there are still more creative ways in which to view the gift of glossolalia. Pentecostal theologians continue to explore new avenues and develop their ideas in continuity with Scripture, Christian tradition broadly conceived, and contemporary spiritual practices.

References and Suggestions for Further Reading

Cartledge, Mark J. 2002. *Charismatic Glossolalia: An Empirical-Theological Study.* Aldershot, UK: Ashgate.

———. 2005. *The Gift of Speaking in Tongues: The Holy Spirit, the Human Spirit, and the Gift of Holy Speech.* Cambridge: Grove Books.

———, ed. 2006. *Speaking in Tongues: Multi-disciplinary Perspectives.* Milton Keynes, UK: Paternoster.

Hovenden, Gerald. 2002. *Speaking in Tongues: The New Testament Evidence in Context.* Sheffield: Sheffield Academic Press.

Macchia, Frank D. 1992. "Sighs Too Deep for Words: Towards a Theology of Glossolalia." *Journal of Pentecostal Theology* 1(1): 47–73.

Godly Love

MATTHEW T. LEE

✘   Godly Love is defined as the dynamic interaction between perceptions of divine and human love that enliven and expand benevolence. The phrase has recently been used in a book by sociologist Margaret Poloma and psychologist Ralph Hood, Jr., that presented the case study of a Neo-Pentecostal social ministry to the homeless in Atlanta, Georgia. Poloma and her colleagues have since applied the phrase to other Pentecostal groups. Although not necessarily limited to Pentecostalism, the early conceptual refinement of Godly Love has occurred entirely within a Pentecostal context. Because frequent religious experiences are normative within Pentecostalism, this Christian tradition has served as an especially fruitful context for the study of Godly Love. In fact, as Frank Macchia points out, the distinctly Pentecostal experience of Spirit baptism has often been referred to as a "baptism of Love." A dynamic interaction with God, which involves loving God and being loved by God, is capable of serving as the emotional engine that drives benevolent service to others, especially given the Pentecostal emphasis on powerful experiences of God through praying in tongues, divine healing, and prophecy. Pentecostal rituals have sought to institutionalize such dynamic interactions (see the other entries in this volume on Revival and Prophecy).

Social scientific research on Godly Love has been informed by Pentecostal theology, but at the same time it has focused on perceived interactions with God, in keeping with the focus of the scientific method on observable data. The writings of the Pentecostal theologian Frank Macchia have been of particular heuristic value as they provide insight into the shape that Godly Love takes in the broadly defined Pentecostal tradition. With his focus on Spirit baptism, Macchia posits the Holy Spirit as empowering the benevolent ministry of the Pentecostal believer through a reciprocal relationship between the kingdom of God and personal spiritual transformation. The work of the Holy Spirit in ushering in the kingdom leads to spiritual transformations among individuals and within the church as a collective entity, inspiring action to make the kingdom appear on earth as it is in heaven. On the other hand, a series of spiritual transformations provides the motivation for action as well as a source of visions of the kingdom of God. The unifying force of these relationships is love: the idea that the kingdom of God is "a reign of self-sacrificial love" and the "Holy Spirit is the Spirit of holy love" (Macchia 2006, 258). Empirical studies of Godly Love have attempted to put empirical flesh on this theological skeleton in the often messy lives of real people.

The perceived interaction between divine and human love provides the framework for a scholarly investigation of the Great Commandment to love God and to love one's neighbor as one's self. Godly Love is not a synonym for God's love. It is rather an attempt to capture a process of interactions between an individual's "vertical" relationship with God and "horizontal" relationships with other people in which benevolent service becomes an emergent property. This is not to suggest that all benevolent service necessarily requires a vertical dimension. But God is a "significant other" for Pentecostals, and perceived interactions with God play an important role in the nature and extent of their expression of compassionate love. In a recent book by Lee and Poloma (2009) on exemplary Pentecostals, the concept of Godly Love was displayed as a Diamond Model (see Figure 1).

FIGURE 1—THE DIAMOND MODEL OF GODLY LOVE

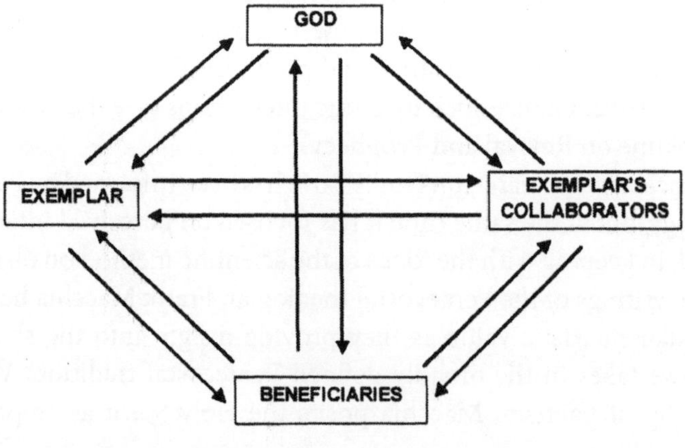

In this ideal type, an "exemplar" of Godly Love establishes a ministry to serve a group in need (that is, beneficiaries) with the help of collaborators and the empowerment of a sustaining relationship with God. The arrows indicate the reciprocal nature of these interactions. Of course, in the real world, some of these arrows would be thicker than others (to indicate frequency or intensity of interactions) and some would be nonexistent (the exemplar who has no immediate contact with any beneficiaries, for example). But as a heuristic device, this model has been invaluable for describing variations in the experience and expression of Godly Love.

The interdisciplinary science of Godly Love is an emerging field of study involving cross-disciplinary dialogue among theologians and social scientists of all stripes. It has been especially successful in documenting and explaining the myriad ways in which Pentecostals have lived out the Great Commandment that is at the heart of the Christian tradition. Research is presently under way to examine the role that Godly Love plays in other Pentecostal organizations and ministries including the Church of God (Cleveland, Tennessee), the Dream Center (a Pentecostal social ministry based in Los Angeles), soaking prayer, healing practices, and risk-taking behavior in Christian outreach. Empirical findings have provided much food for thought for Pentecostal theologians, administrators, pastors, and church members. Thanks to this scholarship, future research on benevolent ministries within the Pentecostal tradition has a solid foundation of theory and empirical results upon which to build.

References and Suggestions for Further Reading

Flame of Love Project. 2010. http://www3.uakron.edu/sociology/flameweb/index.html.

Lee, Matthew T., and Margaret M. Poloma. 2009. *A Sociological Study of the Great Commandment in Pentecostalism: The Practice of Godly Love as Benevolent Service*. Lewiston, NY: Edwin Mellen.

Macchia, Frank D. 2006. *Baptized in the Spirit: A Global Pentecostal Theology*. Grand Rapids, MI: Zondervan.

Poloma, Margaret M., and John C. Green. 2010. *The Assemblies of God: Godly Love and the Revitalization of American Pentecostalism*. New York: New York University Press.

Poloma, Margaret M., and Ralph W. Hood, Jr. 2008. *Blood and Fire: Godly Love in a Pentecostal Emerging Church*. New York: New York University Press.

Healing

KEITH WARRINGTON

Pentecostals believe in the possibility of divine healing as a legitimate expression of the ministry of the church, entrusted to it by Jesus, and mediated through the power of the Holy Spirit. Pentecostal beliefs concerning healing are mainly based on the healing ministry of Jesus, the charismatic gifts of healings referred to by Paul (1 Cor 12:9), and the guidelines found in James 5:13–18. These, as well as the healing references in the book of Acts, have formed the basis for the belief that supernatural healing may still occur today. The biblical data may be summarized thus: (1) the Old Testament presents God as the healer of people, and this helps define him as God; (2) the Gospels present Jesus as the healer of people. As such, he is identified as the Son of God, Messiah, and Savior who came to initiate the kingdom of God. The Gospel writers present Jesus as a healer who has no peer. However, to conclude that this is all they have to say about Jesus as a result of his healings is to make a fundamental mistake. The physical restorations, although important to those healed, also reveal truth about the healer. The healing narratives were intended to result in the question, "Who is this man?" to be closely followed by the more spectacular question, "Is he God?" As well as relieving suffering, the healing ministry of Jesus is thus to be recognized as demonstrating his Messiahship but also, much more important, his deity.

Although Jesus did not establish a set methodology, there are aspects of his ministry, including his sensitivity and grace, that should be emulated. However, there are motifs integral to his healing ministry that confirm its uniqueness. Jesus is to be distinguished from other healers in the church, because his mission is unique and thus inevitably different from the mission of his followers. Central aspects of Jesus' healing ministry are many. First, Jesus healed all who came to him for healing. Second, he never prayed for guidance, approval, or authority before healing people. Third, he never unambiguously related sickness to the personal sin of the sufferer (contrast Lk 1:20; Acts 5:1–11, 13:8–12; Jas 5:15–16). Fourth, Jesus never indicated that sickness had pedagogical value to the sufferer (contrast Acts 5:11, 13:12; 2 Cor 12:7–10; Gal 4:13). Fifth, his healings had a pedagogical function. They demonstrated his authority to heal sicknesses (Mt 8:14–16, 15:29–31). His healings prove he has authority over the Jewish Law, including the Sabbath (Lk 14:1–6; Jn 5:1–14), purity laws (Mt 8:2–4), and the temple (Mt 21:14). They reveal his authority to reinstate outcasts (Mt 15:21–28; Lk 13:10–17) and to initiate the kingdom (Mt 4:23–24, 10:1, 8). Jesus' healings also fulfill prophecy concerning the Messiah (Mt 12:15–21). Most important, they demonstrate Jesus' authority to forgive sins (Mt 9:1–8), and they provide opportunities to develop a more accurate perception of his identity (Jn 4:46–54, 5:2–47). Sixth, the book of Acts provides examples of the ongoing healing ministry in the early church, mainly through Peter and Paul. Furthermore, it presents Jesus as still healing, and the apostles and others healing in ways that are reminiscent of Jesus in his healing activity. The ascended Christ is not absent; he is still seen to be present in the church. Seventh, the letters of Paul impart information about the charismatic and spontaneous nature of the gifts of the Spirit as they relate to healing. Paul reflects the interim period between the initiation and consummation of the kingdom. Although healings still occur, suffering is also present and not all illness is removed. Nevertheless, on occasions, God still heals via the gift of healing (1 Cor 12:9). When God chooses not to bring restoration, the promise of 2 Corinthians 12:9—"My grace is sufficient for you, for my power is made perfect in weakness"—is a strong support for all believers. Eighth, the letter of James (5:13–18) provides guidelines for healing praxis to be undertaken by members of the local church.

The issue of the conditional nature of divine healing is an area that has experienced a noticeable change within Pentecostalism. Although some believe it is always God's will to heal, most assert that although God has the power to heal, he does not always choose to heal. Similarly, because people are not always healed despite prayer being offered, many Pentecostals offer practical guidance to benefit those who remain sick. This includes asking God for guidance as to how to pray, counseling those suffering to realize the presence of God despite their continued sickness, helping to remove any unnecessary sense of guilt, reminding them of their ability to reflect God authentically in their circumstances, and teaching them that God is more concerned about their eternal destiny than their physical well-being. Increasingly, Pentecostals recognize that they exist in an era that does not experience all that God has available for Christians.

In the New Testament, healing miracles encouraged unbelievers to place their faith in Jesus. The description of the ministry of Jesus to the sick (Mt 9:35) is identical to his commission to the disciples in their ministry to the sick (Mt 10:1). The implication is that what their Master has done, they are to do likewise. The Synoptists record that Jesus commissioned the disciples to engage in a ministry of healing alongside their announcement of the kingdom of God (Mt 10:6–7; Mk 6:12), and many Pentecostals take seriously the suggestion that they should also take up the mandate given to the disciples by Jesus.

Pentecostals have always affirmed the importance of prayer in relation to the practice of healing. Increasingly, however, prayer has been recognized as an opportunity not only for requesting healing but also for listening to divine guidance as to how one should pray. When prayer is offered, an attempt should be made to ascertain the will of God in order to pray most appropriately (Jas 1:5–6).

It is a well-established belief among Pentecostals that sickness may be the result of divine judgment or chastisement because of personal sin (Ex 9:14; Nm 14:37; 1 Sm 25:36–39). However, most Pentecostals reject the equation that illness is always linked to individual sin, though personal sin has been cautiously recognized as a reason for a healing not occurring, as reflected in the New Testament (Acts 5:1–11; 1 Cor 11:29–30; Jas 5:16).

The use of the name of Jesus in prayer for healing is common in Pentecostal praxis, deriving from the practice as recorded in the book of Acts (3:6, 16, 4:10). However, to assume that the name of Jesus automatically releases power is inappropriate. The name of Jesus reminds a person of the power of the name bearer; but more important, the will of the owner of that power is of paramount significance. Thus, the name of Jesus is appropriately used when the prayer incorporating it is sanctioned by him, for then it will effect a change.

As well as laying hands on the person receiving prayer for healing, anointing with oil has retained an important place in the context of prayer for the sick in Pentecostal practice. For many, the oil represents the presence and activity of the Holy Spirit. However, it has a much wider symbolic value, signifying to the original readers an infusion of the power of God in whose name the person was anointed. Furthermore, the oil was valued as an indication of love felt for the one who was anointed. As such, it offers hope and encouragement to sufferers, reminding them that they are in the presence of God who loves them and will strengthen them.

REFERENCES AND SUGGESTIONS FOR FURTHER READING

Brown, Michael L. 1995. *Israel's Divine Healer.* Grand Rapids, MI: Zondervan.

Kydd, Ronald A. N. 1998. *Healing through the Centuries: Models for Understanding.* Peabody, MA: Hendrickson.

Twelftree, Graham H. 1999. *Jesus the Miracle Worker: A Historical and Theological Study.* Downers Grove, IL: InterVarsity Press.

Warrington, Keith. 2000. *Jesus the Healer: Paradigm or Unique Phenomenon.* Carlisle, UK: Paternoster.

———. 2005. *Healing and Suffering. Biblical and Pastoral Reflections.* Carlisle, UK: Paternoster.

Hebden Mission

ADAM STEWART

✖   The East End Mission—or as it was more commonly known, the Hebden Mission—was the most important early center of Pentecostalism in Canada. It was established on 20 May 1906 by English immigrants James and Ellen Hebden. James Hebden was born into a working-class family in the industrial town of Mexborough, South Yorkshire, England, on 6 December 1860; Ellen Wharton was born on 15 January 1865 and was reared in a solidly middle-class family in the small village of Gayton, Norfolk, England. Ellen underwent an emotive conversion and sanctification experience at the age of fifteen at the same time that the Keswick movement was sweeping across England. Before the emergence of Pentecostalism in the first decade of the twentieth century, many adherents within both the Holiness and Keswick movements referred to the experience of sanctification as "the baptism in the Holy Spirit." As a result, Ellen initially described her early sanctification experience as a baptism in the Holy Spirit. Ellen's father was a staunch High Church Anglican, and he discouraged Ellen's developing spirituality, which led her to leave home and move in with her older sister's family where she could practice her newfound faith unhindered. Ellen subsequently left her sister's home in Gayton in order to work under the tutelage of the renowned faith healer

Elizabeth Baxter at her Bethshan healing home in London. It was while she was being mentored by Baxter in London that a vision began to form deep in Ellen's heart that some day she would establish her own mission, where people could receive prayer for divine healing and be called to the foreign mission field.

After finishing her time apprenticing with Baxter, Ellen met James Hebden, a glassworks laborer and, like Ellen, an aspiring missionary who was raising his two children after the recent death of his wife. Ellen and James were soon married on 24 July 1893, had four more children together, and spent the next ten years living and working in Swinton, South Yorkshire, England. In 1903, after a hurricane devastated the Caribbean island of Jamaica, James and Ellen believed this was their much-anticipated opportunity to begin their missionary career. Along with their four youngest children, the couple boarded a ship for Kingston, Jamaica, where they established a mission. Jamaica, however, proved too dramatic a change for the Hebdens, and in December of 1904, the family relocated to Toronto, Ontario, with the hopes of beginning a more permanent ministry. It is difficult to know the exact reasons the Hebdens left Jamaica; it could have been the climate, the difference in culture, fears of safety, the inability to make friends, or even the lack of amenities. It is also possible, however, that the Hebdens were unable to carve out a sufficiently distinct niche in the already dynamic religious environment of Kingston. Edwardian Toronto may have provided just the right degree of tension in order to allow the Hebdens' mission to stand out from the competition. Nevertheless, it took James and Ellen almost a year and a half to secure a former three-storey bakery and tenement building at 651 Queen Street East in Toronto, where they would finally realize their vision (more than a decade old now) of establishing their own healing mission. The main floor of the new building was used as the mission's meeting hall, the second floor was converted into the Hebden family's personal residence, while the third floor of the mission was either rented out to tenants or used to house visitors to the mission without cost. A typical week at the Hebden Mission included morning, afternoon, and evening services on Sunday, a Bible study class on Monday evening, an all-day prayer meeting on Wednesday, and a divine healing service on Friday evening.

On the evening of Saturday 17 November 1906, six months after the establishment of the mission, something dramatic happened that would forever change the course of James and Ellen's ministry as well as the very shape of the Canadian religious landscape. After being prompted by God to get out of bed and pray for improved power in order to heal the sick, Ellen claimed that she underwent a baptism of the Holy Spirit accompanied by speaking in tongues, an event totally unlike her sanctification experienced at the age of fifteen. Ellen then returned to bed, and when she awoke the next morning, explained to her husband what had happened to her the night before. Given that it was a Sunday, she also recounted her experience to those gathered at the mission's morning, afternoon, and evening services, during which she again exhibited supernatural manifestations. Within a month, James also received the baptism of the Holy Spirit accompanied by speaking in tongues, and within five months between seventy and eighty others also shared in the experience. In time, Ellen would claim that God enabled her both to speak and to write twenty-two different languages. Ellen's experience in November 1906 makes her the first historically confirmed individual to have received the Pentecostal Spirit baptism in Canada. What is more interesting, and which makes the Hebden Mission particularly important, is that there is no historical evidence to suggest Ellen had any previous knowledge of the revival that had already begun in April 1906 at William Seymour's Apostolic Faith Mission in Los Angeles, California. In other words, both Ellen's Spirit baptism and the beginning of Pentecostalism in Canada appear to have originated independently from the influence of Pentecostalism in the United States.

Before long, news of what had happened at the Hebden Mission spread across the city of Toronto and throughout the Holiness and emerging Pentecostal networks in Canada and the United States. Soon throngs of people from across North America began to visit the mission in order to experience the new Pentecostal baptism, and early Pentecostal leaders such as Daniel Awrey, Frank Bartleman, William H. Durham, and Aimee Semple McPherson visited and spoke at the mission. This radical religious experience led James and Ellen to transform their mission from the healing home ministry paradigm learned from Baxter in London to a newly emerging Pentecostal ministry paradigm, which viewed healing as more of a crisis-event than a gradual process. Completing the transition from a healing home to a Pentecostal mission, the Hebdens transformed the third floor of the mission from a place for spiritual retreat and respite for the sick to an "upper room," common in many Pentecostal missions, where visitors could pray and wait for the baptism of the Holy Spirit.

While the Hebdens' ministry was one of many firsts for Canadian Pentecostalism, their most enduring influence stemmed from the many evangelists whom they equipped and sent out across Ontario in order to establish new Pentecostal churches and missions. One of these evangelists, Robert Semple, would convert—and later, marry—a young woman who had initially visited one of the Hebden-inspired missions in order to jeer at its fanatical devotees. This young woman, however, was mesmerized by both the religious praxis and the evangelist she witnessed at the mission and later became one of the most important Pentecostal evangelists of the twentieth century, Aimee Semple McPherson.

In 1908, the Hebdens moved their personal residence from the second floor of the mission on Queen Street East to a large home that they purchased at 191 George Street in Toronto. Ellen believed that God, through a glossolalic utterance, gave her a name for their new home, "Lama Gersha," which she interpreted as meaning "a place of spiritual teaching." The mission on Queen Street East then began to operate more as a church, while, in addition to serving as the family's residence, the home at 191 George Street was used to hold daily prayer meetings and to house guests who were visiting the mission in order to seek the baptism of the Holy Spirit and divine healing. In 1909, the same year that Seymour's mission in Los Angeles began to experience significant organizational setbacks, the Hebden Mission, ironically, also encountered a series of organizational challenges that would have significant consequences for the future of James and Ellen's ministry in Toronto.

First, a number of Canadian Pentecostal leaders gathered in Markham, Ontario, in June 1909 in order to discuss the possibility of joining the English Anglican vicar Alexander Boddy's Pentecostal Missionary Union. The Hebdens, however, were adamantly opposed to any kind of official religious organization as they believed that it would stifle the spontaneous leading of the Holy Spirit, a view not uncommon among Pentecostals even to this day. The Hebdens' fierce opposition to denominationalism and organization—not to mention the fact that the primary leader of the mission, Ellen, was a woman—created a fissure between the Hebdens and the emerging body of overwhelmingly male Canadian Pentecostal leaders.

A second set of events also contributed to the increasing instability of the Hebden Mission. James decided to leave Toronto in March 1910, in order to help establish a mission in Algiers. Ellen, in the absence of her husband, decided to sell the building at 651 Queen Street East and leave for an extended trip to England. Both James and Ellen made these departures from the mission in the midst of fund-raising for a new church building. Even though Ellen was the mission's primary leader, her authority would have surely suffered with the absence of her husband's support. Furthermore, without James or Ellen at the mission, which was then meeting in their home at 191 George Street, and with their absences lasting several months, a schism arose within the mission due to concerns over how the Hebdens were spending the mission's funds.

Despite a failed lawsuit in which the Hebdens attempted to secure some funds that were taken from the mission by a group of dissenting members, and a series of unfavorable articles about the mission in the *Toronto Daily Star*, the Hebdens succeeded in building their new church at 115 Broadway Avenue in the spring and summer of 1913. The new church, which they named the Church of God, was located just one block north of the previous mission on Queen Street East. The Hebdens, probably suffering a significant financial loss from the recent schism, sold their large home at 191 George Street and moved into a second-floor apartment above the new church. In 1917, they moved their family to a modest home at 48 Westlake Avenue and continued to pastor the small church until their retirement in 1921, thus ending their fifteen years of ministry in the city of Toronto. Ellen Hebden died on 1 May 1923 at the age of fifty-eight and was buried in Toronto. The time and place of James's death is not clear.

The Hebden Mission is important for two reasons. First, Ellen's independent experience of the baptism of the Holy Spirit provides important evidence for understanding the multiple origins of the global Pentecostal movement. This experience is often overlooked within the dominant American literature on early Pentecostal historiography, which suffers from a sometimes myopic focus on the events at William Seymour's Azusa Street Mission in Los Angeles. Second, the Hebden Mission was the first and most important early center of Canadian Pentecostalism. The Hebden Mission was responsible for bringing one of Pentecostalism's most important leaders and evangelists, Aimee Semple McPherson, into the Pentecostal fold. It also initiated the first Canadian Pentecostal periodical, *The Promise*; held the first Canadian Pentecostal camp meeting, which was located outside of Simcoe, Ontario; organized the first Canadian Pentecostal convention; sent the first Canadian Pentecostal missionary, Charles Chawner, to a foreign field; and was instrumental in establishing the first Pentecostal mission to Native Americans near Brantford, Ontario.

References and Suggestions for Further Reading

Miller, Thomas William. 1986. "The Canadian 'Azusa': The Hebden Mission in Toronto." *Pneuma* 8(1): 5–30.

Sloos, William. 2010. "The Story of James and Ellen Hebden: The First Family of Pentecost in Canada." *Pneuma* 32(2): 181–202.

Stewart, Adam. 2010. "A Canadian Azusa? The Implications of the Hebden Mission for Pentecostal Historiography." In *Winds from the North: Canadian Contributions to the Pentecostal Movement*, ed. Michael Wilkinson and Peter Althouse, 17–37. Leiden and Boston: Brill.

Wilkinson, Michael. 2010. "Charles Chawner and the Missionary Impulse of the Hebden Mission." In *Winds from the North: Canadian Contributions to the Pentecostal Movement*, ed. Michael Wilkinson and Peter Althouse, 39–54. Leiden and Boston: Brill.

Hermeneutics

KENNETH J. ARCHER

Hermeneutics is the study of the methodological principles of interpretation. The various activities associated with this include explaining, translating, evaluating, and judging the value and the truthfulness of the claims being made in the communicative event. In hermeneutics, scholars can define the theories associated with interpretation and also describe the phenomenon of understanding.

Hermeneutics can also be seen as the art and science of interpretation, with the primary goal of coming to a proper understanding. As a science it is concerned with methods, procedures, and linguistic rules governing communication. Scholars use particular strategies in order to get at the meaning of the communicative event. Linguistic rules help to reduce misunderstanding and to establish possible legitimate meanings involved in the interpretation process. But simply following the rules is not enough to arrive at a proper interpretation. Hermeneutics cannot be reduced to just the rules, even though it is governed by certain rules; it is the process of interpretation, and therefore, it is also an art.

Hermeneutics as an art affirms the necessity of human involvement. There is a need for the listener to demonstrate sensitivity and patiently engage in active, reflective listening skills. Such sensitivity recognizes that one person desires to communicate something to another. Hermeneutics encourages awareness, in order to recognize the other person's intention to communicate, and affirms the responsibility of the one interpreting to listen attentively to the other person's act of communication, on that person's terms.

Also, awareness of one's own involvement in the communicative process, along with the particular concerns of the interpreter, is an essential contribution to human understanding. Even though hermeneutics claims to be a science, interpretation is never neutral, nor a purely objective procedure. Contemporary discussions concerning hermeneutics have demonstrated that the way in which communication takes place, how communication functions, and the understanding arrived at through the communicative event often perpetuate certain biases on behalf of both the sender (which are embedded in the text) and the receiver (who determines the true meaning of the text). Hermeneutics is the art of understanding as well as the rules for interpretation. It denotes the academic critical reflection upon the processes of human interpretation and understanding.

The particular focus of hermeneutics has traditionally been upon religious texts, especially those originating in a different culture and language from those of the scholars wishing to interpret the text. The goal is to discern and transfer proper understanding of the text from its original senders to its current receivers—from one place, time, or language to another. The practice of interpreting recognizes the distance between the text and the reader in terms of language, cultural influences, customs, and worldview. Furthermore, this becomes more challenging with the historical passage of time.

Eventually, with the aid of philosophical hermeneutics, scholars of contemporary hermeneutics address this distance through the notion of horizon. The term "horizon" denotes the distance from the then-and-there to the here-and-now. The first horizon refers to the particular origin, location, language, and point of view of the text. The second horizon refers to the perspective or particular point of view of the receiving individual, limited by his or her location in time and space, rooted in a particular culture, and shaped by life experiences. The interpreters engage in dialogue with the text allowing it to fulfill its contribution to the communicative event. The interpreter's horizon of understanding can be expanded as a result of interpreting the text. Furthermore, I would make a clear distinction between the terms "meaning" and "understanding." I can understand atheistic writings, for example, but they may not be meaningful for me. "Meaning" here has to do with incorporating real understanding into one's interpretation of ultimate reality, which influences the way one lives one's life. Hermeneutics as a form of study, therefore, is a way of life, a learning, an expansion, and an apprehension of understanding. Hermeneutics is concerned with communication, historical distance, linguistic significance, and epistemological issues pertaining to the meaning of texts.

The academic discipline of hermeneutics has been enriched considerably by biblical hermeneutics, which is concerned with interpretation of a specific corpus of texts contained in the Bible. Biblical interpretation arose out of the Jewish and Christian communities' desire to interpret Scripture correctly. Biblical hermeneutics draws upon various disciplines, but its primary goal is to arrive at a proper understanding of the text, so its scholars investigate the various ways in which we read, understand, apply, and respond to biblical texts.

The terms "exegesis" and "application" are often used in discussing biblical interpretation. "Exegesis" means exposition or explanation, especially an explanation or critical interpretation of a text. Acceptable exegetical methods might be used to arrive at the meaning of the text, generally in an attempt to get at what the author intended the text to mean, with the goal of exegesis being to discover what the text means. For Christian readers of the Bible, this is not enough. Christians desire to live their lives in light of the sacred Scriptures. Thus, one has to apply the past meaning of the text to one's present situation.

Current discussions of biblical hermeneutics appreciate that arriving at an understanding of a text has a lot to do with where the interpreter locates meaning. Should meaning be located in the mind of the author of the text, in the text itself, in the mind of the reader, or in a combination of all of these? If one understands meaning to be located in the author's intention, then one uses academic, historical-critical methods to find what lies behind the text, and the Bible is viewed, then, as an ancient artifact. If one locates meaning within the text itself, one uses literary methods, and the Bible is viewed as a work of art. If one locates meaning in the mind of the reader, then one uses reader-response methods, and the Bible is viewed as an ongoing conversation. All these methods have merit, but they are never void of the interpreter's pre-understandings, nor are they all equally concerned with arriving at a present, meaningful appropriation of the text.

When discussing biblical hermeneutics, the interpreters, the methods, and their interpretation should all be critically considered. What is essential to this process is that it is an activity of communication. The text intends to communicate to its readers; thus, basic communication theory, grammatical rules of the languages, distance, and the pre-understanding of the interpreter, all contribute to the process of understanding the text. The notion of the two horizons discussed above is as helpful to the process of biblical interpretation as it is to the more philosophical concerns of human understanding.

Pentecostal identity, experience, and theology are all directly connected to the book of Acts. Simply put, if the book of Acts was not in the Bible, there would be no modern Pentecostal movement. The importance of Luke-Acts and its proper interpretation became the exegetical battleground for Pentecostals. The belief in the baptism in the Holy Spirit accompanied with the biblical evidence of speaking in tongues was one of the most debated features of the Pentecostal movement.

The development of Pentecostal biblical hermeneutics has moved through three stages: an early pre-critical period (1900 into the 1940s), the modern period (1940s into the early 1980s), and the contemporary period (1980s through the present). Although this discussion proceeds in a linear fashion, the three stages in the process do overlap. The pre-critical period describes the hermeneutic employed by early Pentecostal leaders. It was in the modern period that Pentecostals began to earn degrees more frequently from accredited post-secondary institutions where they were first exposed to academic concepts of biblical interpretation. The contemporary period describes the current state of Pentecostal biblical hermeneutics, which is defined by the work of formally educated and academically trained Pentecostal interpreters of Scripture.

The first stage of Pentecostal interpretation was the Bible reading method, the same interpretive procedure as was used by the Holiness traditions. This was a pre-critical, commonsense interpretive approach, which assumed that the Bible could be read in a straightforward manner and could be understood by the common person. The Bible reading method relied upon inductive and deductive interpretive reasoning. The inductive approach focused upon the text. A verse of Scripture was interpreted in its immediate literary context, then within the larger context (such as the chapter), and then within the book, and so on. Deductive interpretation required that all the biblical data available on a particular topic, such as Spirit baptism, be examined. The information would be harmonized into a cohesive synthesis. The deductive process involved looking up a specific word in an English Bible concordance, compiling an exhaustive list of the verses where the word appeared, and deducing a biblical truth based on the reading of the texts. The Bible reading method encouraged a synchronic interpretive strategy, which removed all the verses that related to a particular word or topic from their original contexts and placed them together where they could be studied as a unified whole. This method, along with their non-cessationist worldview (the idea that the gifts of the Spirit did not end with the early church), enabled Pentecostals to affirm that Spirit baptism signified by speaking in other tongues was for today. This experiential biblical doctrine was based upon a careful—yet pre-critical—inductive-deductive interpretation of the book of Acts. The Bible reading method was the primary interpretive method used by early Pentecostals for preaching and the formation of doctrine.

The second stage of Pentecostal biblical hermeneutics began as Pentecostals entered the academic arena. They were educated in accepted, modernistic, biblical interpretive practices. There was a shift away from the Bible reading method to historical-critical methodologies. Pentecostals became more modern in their academic education and more mainstream evangelical in their interpretive practices. The modern historical-critical methods raised issues pertaining to the historical accuracy of the Bible and its presentation of God. The focus was on the world behind the text. The historical events that gave rise to the text, the written sources, and oral forms of information incorporated into the text, all became the focus. The historical-critical methods were to be scientifically based and historically verifiable. Truth had to meet the epistemological standards of the day. Only what could be scientifically and historically verifiable would be considered true.

Pentecostals accepted many of the basic principles of historical criticism, yet they rejected the naturalistic worldview of modernity. When interpreting the final form of the biblical text, Pentecostals used an interpretive approach called the historical-grammatical method. This methodology, and the presuppositions guiding it, had been practiced by evangelicals. Historical-grammatical exegesis was an adaptation of historical criticism. The interpreter was trained in exegetical interpretation, was able to read the Bible in its original languages, and could translate the original into the receptive language, a kind of streamlined exegetical process. He or she was capable of identifying the sociohistorical influences upon the author, and possibly some of the circumstances that led to the production of the text. The goal was to arrive objectively at the author's intended meaning. Once readers discovered the author's meaning, as communicated through the text, then they would apply it to their current situation. They affirmed a clear distinction between what a text meant for the original or first audience (the past understanding of the text), and what it meant for their own Christian community (the present application). The present application was based upon a deduced principle. The text had one past determinate meaning. The one past meaning, however, had multiple applications.

The historical-grammatical method did not resolve the issues that some Pentecostals had concerning Spirit baptism. Prior to this stage, some Pentecostals had rejected tongues as the initial sign of Spirit baptism while still maintaining that Spirit baptism was a distinct and separate experience following regeneration. The modern academic interpretive methods moved some Pentecostal scholars to abandon tongues as initial evidence. Some would abandon Spirit baptism as a subsequent experience altogether.

A corollary was that most academic evangelical scholars, including some Pentecostals, argued that the book of Acts was simply a historical narrative. As a historical narrative, it was a descriptive account of the early church. Because it was a descriptive historical narrative, they argued, Christian doctrine should not be based upon it. Thus, even though Acts highlights Spirit baptism as a subsequent experience to regeneration, it is not an experience intended for today. The story of Acts was about the past, and how the Gentiles came to be included in the Christian community. Yet, other academically educated Pentecostals—using the same method— have maintained the traditional Pentecostal doctrines. The question raised is what kind of genre a biblical book needed to be in order to base doctrine upon it. Not only was the interpretive method under consideration but now the very book from which Pentecostals based their experiential identity was under question.

The historical-grammatical method (exegesis) became the primary method used by many Pentecostals. A notable advancement within historical methods was the development of redaction criticism. Unlike the other historical-critical methods, redaction criticism emphasizes a close reading of the final form of the biblical book with the goal of discerning the theological intention of the author. This method was applied to Luke and Acts with fruitful results. Using redaction criticism, some argued that Luke's theology of Spirit baptism as articulated in the Gospel of Luke and Acts is different from Paul's understanding as presented in his letters. For Pentecostal scholars it was important to show how the two understandings were complementary and not contradictory. Redaction criticism also affirmed the value of Acts as a theological document. Acts, like the Gospels, was both descriptive and prescriptive; thus, narrative (the genre of Acts) as well as the New Testament epistles could be utilized for the development of contemporary Christian doctrine.

The modern stage demonstrated that Pentecostals could fully engage in critical academic methods and yet still maintain traditional Pentecostal doctrine. For Pentecostals, a correct interpretation of Scripture was essential to Christian faith and practice. During the modern period, Pentecostals engaged in textual criticism, began writing academic commentaries, and produced more formal theological textbooks.

The modern stage of Pentecostal interpretation of the Bible paralleled the stages of development in academic universities. Literary interpretation of Scripture began to emerge in university biblical studies departments. Literary methods such as redaction criticism are concerned with the interpretation of the final form of the biblical text. The location of meaning moved from the author's world to the world of the text. Literary methods can be concerned with historical questions, but the focus is always on the text. Some Pentecostal biblical scholars embraced literary methods. They welcomed the newer methods associated with literary approaches because these engaged the text.

The issue of a distinct Pentecostal hermeneutic and experience also came to the forefront of discussions during this time. Although the literary methods and the initial quest for a distinctly Pentecostal interpretive method was part of the later modern age, in a broad way this signaled a new stage of development in Pentecostal biblical interpretation. The stages do overlap, especially the later modern and early contemporary periods.

The present, contemporary stage of development embraces more post-critical and postmodern approaches. Literary approaches (what the text is communicating and how it is communicating this), reader-response approaches (what impact the text has upon the reader community), and advocacy hermeneutics (how the socioeconomic and ethnic makeup of interpreters leads to "seeing" and "hearing" things in the text that others miss), all can be combined in a number of different ways. Various methodologies, especially those that focus on the final form of the text, have proved beneficial to Pentecostal academic communities and are more in step with the Pentecostal pre-critical stage.

During the contemporary stage, Pentecostals also had the opportunity to engage in broader issues of hermeneutics. No longer was there a quest for identifying "one" proper interpretive method. Although methodology is indeed important to the interpretive process, method alone is insufficient to arrive at a proper understanding of the meaning of a text. Methods serve various purposes. By its very nature a method can only achieve the particular function it serves. The broader concerns of hermeneutics have led to a reexamination of Pentecostal identity and the role this identity plays in the interpretive process. One can no longer dismiss the current, particular horizon of the interpretive community. This leads to an examination of the interpreters and the role of experience—and how these might point to methodologies that are more conducive to the community's needs and experiences.

Current Pentecostal debates about hermeneutics recognize the importance of the interpretive community. Who is reading and listening to the biblical text? What redemptive experiences have they had or not had? Equally important is the role of the Holy Spirit. How does the community go about discerning the voice of God in the interpretive process? The Spirit is still speaking and has more to say than simply quoting a verse of Scripture. Thus, pneumatological interpretation, human experiences, the importance of Luke-Acts as guiding Pentecostal theology, and theological methodology, all remain contemporary hermeneutical concerns.

I have argued that a distinct Pentecostal interpretive method does not exist. Pentecostals have used various interpretive methods and maintained basic core Christian doctrines. The distinction does not lie so much in the method as in the community using the method. A distinct Pentecostal hermeneutic does exist, because there are Pentecostal readers and interpreters. Pentecostals' common story, shared charismatic experiences, and expressive dynamic worship practices, all generate a particular hermeneutical community. I have also argued that a Pentecostal hermeneutical strategy would want to negotiate the meaning of a text through a conversation between the Holy Spirit, community, and Scripture.

Pentecostals have always believed that the Bible cannot mean whatever one wants it to mean. Many people, including Pentecostals, have misunderstood Scripture. An interpretive exegetical method that pays close attention to the final form of the text—and in conversation with the reading community—is the most beneficial for Pentecostal hermeneutics. In this way the text's intention to communicate to its readers is affirmed, while simultaneously, the community's responsibility to participate in the process is also affirmed. The goal is to understand the text as the Spirit inspires the community to discern the meaning for today. The heart of Pentecostal hermeneutics is conversation with God, Scripture, and the community. The goal is to nurture virtuous reading communities that can discern the leading of the Spirit. The desire has always been to be faithful followers of Jesus ministering to the world through the powerful presence of the Holy Spirit. A Pentecostal hermeneutic is concerned with properly interpreting Scripture as it proclaims and incarnates the full gospel of Jesus Christ.

References and Suggestions for Further Reading

Archer, Kenneth J. 1996. "Pentecostal Hermeneutics: Retrospect and Prospect." *Journal of Pentecostal Theology* (4)8: 63–81.

———. 2004. *A Pentecostal Hermeneutic for the Twenty-First Century: Spirit, Scripture and Community.* London: T&T Clark.

Gorman, Michael J. 2001. *Elements of Biblical Exegesis: A Basic Guide for Students and Ministers.* Peabody, MA: Hendrickson.

McKnight, Scott. 2008. *The Blue Parakeet: Rethinking How to Read the Bible.* Grand Rapids, MI: Zondervan.

Mittelstadt, Martin William. 2010. *Reading Luke-Acts in the Pentecostal Tradition.* Cleveland, TN: CPT Press.

Tate, W. Randolph. 1997. *Biblical Interpretation: An Integrated Approach.* Revised edition. Peabody, MA: Hendrickson.

Thiselton, Anthony C. 2009. *Hermeneutics: An Introduction.* Grand Rapids, MI: Eerdmans.

Thomas, John Christopher. 2009. "'Where the Spirit Leads'—the Development of Pentecostal Hermeneutics." *Journal of Beliefs and Values* 30(3): 289–302.

Holiness Movement

ADAM STEWART

✂ The Wesleyan Holiness movement, arising out of American Methodism, made what was probably the most important contribution to the development of Pentecostal Christianity. The Holiness movement forms one part of a wide collection of movements within what can be called nineteenth-century "Higher Life" revivalism, also including Charles Finney's Oberlin School of Perfectionism (in addition to the thought of Oberlin College's first president, Asa Mahan), and the Keswick movement, which both emphasized a transformative spiritual experience following conversion and leading to moral purity and victory over sin. While these and other movements certainly did influence (just as they themselves were influenced by) the Holiness movement, they are best thought of as distinct, rather than synonymous, religious movements. Oberlin Perfectionism and the Keswick movement, for instance, are distinguished from the Holiness movement, as Donald Dayton writes, by their "context in Reformed theology" and "emphasis on gradual rather than instantaneous sanctification" (Dayton 1985, 23). Because of the significant historical and theological differences between these and other Higher Life movements, the focus here is on this distinctive Wesleyan Holiness movement. Readers interested in learning more about these Reformed expressions of Higher Life revivalism are directed to Allan Anderson's essay on the Keswick movement also found in this volume.

The Holiness movement has complex beginnings, but its genesis is found in the thought of the founder of Methodism, John Wesley (1703–1791). Wesley taught that after conversion (a first work of grace in the order of salvation), the Christian can undergo a second work or "blessing," called sanctification, through which God is able to eradicate the desire to sin, thus enabling the Christian to live a life of "perfect love" toward God and others. Wesley believed that this work was both a process of gradual growth in holiness and a distinct event, during which the individual achieves perfection from sin in an instantaneous crisis experience. Often the more gradual process of growth in holiness held to within mainstream Methodism is simply called sanctification, while the crisis experience that predominated within the Holiness movement is referred to as "entire sanctification." Although Wesley strived for this second blessing himself, he nowhere claims to have experienced it; he also believed that many people do not receive this experience until just prior to death.

In the decades following Wesley's death, many Methodist teachers and preachers—most notably, perhaps, Timothy Merritt (1775–1845)—continued to purvey the doctrine of entire sanctification or perfect love. It was not, however, until the 1830s that this aspect of Wesley's holiness doctrine became a mainstream religious concept and was subsequently exported throughout revivalist networks in the United States, Canada, and Great Britain. The most important early proponent of holiness theology was Phoebe Palmer (1807–1874), a Methodist and physician's wife. Palmer was introduced to the experience of entire sanctification (or, as she initially called it, "rest of soul") through her sister Sarah Lankford, who received the second blessing on 21 May 1835 and subsequently began to hold prayer meetings in her home in New York City, which became known as the Tuesday Meetings for the Promotion of Holiness. It was at one of these prayer meetings that Palmer herself experienced the second blessing on 26 July 1837. Before long, news of the Tuesday Meetings spread throughout the city, sometimes attracting hundreds of participants and necessitating a change in venue. Palmer emerged from these meetings as one of the most sought-after speakers and popular evangelists in Anglo-America.

What made Palmer's theology unique on the nineteenth-century religious landscape was her teaching that sanctification was not something that took a lifetime of prayerful persistence to achieve but, rather, that the New Testament (Mt 23:19; Heb 13:10) promised sanctification could be received in an instant upon "the altar" where one can ask and receive this second blessing with assurance. An example of Palmer's "altar theology" reads, "On everyone who will specifically present himself upon the altar . . . for the sole object of being ceaselessly consumed, body and soul in the self-sacrificing service of God, He will cause the fire to descend. And . . . he will not delay to do this for every waiting soul, for He standeth waiting, and the moment the offerer presents the sacrifice, the hallowing, consuming touch will be given" (quoted in Dieter 1996, 24). Palmer's adaptation of Wesley's theology eventually came to comprise the dominant, though certainly not uncontested, understanding of how to achieve the second blessing of entire sanctification within both the Holiness and the broader Methodist movements.

The renewal of the crisis or instantaneous component of Wesley's doctrine of sanctification was successfully diffused across Anglo-American Christianity through the work of Palmer and other Holiness evangelists and teachers during the early to mid-nineteenth century. The Holiness movement, however, achieved a level of prominence following the American Civil War (1861–1865), and lasting until about the end of the nineteenth century, that greatly surpassed these earlier decades. The conclusion of the war saw the organization of a ten-day camp meeting in Vineland, New Jersey, beginning on 17 July 1867, with the purpose of promoting the teaching of entire sanctification. The camp meeting was spearheaded by the Methodists William Osborn (1832–1902) and John Inskip (1816–1884) and drew thousands of visitors from across the United States and Canada. Given the success of the first camp meeting, a committee was subsequently formed to organize a future meeting, which resulted in the formation of the National Camp Meeting Association for the Promotion of Holiness, and the selection of Inskip as its president. A total of fifty-two national camp meetings were held by the association between 1867 and 1883, some of which were attended by as many as twenty-five thousand participants.

It is important to note that, in the postbellum period, Holiness theology was widely adhered to within most segments of Methodism and many other Christian denominations. Many prominent individuals were often in attendance, such as U.S. President Ulysses Grant, who attended the camp meeting held in Round Lake, New York, in 1874 (Synan 1997, 26). The National Camp Meeting Association for the Promotion of Holiness was more than merely a camp-meeting committee. It eventually became a full-fledged interdenominational Holiness organization, which sent out foreign missionaries, operated its own press, and encouraged the development of a plethora of state and regional Holiness associations through the United States and Canada. The organization would later change its name to the National Holiness Association and, more recently, to the Christian Holiness Association, in order to reflect these broader institutional objectives.

Several decades before the emergence of Pentecostalism in the twentieth century, Holiness adherents referred to the second blessing of entire sanctification using the "Pentecostal" term "the baptism of the Holy Spirit." By using this terminology, however, these Holiness Christians were not implying (as would today most likely be assumed) that this second blessing necessarily included the experience of speaking in tongues. To be clear, some members of the Holiness movement did indeed speak in tongues, but they did not make an explicit evidentiary connection between the second blessing and tongues speech. It was the Canadian Holiness preacher R. C. Horner who was primarily responsible for suggesting that the two terms Holiness adherents frequently used to refer to the second blessing— "sanctification" and "the baptism of the Holy Spirit"—actually formed their own distinct works of grace. Horner remained firmly committed to the traditional Methodist belief that the second blessing of sanctification provided perfection from sin. But he also believed that a third blessing following sanctification could provide the believer with power for evangelistic service, resulting in three distinct works of grace: (1) conversion or justification, (2) sanctification, and (3) the baptism of the Holy Spirit. This was one of the most important theological developments that contributed to the eventual formation of Pentecostalism, as it established the baptism of the Holy Spirit as a distinct event in the life of the believer, which needed only to include the condition of speaking in tongues as a means of assurance in order to distinguish itself theologically from Methodism and the Holiness movement (Dayton 1987, 98–100).

The Holiness movement enjoyed nearly three decades of renewed popularity between the years 1867 and 1894. Beginning in the 1880s, however, a growing number of Methodist leaders became uncomfortable with the Holiness movement, partly because of the autonomous nature of the National Holiness Association, which sidestepped the authority of Methodist Church officials, and the preponderance of heterodox teaching and practice among some Holiness teachers and adherents (Synan 1997, 35–37). In the mid-1890s, this uneasiness culminated in many Methodist denominations' either discouraging or condemning altogether the Holiness teaching of entire sanctification, which spurred the development of several new Holiness denominations. These included the Church of the Nazarene, formed in 1895 by Phineas Bresee (1838–1915) and Joseph Widney (1841–1938), and the Pilgrim Holiness Church, founded in 1897 by Martin Knapp (1853–1901), which, along with the Alliance of Reformed Baptists of Canada, later joined the Wesleyan Church, founded in 1843 by Orange Scott (1800–1847) under the original name of the Wesleyan Methodist Connection. It should now be clear that, as Donald Dayton notes, "Pentecostalism cannot be understood apart from its deep roots in the Methodism experience" (2009, 171). The Holiness movement and its many advocates provided not only the terminology, theological concepts, and religious practices but also many of the earliest adherents that made up the Pentecostal movement and contributed to its success as a global religion in the twentieth and twenty-first centuries.

REFERENCES AND SUGGESTIONS FOR FURTHER READING

Dayton, Donald W. 1985. "The American Holiness Movement: A Bibliographic Introduction." In *The Christian Higher Life: A Bibliographic Overview*, ed. Donald W. Dayton, 1–56. New York: Garland.

———. 1987. *Theological Roots of Pentecostalism*. Peabody, MA: Hendrickson.

———. 2009. "Methodism and Pentecostalism." In *The Oxford Handbook of Methodist Studies*, ed. William J. Abraham and James L. Kirby, 171–87. New York: Oxford University Press.

Dieter, Melvin Easterday. 1996. *The Holiness Revival of the Nineteenth Century*. Second edition. Lanham, MD: Scarecrow Press.

Kostlevy, William. 2009. *Historical Dictionary of the Holiness Movement*. Second edition. Lanham, MD: Scarecrow Press.

Stephens, Randall J. 2008. *The Fire Spreads: Holiness and Pentecostalism in the American South*. Cambridge, MA: Harvard University Press.

Synan, Vinson. 1997. *The Holiness-Pentecostal Tradition: Charismatic Movements in the Twentieth Century*. Second edition. Grand Rapids, MI: Eerdmans.

Holy Spirit

KEITH WARRINGTON

✄   In both the New and Old Testaments the Holy Spirit is particularly identified in relationship with believers. Since the Spirit indwells Christians and is God (Rom 8:27), he relationally bonds them to God (Eph 2:18), functioning with Jesus as a mediator (1 Tm 2:4–5) between them and God. Thus, the Holy Spirit inspires and fills, empowers and encourages, supports and affirms all Christians in an immanent and ongoing interchange. Although he is supraspatial and supratemporal, he is also intimately present with every Christian. Of fundamental importance to Pentecostals is the fact that the Spirit is to be encountered and experienced. When Paul sought to remind his readers of the validity of their salvation, he reminded them of the activity of the Spirit in their lives (Gal 3:2). Similarly, Paul asked the Ephesian disciples whether they had received the Spirit (Acts 19:2), indicating that he expected them to know whether this was the case or not.

The following aspects of the Spirit and, in particular, his experiential and empowering dimensions are of importance to Pentecostals, though most of these are also held in common with other Christians:

(1)   The Holy Spirit is a separate person in the Godhead (Mt 28:19; Lk 1:35), worthy of worship, equal in honor with the Father and the Son, independent and interdependent, functioning separately on occasions, though in harmony and unity at all times. As such, the Spirit is involved in a number of significant occasions, including creation (Gn 1:2; Ps 104:30), regeneration and renewal (Ti 3:5), and eschatological renewal (Is 44:3–5). Although a variety of descriptions are offered for the Spirit such as Spirit of God (1 Cor 2:11), Holy Spirit (Acts 16:6), Holy Spirit of God (Eph 4:30), and Spirit of Jesus (Acts 16:7), only one person is being referred to.

(2)   The Holy Spirit is by definition set apart, the term "holy" (*hagios*) best being translated as a reference to his uniqueness, rather than merely his sinlessness.

(3)   The coming of the Spirit at Pentecost (Acts 2:1–4) was a vitally significant event. Although the Spirit functioned in the lives of people in the Old Testament era (Ps 51:11) and lived with believers before Pentecost (Jn 14:16–17), he did not empower the church as a whole until the day of Pentecost. The ministry of the Spirit on behalf of and through believers is much more comprehensive after Pentecost than before (Eph 1:3, 13–14).

(4)   The Spirit exalts and inspires worship and belief in Jesus (Jn 4:23–24; 1 Jn 4:2, 6).

(5)   The Spirit is a personal, immediate, dynamic, and perfect guide. He speaks—and so must be listened to. This demands developing a

personal relationship with him, learning to recognize and respond to his guidance (Jn 14:16–17, 26, 15:26, 16:7). Reliance on a relationship with the creative, dynamic, and personal Spirit demands trust, honesty, maturity, and a determination to listen to the rarely silent Spirit. In Ephesians 1:17, Paul also describes the role of the Spirit as enabling believers to know, accurately and experientially, certain aspects of truth concerning God, particularly relating to their salvation.

(6) The Spirit is involved in the process of salvation (1 Cor 6:11, 12:3, 13), convicting people of sin (Jn 16:8, 9), and setting believers apart (1 Pt 1:2). The Spirit releases the believer from the power of sin and death (Rom 8:2; as forecast in Ez 36:26–28) and enables people to enter the kingdom of God (Jn 3:5–7), and to participate in eternal life (Jn 4:14).

(7) The Spirit affirms the believer in a variety of ways. As in the Old Testament, the Spirit authenticates those he chooses (Nm 11:25; 1 Sm 19:18–24), enabling believers to know they are adopted as children of God (Rom 8:9, 14–17; Gal 4:6).

(8) He proactively transforms believers ethically (2 Cor 3:16–18, 6:6–7), which results in their exhibiting godly lifestyles (Gal 3:3, 5:16–25; 1 Pt 1:2).

(9) The Spirit is a limitless resource for believers with regard to their spirituality. One of the keywords relating to Pentecostals is "power," and one of the most important verses for them (Acts 1:8) identifies "power" as that which follows an experience with the Spirit. Pentecostals have recognized that a specific empowering role of the Spirit is prophecy, or proclamation, sometimes in evangelism (Mk 12:35–37; Acts 2:4, 4:8). The Spirit provides resources for all believers and expects these to be used, and used sensitively, for every task he sets. Thus, he diversely distributes gifts (Rom 1:11, 12:6–8) for the benefit of all in the development of the church, both inspiring and initiating evangelism (Acts 1:8, 4:8, 6:10), preaching (Lk 4:14–19), prophecy (Lk 1:41–45, 67–79, 2:25–32), and other charismata (1 Cor 12:4–11, 27–31) including strength (Jgs 14:6, 19), leadership (Gn 41:38), military authority (Jgs 6:34), skill (Ex

31:3–4), and wisdom (Dn 5:14). Not only are the gifts of the Spirit bestowed by the Spirit to believers, but he also manifests himself through those gifts. They are not derived remotely from a distance as a result of divine initiation from heaven so much as resulting from his being present in believers.

(10) The Spirit is the source of spiritual cleansing (Rom 15:16; 1 Cor 6:11) and righteousness (Rom 2:29, 14:17). The Spirit expects believers to be active in improving their lifestyles (Eph 5:18–19). If they are controlled by him, they will benefit from his influential presence, his fruit being personally and corporately experienced, and their lifestyles will increasingly become reflective of his character (Gal 5:22–6:1). It is the pathway of Paul who also encourages his readers to "live by the Spirit" (Gal 5:25), "walk by the Spirit" (Gal 5:16, 25), and "be filled with the Spirit" (Eph 5:18), as a result of which they will develop godly lifestyles.

(11) The Spirit, who establishes the church as a body (1 Cor 3:16–17), is committed to unity (Phil 1:27, 2:1–2), and believers are to maintain unity, recognizing that the aim of the Spirit is to welcome people from all backgrounds, and to shed the love of God through each one (2 Cor 13:14; Eph 4:3). As such, the Spirit establishes a new community. The Day of Pentecost provided the basis for a nationally undivided community, demonstrated by the expansion of the Christian community to include Samaritans and even Gentiles; those outside have now been included. The gift of tongues and the sign of fire, exhibited on the day of Pentecost, served to set believers apart and identify them as appropriate recipients of the promise of Joel 2:28–32. The Spirit affirmed those whom others were wishing to exclude.

Where Paul describes the proximity of the Spirit to the believer (Eph 2:18), his expectation is that the readers will realize they are constantly in the presence of God and will learn to enjoy it experientially. It is the Spirit who makes this possible. His desire is to empower and affirm believers, enabling them to serve God and each other more successfully, but also to help them to realize their status, in relationship to God, more accurately.

REFERENCES AND SUGGESTIONS FOR FURTHER READING

Fee, Gordon D. 1994. *God's Empowering Presence: The Holy Spirit in the Letters of Paul.* Peabody, MA: Hendrickson.

Macchia, Frank D. 2006. *Baptized in the Spirit. A Global Pentecostal Theology.* Grand Rapids, MI: Zondervan.

Menzies, Robert P. 1991. *The Development of Early Christian Pneumatology.* Sheffield: Sheffield Academic Press.

Warrington, Keith. 2005. *Discovering the Spirit in the New Testament.* Peabody, MA: Hendrickson.

——. 2009. *The Message of the Holy Spirit.* Leicester, UK: IVP.

Initial Evidence

ROGER J. STRONSTAD

❧   The doctrine of "initial evidence" is the corollary to the doctrine of baptism in the Holy Spirit. The data about initial evidence is found in the context of Luke's reports that Jesus baptized his followers in the Holy Spirit (Acts 1:4–2:21, 8:14–17, 10:1–11:17, 19:1–7). In three of the four Spirit baptism episodes in Acts, Luke reports that when the Spirit was poured out, the disciples "began to speak in other languages, as the Spirit gave them ability" (2:4), were heard "speaking in tongues and extolling God" (10:46), or "spoke in tongues and prophesied" (19:6). Luke uses the term "sign" to describe the purpose or function of speaking in tongues (Acts 2:19).

The term "sign" (*sēmeion*) echoes the sign theme in the Hebrew Scriptures. One function of the sign theme is to attest either to the inauguration of leadership or to the transfer of leadership from an incumbent to a successor. The anointing of Saul, son of Kish, to be Israel's first king is an example of the former. On the day that Samuel anoints Saul as king, Saul's anointing is attested by three signs. The most dramatic of the signs is that the Spirit of God comes upon him powerfully with the result that he prophesies (1 Sm 10:1–13). For Saul, the sign means that God is with him (1 Sm 10:7). The transfer of secondary leadership responsibility from Moses to the seventy elders of Israel also involves the transfer of the Spirit from Moses to the elders. The sign that this transfer is divinely sanctioned is that, when the Spirit rested on the elders, they prophesied (Nm 11:25). The commissioning of the seventy and of Saul illustrates that in Old Testament times prophecy is a typical sign of commissioning, or empowerment (by the Spirit).

What is true of these and other examples of Old Testament commissioning is also true of Luke's theme of Spirit baptism or sign. For example, when Jesus baptizes his followers in the Spirit in Jerusalem to commission them to be worldwide witnesses, they speak in other tongues as the Spirit inspires them (Acts 1:5, 8, 2:4). This sign and the two signs of theophany (the wind and the fire; Acts 2:2–3) attract the attention of a large crowd of international Jewry, who are "bewildered," "amazed," "astonished," and "perplexed" because Jesus' disciples (who are Galileans) are speaking in the "native language" of this international Jewry (Acts 2:5–8). Seizing the opportunity, Peter identifies the sign to be one type of prophecy, which the prophet Joel prophesied about (Acts 2:14–21). Thus, on the day of Pentecost, Jesus has transferred leadership from himself to his disciples, which is attested by the sign of tongues-speaking and prophecy. In other words, on the first post-Easter day of Pentecost, Jesus baptizes his disciples in the Holy Spirit, commissioning, empowering, and "signing" them for their worldwide witness.

In his Acts narrative, Luke illustrates that the Spirit-baptized "commissioning-empowerment-sign" theme is coextensive with the spread of the gospel throughout the empire. For example, Jesus baptizes a household of Gentile believers in Judea (that is, Caesarea Maritima) in the Spirit—attested by the same sign as earlier, on the day of Pentecost, namely, speaking in tongues (Acts 10:44–48, 11:15–16). That this Spirit baptism–speaking in tongues is a commissioning-empowerment experience and not a conversion-initiation experience is confirmed by Peter's insistence that Cornelius and his household of faith have now experienced the same vocational gift as Jesus poured out on the day of Pentecost (11:17).

Luke's day of Pentecost and Cornelius's reports illustrate the following principle. When Jesus announces that he will baptize his followers in the Holy Spirit, the sign that this has happened is that they speak in other tongues, that is, they prophesy (Acts 1:5, 2:4, 17). On the other hand, when disciples such as Peter hear the sign of speaking in tongues, they conclude that a Spirit baptism has taken place (Acts 10:44–48, 11:15–17). Therefore, when Luke reports that believers in Samaria have received the Holy Spirit and also reports that an observer "saw" a sign that this happened, his readership is justified in concluding that a Spirit baptism has taken place, and also that the sign is that they have spoken in tongues. Similarly, when Luke reports that believers in Ephesus have spoken in tongues and prophesied, the same thing that the disciples experienced on the day of Pentecost, Luke's readership is justified in concluding that the sign means, once again, that Jesus has baptized his followers in the Holy Spirit.

These data show that the doctrine of initial evidence does not stand alone. It is the third element in divine commissioning, which includes (1) anointing/baptizing, (2) empowering, and (3) an authenticating sign. Saul is an Old Testament example of this commissioning process. First, Samuel anoints Saul (1 Sm 10:1); second, the Spirit of God empowers Saul (1 Sm 10:10a); and third, Saul prophesies (1 Sm 10:10b–13). Similarly, in New Testament times, the Lord commissions Jesus, anointing him (Lk 4:18), empowering him (Lk 4:14), and authenticating his Messiahship (Lk 3:21–22). The same is true of disciples on the day of Pentecost. Thus, Jesus commissions them, first by baptizing them in the Holy Spirit (Acts 1:5), then by empowering them (Acts 1:8), and finally by authenticating their commissioning with the sign of speaking in other tongues. Luke's subsequent examples in Samaria, Caesarea, and Ephesus, in whole or in part, illustrate that these commissioning elements extend beyond Jesus and his initial disciples to their converts. Peter did get it right. The Father's promise of being baptized in the Holy Spirit (Acts 1:4–5) is for the first generation, their children, and for all who are far off (Acts 2:38)—even extending to global Christianity in the twenty-first century.

References and Suggestions for Further Reading

Blumhofer, Edith L. 1993. *Restoring the Faith: The Assemblies of God, Pentecostalism, and American Culture.* Urbana: University of Illinois Press.

McGee, Gary B., ed. 1991. *Initial Evidence: Historical and Biblical Perspectives on the Pentecostal Doctrine of Spirit Baptism.* Peabody, MA: Hendrickson.

Menzies, William W., and Robert P. Menzies. 2000. *Spirit and Power: Foundations of Pentecostal Experience.* Grand Rapids, MI: Zondervan.

Palma, Anthony D. 2001. *The Holy Spirit: A Pentecostal Perspective.* Springfield, MO: Logion Press.

Wyckoff, John W. 2007. "The Baptism in the Holy Spirit." In *Systematic Theology: A Pentecostal Perspective.* Revised edition, ed. Stanley M. Horton, 423–55. Springfield, MO: Logion Press.

Keswick Movement

ALLAN HEATON ANDERSON

The Keswick Convention, which began annual gatherings in the En-glish Lake District in 1875, recognized two distinct experiences—the "new birth" and the "fullness of the Spirit"—and represented a major influence on Pentecostalism. Although the "fullness of the Spirit" was seen in terms of "holiness" (as the Holiness movement saw it) or the "higher Christian life" (a popular term within the convention), Keswick was more affected by Anglican evangelicalism and the influence of Reformed teachers such as the American Presbyterian A. T. Pierson, and the South African Dutch Reformed revivalist Andrew Murray, Jr., who, for example, taught that sanctification was a possible but progressive experience. Being filled with the fullness of God, Murray wrote, was "the highest aim of the Pentecostal blessing" and was attainable by the believer who prepared for it in humility and faith. Although Murray continued to link the "fullness of the Spirit" with purity and "overcoming sin," he added the new Keswick emphasis on power for service to others, which he called "the full blessing of Pentecost" (Murray [1907] 1954). He described his expectations regarding the restoration of spiritual gifts to the church:

> On the day of Pentecost the speaking "with other tongues" and the prophesying was the result of being filled with the Spirit. Here at Ephesus twenty years later, the very same miracle is again witnessed as the visible token and pledge of the other glorious gifts of the Spirit. We may reckon upon it that where the reception of the Holy Spirit and the possibility of being filled with Him are proclaimed and appropriated, the blessed life of the Pentecostal community will be restored in ALL its pristine power. (Murray 1909)

Increasingly in Holiness and revivalist movements such as Keswick, the phrase "baptism with the Spirit" was used to indicate the "second blessing" that had previously referred to the experience of sanctification. By the end of the nineteenth century, however, Spirit baptism in Keswick and elsewhere was no longer understood primarily in terms of holiness but also as empowering for mission service. Keswick meetings became international events and always featured prominent missionary speakers (including Pandita Ramabai from India), emphasizing the need for the "higher Christian life" in missionary service. Murray, Pierson, and other leaders wrote regular reports to the Christian press on the work of missions. Pierson as editor of the *Missionary Review of the World* was one of the most influential mission motivators in the Western world, regarding missions as the indispensable proof and fruit of all spiritual life. In particular, the change of emphasis was taught by Reuben Torrey, D. L. Moody's junior associate and successor, who wrote that "the Baptism with the Holy Spirit" was a definite experience "distinct from and additional to His regenerating work" and "always connected with and primarily for the purpose of testimony and service" (Torrey 1927, 112, 117). Torrey wrote further that Spirit baptism was "not primarily for the purpose of making us individually holy," and that the power received during Spirit baptism varied according to "a wide variety of manifestations of that one Baptism with that one and same Spirit" (ibid., 119, 122).

Although Torrey endorsed the belief that Spirit baptism would be accompanied by "manifestations" or gifts of the Spirit, he (like Keswick and many others in evangelical revivalist circles) reacted negatively to the new Pentecostal movement and declared that "the teaching that speaking with tongues was the inevitable and invariable result of being baptised with the Holy Spirit" was "utterly unscriptural and anti-scriptural" (ibid., 123). Nevertheless, Torrey's influence on the doctrine of Spirit baptism as being distinct from and subsequent to conversion (the central and most distinctive theme of Pentecostal doctrine) was considerable, and his writings were quoted widely (if selectively) by Pentecostals. By the end of the nineteenth century, the idea had grown that there would be a great outpouring of the Spirit throughout the world before the second coming of Christ—and it was hoped, at the beginning of the twentieth century—and that those upon whom the Spirit had fallen were to prepare for this by offering themselves for missionary service. Mission was thereby given a new pneumatological and eschatological dimension that was to become the preoccupation of early Pentecostals.

By the turn of the century, there were three distinct groups of Holiness adherents. First, there was the Wesleyan Holiness position typified by Phoebe Palmer, who said that "entire sanctification" or "perfect love" was the "second blessing," or baptism with the Spirit, and identified it with moral purity. Second was the Reformed and Keswick position, best expressed by Torrey, who held that the baptism with the Spirit was an enduement with power for service. Torrey would add that there would be evidence of some manifestation of the Spirit—a position with which Pentecostals heartily agreed. Third was the "third blessing." This was a radical fringe position, which had both the "second blessing" of sanctification and a "third blessing" of "baptism with fire"—again an enduement with power. The first American Pentecostals were to follow this third position, but they equated the "third blessing" with "baptism with the Spirit," usually evidenced by speaking in tongues. All these different Holiness and evangelical groups made mission service their highest priority. They were the sources out of which Pentecostalism gradually surfaced as a distinct movement.

REFERENCES AND SUGGESTIONS FOR FURTHER READING

Dayton, Donald W. 1987. *Theological Roots of Pentecostalism*. Peabody, MA: Hendrickson.
Faupel, D. William 1996. *The Everlasting Gospel: The Significance of Eschatology in the Development of Pentecostal Thought*. Sheffield: Sheffield Academic Press.
Murray, Andrew. [1907] 1954. *The Full Blessing of Pentecost*. Basingstoke, UK: Marshall Morgan and Scott.
———. 1909. *The Upper Room*, June.
Robert, Dana. 2003. *Occupy until I Come: A. T. Pierson and the Evangelization of the World*. Cambridge, UK: Eerdmans.
Torrey, R. A. 1927. *The Holy Spirit: Who He Is and What He Does*. Westwood, NJ: Fleming H. Revell.

Latin American Pentecostalism

CALVIN L. SMITH

✖   In his *Introduction to Pentecostalism*, noted Pentecostal historian Allan Anderson (2004, 63) observes how "the growth of Pentecostalism in Latin America has been one of the most remarkable stories in the history of Christianity." Indeed, explosive growth of Latin American Pentecostalism during the last third of the twentieth century has captivated scholars from across the humanities and social sciences, generating considerable research and an extensive body of scholarly literature. The aim of this brief article is to highlight the history, nature, and diverse political expressions of Latin American Pentecostalism.

Protestantism arrived late in Latin America, because it was regarded by Spain as a subversive political ideology that threatened her hold over her colonies. Yet with independence, liberal elites across the continent—keen to emulate the advancement of liberal Anglo-Saxon nations (particularly the United States) and curb the societal role of the Roman Catholic Church—introduced religious reforms that ultimately opened up the continent to Protestantism, which liberal leaders regarded as a religion of progress.

The arrival of Protestant missionaries at the beginning of the twentieth century coincided with the emergence of the new Pentecostal movement in the United States. Pentecostalism's symbiosis of pneumatology (theology of the Holy Spirit) and eschatology (theology of the end times) contributed to an urgent evangelistic movement, which sought to spread the gospel before the imminent return of Christ. Given Latin America's proximity to the United States, it was inevitable that the new Pentecostals should urgently set about evangelizing the region, and soon small groups of missionaries began arriving in different countries across the continent.

Initially, growth was slow, hampered by fierce Catholic resistance and persecution. Yet by the middle of the century, modest Pentecostal gains were being consolidated, while citywide evangelization campaigns in the 1950s and 1960s contributed to further growth. The Second Vatican Council (1962–1965) softened Catholicism's antagonism toward Protestantism, consequently conversions to Pentecostalism attracted less social stigma than before, which resulted in yet further growth. By the 1980s the exponential growth experienced by the movement captured the current academic interest in the phenomenon.

Statistics highlighting Pentecostalism's success in Latin America are startling. For example, Pentecostals are believed to represent around 13–15 percent of the total population in Mexico, and about 20 percent in Nicaragua, while several surveys suggest that renewalists (Pentecostals, Charismatics, and Neo-Pentecostals combined) in Chile and El Salvador may represent over 30 percent of the population. Brazilian Pentecostals have been estimated at nearly 50 percent—and in Guatemala, a massive 60 percent. At this stage it is important to note how some of the more spectacular statistics have been challenged on the basis of the methodology underpinning them (that is, an overreliance on extrapolations, or how one actually defines a Pentecostal), while both triumphalism and exaggeration for political reasons also contribute to inflation. Yet rogue statistics aside, there can be no doubt of Pentecostalism's numerical strength and success in Latin America, home to some of the world's largest megachurches, and with templos in almost every poor barrio across the continent.

For Catholic leaders and Marxist analysts, mushrooming Latin American Pentecostalism represents an ideological and cultural invasion, even a social prop for regimes supported by Washington, thus accounting for considerable North American funding. Yet such an analysis ignores how early liberal leaders contributed to the rise of Protestantism, which is as much an endogenous as an exogenous phenomenon. Neither was there ever a Pentecostal invasion in the true sense of the word. Rather, the evidence suggests a small influx of missionaries, often individuals or man-and-wife teams, barely surviving on subsistence-level funding, while the seminal work on Latin American Protestantism by David Stoll argues that the funding argument is inadequate and overstated (1990). Moreover, if Pentecostals represented a social prop for some military or pro-Washington regimes, they seemed to get very little in return (for example, consider Nicaragua, where the Somoza regime failed to protect Pentecostals from Catholic persecution). Finally, such arguments ignore the emergence of autochthonous Pentecostalism that originated locally, which contributes to an understanding of the diverse political expressions of the movement across Latin America (discussed below).

It is important to differentiate between classical Pentecostalism arising out of the Azusa Street revival in Los Angeles (1906–1909), which is often found in the poorer barrios, and the urban, middle-class Neo-Pentecostals. Church services held by the former are often noisy and exuberant, drawing on music incorporating Latin beats, while a culture of orality represents an important defining feature of Latin American Pentecostalism. Meanwhile, the Neo-Pentecostal churches in countries such as Guatemala "are not the product of an oral culture, but are a far more literate style of worship and community with greater rationalization and individualization" (Schultze 1994, 69). Worship is more structured, quite often emulating a North American model.

It is also important to differentiate between Latin American Pentecostals traditionally influenced by North America and autochthonous (indigenous, national, or "homegrown") expressions of Pentecostalism, notably in countries such as Chile and Brazil, which contribute to our understanding of the diverse expressions that make up Latin American Pentecostalism. Because autochthonous Pentecostals have developed separately from their U.S. counterparts, they sometimes exhibit different theological features or emphases and notably different political responses from North American classical Pentecostals. For example, where U.S. influence is strong, Latin American Pentecostals hold firmly to the doctrine of speaking in tongues as the initial evidence of having received the baptism of the Holy Spirit. Yet among autochthonous Pentecostals in Chile, speaking in tongues is not promoted in this way; it is regarded simply as one of various evidences of Spirit baptism. Meanwhile, some autochthonous Pentecostal churches in Latin America are heavily involved in ecumenical dialogue, unlike some of their United States–influenced classical counterparts.

As a result, across Latin America one will find theological divergences, though it is important at this stage to note that Latin American Pentecostalism is also not theologically heterogeneous. Local factors have contributed to different theological expressions of the movement, but a symbiosis of pneumapraxis (experience of the Spirit) and eschatological urgency lies at the core of Latin American Pentecostalism. This is somewhat less so among Charismatics.

More diverse are the various expressions of Latin American Pentecostalism's political responses. For example, in revolutionary Nicaragua, about two-thirds of classical Pentecostals with close ties to North America were suspicious of the Sandinista revolutionary project, while the other third enthusiastically supported it. During the 1970 election in Chile, Pentecostal leaders generally opposed the leftist Salvador Allende, whereas many grassroots Pentecostals voted for him. Meanwhile, in El Salvador, moral conservatism among Pentecostals does not necessarily translate into political conservatism. Thus, Pentecostals have exhibited a range of political views—and indeed, even expressions of liberation theology have emerged in parts of Latin America, demonstrating that while Pentecostalism exhibits a core theology and modus operandi, politically it is far less homogenous.

Latin American Pentecostals have firmly left behind the previously emphasized rigid separation of church and state in order to form new political parties and even stand for election at the local and national levels.

However, this kind of overt, or explicit, political activity has had mixed fortunes in Latin America, with Neo-Pentecostals capturing national power in Guatemala but failing dismally elsewhere. For example, in the 1997 elections, former Nicaraguan Assemblies of God minister Guillermo Osorno came third with just 4 percent of the vote. Other expressions of social and political activity among Pentecostals include forming pressure groups with strong involvement in social projects such as literacy, helping the poor, orphanage work, and drug rehabilitation. Douglas Petersen details at length an increasing and sustained Pentecostal engagement with the social sphere in a seminal work that aroused considerable interest when it was published (1996).

Just as important, however, is how Pentecostal beliefs, practices, and distinct worldview have had an implicit social and political impact (Smith 2009). Pentecostalism attracts the poor and provides a strong sense of community. Meanwhile, the displaced and marginalized find a home stressing their self-worth, while a focus on spiritual gifts and empowerment for service allows every Pentecostal member of the local templo to participate and feel they have a worthwhile role to contribute within the local body of Christ. Pentecostalism also transforms lives and socioeconomic circumstances by discouraging gambling or spending money on alcohol, while different spending priorities may contribute to social upward mobility. Hence, new converts to Pentecostalism begin to see positive effects almost immediately. Latin American Pentecostalism empowers Latin American women, emphasizing self-worth and autonomy in a machismo culture by providing them with a role and a function in the local church by virtue of their spiritual gifts and callings.

Pentecostalism, then, has had a major impact upon Latin America, not only in terms of ushering in a new religion that has strongly and successfully challenged Catholicism's religious hold in the region (leading David Stoll to argue that the rise of Latin American Pentecostalism has been no less profound than the Reformation in sixteenth-century Europe) but also through its social and political impact, both overtly and implicitly. Meanwhile, Pentecostalism has also strongly influenced other Latin American religious expressions, leading several commentators to speak of "Pentecostalized religion" across the continent. Thus, ironically, in a bid to challenge the very sectas they oppose, some Catholic churches draw on Pentecostal-style worship to attract new members and to challenge and seek to reverse its success.

REFERENCES AND SUGGESTIONS FOR FURTHER READING

Anderson, Allan. 2004. *An Introduction to Pentecostalism: Global Charismatic Christianity.* Cambridge: Cambridge University Press.

Cleary, Edward L., and Hannah W. Stewart-Gambino, eds. 1998. *Power, Politics, and Pentecostals in Latin America.* Boulder, CO: Westview Press.

Petersen, Douglas. 1996. *Not by Might Nor by Power: A Pentecostal Theology of Social Concern in Latin America.* Oxford: Regnum.

Schultze, Quentin J. 1994. "Orality and Power in Latin American Pentecostalism." In *Coming of Age: Protestantism in Contemporary Latin America*, ed. Daniel R. Miller, 65–88. Lanham, MD: University Press of America.

Smith, Calvin L. 2009. "Pentecostal Presence, Power, and Politics in Latin America." *Journal of Beliefs and Values* 30(3): 219–29.

———, ed. 2010. *Pentecostal Power: Expressions, Impact, and Faith of Latin American Pentecostalism.* Leiden and Boston: Brill.

Stoll, David. 1990. *Is Latin America Turning Protestant? The Politics of Evangelical Growth.* Berkeley and Los Angeles: University of California Press.

Latter Rain Movement

MARTIN W. MITTELSTADT

✳ The New Order of the Latter Rain, a revival with affinities to classical Pentecostalism and a precursor to the Charismatic movement, originated at the Sharon Orphanage and Schools in North Battleford, Saskatchewan, Canada. The movement began in 1947, spread quickly to the United States, Europe, and around the world, and finally merged with the Charismatic movement. In the spring of 1947, the principal proponent and primary facilitator, George Hawtin, officiated a series of controversial meetings. Marked by an apparent "unrestrained zeal," the meetings led to an organizational schism. By the fall of 1947, Hawtin—a pastor with the Pentecostal Assemblies of Canada (PAOC), as well as founder and faculty member of Bethel Bible Institute in Saskatoon, Saskatchewan—clashed with colleagues and district officials and ultimately resigned from the PAOC. He and his brother Ernest, along with Percy Hunt and Herrick

Holt, moved to North Battleford, where they were followed by a nucleus of returning and incoming Bethel students. Activities continued in a Bible school atmosphere until all attempts to run an educational institution were postponed, and the campus became a retreat center. Beginning on 11 February 1948, Hawtin guided four days of extended chapel services that featured extraordinary prophetic utterances, ecstatic worship likened to a "heavenly choir," revelations concerning demon possession among believers, healings, and a strong emphasis on the imparting of specific spiritual gifts through the laying on of hands (strongly precipitated through the ministry of the controversial healing evangelist William Branham). George Hawtin referred to these special days as the launching of a "new thing" (Is 43:19) and attributed the outpouring to months of sustained prayer and fasting: "After they had spent a day searching the Scriptures, it seemed on Feb. 14 'that all Heaven broke loose upon our souls and heaven above came down to greet us'" (Hawtin 1950, 2).

Although it was founded in a small prairie city, the movement drew immediate interest from all parts of North America. People first began to attend camp meeting conventions under the North Battleford teachers. As visitors returned to their homes, they took the revival with them and invited key proponents for special meetings. New revival centers quickly emerged at Glad Tidings Temple in Vancouver, British Columbia; Bethesda Missionary Temple in Detroit, Michigan; and Elim Bible Institute, at that time located in Hornell, New York. The North American surge led to rapid decentralization and the development of a highly sectarian identity. Although the revival proper subsided quickly, controversy erupted and caused long-term repercussions among established denominations such as the PAOC, Assemblies of God (AG), the Pentecostal Holiness Church, and the United Pentecostal Church. While many participants generally expressed renewed faith and affirmation of prophetic gifts and calling, others found their faith shipwrecked and suffered great pain because of the schismatic teaching; some Latter Rain leaders in western Canada circulated pamphlets on "How to Take a PAOC Church." Even experienced pastors found themselves dropped from the rolls of various ecclesial bodies for their involvement in the revival. For example, Stanley Frodsham, the respected editor of the official publication of the AG, the *Pentecostal Evangel*, felt pressure from leadership within the denomination because of his support of the revival and thus resigned not only his position but also his AG ministerial credentials. As schism continued to make its way through numerous Pentecostal families and churches, the Latter Rain found success outside of Pentecostal denominations through the emergence of independent and autonomous "revival churches." As the years passed, Pentecostals often downplayed the lasting effects of the revival and regularly ignored the movement in their recounting of early Pentecostal history. However, in the ensuing decades, many participants of the Latter Rain became vital contributors to the Charismatic movement in the late 1960s and 1970s.

Concerning propagation of Latter Rain theology, George Warnock published *The Feast of Tabernacles*, the most influential theological work of the movement, which was published in 1951 and widely disseminated over the next several decades. In this book Warnock argued that the already fulfilled Feast of Passover (via the death of Christ) and the Feast of Pentecost (marked by the outpouring of the Holy Spirit as recorded in Acts 2) set the stage for the last of Israel's three typological feasts. The Feast of Tabernacles, yet to be fulfilled, would be ushered in through a Latter Rain revival. Warnock and proponents declared strong expectation of the imminent return of Jesus and believed reestablishment of present-day apostles, prophets, evangelists, pastors, and teachers would herald the last days and find widespread success. According to Warnock, the earlier noted manifestations created excitement and expectation among participants that fulfillment of this final feast was upon them.

In the aftermath, proponents and opponents slowly stepped back for evaluation. First, lessons concerning the theology and practice of the charismata highlighted the controversy. When individuals utilized utterances that moved beyond scrutiny and, in some cases, pronounced personal prophecies such as the choice of a marriage partner, some participants experienced the negative repercussions of unwarranted excess and longed for more balanced and Scripture-based prophetic speech. Second, the movement produced significant discussion on the nature of religious authority. When given a choice between ecstatic speech and exegesis, participants would regularly choose the former, "a direct word from God." As a result, overzealous and inexperienced proponents often laid hands upon various participants, thereby usurping ecclesial and pastoral authority from local church bodies and empowering unrestrained enthusiasm with schismatic results. Still others took pride in the discarding of "former doctrines" and felt that revelation was not yet complete. Although many Pentecostals considered the New Order of the Latter Rain to be a heterodox religious

movement that greatly challenged the authority of Scripture and traditional church leadership, Latter Rain leaders, nonetheless, celebrated the gifts
and call of God upon all believers, a primary impulse of Pentecostalism.
In sum, the history and theology of the Latter Rain movement, generally
forgotten in many Pentecostal and Charismatic circles, remains a valuable test case—not only in the areas of ecclesiology, church governance,
pneumatology, and pastoral theology but also concerning the very nature
of revelation and religious experience in general.

REFERENCES AND SUGGESTIONS FOR FURTHER READING

Hawtin, Ernest. 1949. "How This Revival Began." *The Sharon Star*, August 1.
Hawtin, George. 1950. "The Church—Which Is His Body." *The Sharon Star*,
    March 1.
Holdcroft, Thomas L. 1980. "The New Order of the Latter Rain." *Pneuma* 2(2): 46–60.
Riss, Richard M. 1982. "The Latter Rain Movement of 1948." *Pneuma* 4(1): 32–45.
Warnock, George. 1951. *The Feast of Tabernacles*. North Battleford, SK: Sharon
    Schools.

Charles Harrison Mason

ADAM STEWART

Charles Harrison Mason (1866–1961) was one of the most important leaders within the early Pentecostal movement in the United States.
He founded what would become one of the largest Pentecostal denominations in North America, the Church of God in Christ. Mason was born
to emancipated slaves, Jerry and Eliza Mason, in Bartlett, Tennessee, on
8 September 1866. While he was still a boy, Mason's father, a Civil War
veteran, died; his mother remarried, to John Nelson; and the family moved
to Plumersville, Arkansas. Both the Mason and Nelson families were devoted members of the Missionary Baptist Church and cultivated a deeply
spiritual home life where supernatural experiences, characteristic of the
American slave religion of the time, formed an important part of Mason's
spiritual life. In 1878, at the age of twelve, Mason underwent a profound
conversion experience and was baptized by his stepbrother I. S. Nelson,

who served as the pastor of Mount Olive Missionary Baptist Church near Plumersville. Given his heightened spiritual inclination, it is perhaps not surprising that Mason soon became interested in the burgeoning Holiness movement. He was particularly influenced by the thought of William Christian, an African American Holiness preacher who introduced him to an interracial theology that aimed to counter white European claims of racial superiority and promote racial cooperation and equality. During this time Mason felt increasingly pulled toward a life devoted to Christian ministry; however, this ambition was stalled by his marriage to Alice Saxton in 1890. Saxton objected to Mason's ministry aspirations, and the couple separated in 1893. Mason remained unmarried until Saxton's death in 1905, at which time he married Leila Washington.

The year 1893 saw two important developments in Mason's spiritual formation. The first was his experience of sanctification, which came after reading the autobiography of the important African American Holiness evangelist Amanda Smith. The second was Mason's decision to prepare for ministry by enrolling at Arkansas Baptist College in Little Rock, Arkansas, during the fall. Mason, however, was greatly troubled by the teaching of higher criticism at the college and subsequently withdrew after only three months of study. Armed with the confidence that he was now prepared to instigate the type of interracial ministry he envisioned within the Southern African American Baptist churches, in 1895 Mason began working with other Holiness Baptist ministers (most notably, Charles Price Jones) in organizing Holiness events and promoting the Holiness teaching of the necessity of sanctification as a second work of grace. This, however, caused the leadership of the National Baptist Convention, who did not agree that sanctification formed a second stage in the order of salvation, to eject Mason and his companions from the denomination in 1896. Later that same year, Mason and Jones held a Holiness revival in Jackson, Mississippi, and officially formed their own church, which initially met in an old gin house on the banks of a Mississippi creek. With an official religious body now established, the leaders had to decide upon a name for the new group. While he was walking the streets of Little Rock in 1897, Mason claims, God revealed to him the name of his new denomination, "Church of God in Christ," which was based on the passage from 1 Thessalonians "For you, brothers and sisters, became imitators of the churches of God in Christ Jesus that are in Judea, for you suffered the same things from your own compatriots as they did from the Jews" (1 Thes 2:14). With a new name and the leadership of Mason and Jones the Church of God in Christ was born, and both new and existing churches throughout the American South began to affiliate with the denomination.

The story of the Church of God in Christ, however, was only just beginning. In March 1907, Mason traveled to Los Angeles in order to attend the much talked about revival being led by African American Holiness preacher William. J. Seymour at 312 Azusa Street. While visiting Azusa Street, Mason experienced the baptism of the Holy Spirit with the evidence of speaking in tongues, and he came to believe that this event formed a third necessary experience in the life of the believer, in addition to salvation and sanctification. Mason's companions in ministry were not as enthusiastic about this new Pentecostal doctrine. At the general assembly of the Church of God in Christ held in August 1907, Jones and the assembly asked Mason to leave the Church of God in Christ, and so he, along with a small portion of the ministers and members who also supported the teaching of the Pentecostal baptism, left to form their own denomination. A series of lawsuits ensued in which Mason and Jones fought for control of the name and properties of the organization. Mason changed the date of his denomination's founding to 1907 in order to distinguish it from the earlier Holiness group formed with Jones in 1896, and Mason later won the right to use the name Church of God in Christ, while Jones subsequently changed the name of his organization to the Church of Christ (Holiness) USA.

Mason's commitment to interracial cooperation, as well as the fact that he was one of the only early American Pentecostals who led a legally incorporated denomination, meant that, until 1914, he was personally responsible for ordaining many of the leaders, both black and white, within the early Pentecostal movement in the United States. Several white Pentecostal groups chose to join the Church of God in Christ and submit to Mason's leadership, a highly unusual occurrence given the inherent racism in early twentieth-century America. Under its new Pentecostal banner, the Church of God in Christ was able to continue Mason's interracial vision and also made an important organizational contribution to the burgeoning Pentecostal movement.

Much as at William Seymour's Azusa Street Mission, Mason's interracial experiment within the Church of God in Christ eventually ended in failure. The first major blow to Mason's vision was the plan devised by a number of white ministers who already held their ministerial credentials with the Church of God in Christ to hold a general council of the denomination in Hot Springs, Arkansas, in April 1914, to which only other white ministers were invited. This initiative, spearheaded by Eudorus N. Bell and Howard A. Goss, resulted in the formation of an almost entirely white Pentecostal denomination, the Assemblies of God. In the decades following the formation of the Assemblies of God in 1914, most of the white congregations that remained within the Church of God in Christ slowly withdrew from Mason's denomination until it once again became an almost entirely African American organization.

Regardless of this setback, Mason continued to lead the Church of God in Christ and saw the denomination grow to include nearly five hundred thousand members during his lifetime. Mason died in 1961 at the age of ninety-five in Detroit, Michigan, and his remains are interred at Mason Temple, Mason's former church and the headquarters of the Church of God in Christ located in Memphis, Tennessee, where Martin Luther King, Jr., delivered his famous "I've Been to the Mountaintop" speech the night before his assassination. In the half century since Mason's death, the Church of God in Christ has grown to become one of the largest Pentecostal as well as African American denominations in the United States.

REFERENCES AND SUGGESTIONS FOR FURTHER READING

Church of God in Christ. 2010. "The Founder and Church History." http://cogic. net/cogiccms/default/cogic-history/the-founder-church-history.

Clemmons, Ithiel C. 1996. *Bishop C. H. Mason and the Roots of the Church of God in Christ.* Bakersfield, CA: Pneuma Life.

Daniels, David D. 2002. "Charles Harrison Mason: The Interracial Impulse of Early Pentecostalism." In *Portraits of a Generation: Early Pentecostal Leaders,* ed. James R. Goff, Jr., and Grant Wacker, 255–70. Fayetteville: University of Arkansas Press.

Jacobsen, Douglas. 2006. "Charles Harrison Mason." In *A Reader in Pentecostal Theology: Voices from the First Generation,* ed. Douglas Jacobsen, 213–21. Bloomington: Indiana University Press.

Lincoln, C. Eric, and Lawrence H. Mamiya. 1990. *The Black Church in the African American Experience.* Durham, NC: Duke University Press.

Aimee Semple McPherson

LINDA M. AMBROSE

✹   Aimee Semple McPherson, who is best known for her role as founder of the International Church of the Foursquare Gospel, was born on 9 October 1890, near Ingersoll, Ontario, to James Kennedy, a farmer, and Mildred (Minnie) Pearce, a Salvation Army worker with Methodist roots. By her teenage years, Aimee Kennedy was asking hard questions about reconciling faith and science and, at the same time, was indulging in "worldly" behaviors that included her enjoyment of popular culture such as novels, music, and theatre. When she heard about a series of revival meetings being held by a Pentecostal evangelist, her curiosity piqued, and against her family's wishes she attended a 1907 meeting led by evangelist Robert Semple, who had been sent out from the Hebden Mission in Toronto. Smitten both by the message and by the man himself, Aimee experienced the baptism of the Holy Spirit and promptly fell in love with the young preacher. After their marriage in August 1908, the Semples answered the call to overseas missions, and after spending some time partnering with William H. Durham in his ministry work in Chicago, they traveled to China, arriving in June 1910. Unfortunately, both of them contracted malaria shortly after their arrival, and Robert Semple died in mid-August. Aimee recovered and, just a few weeks later, gave birth to their daughter, Roberta Star Semple, on 17 September 1910. Still only nineteen years of age, Aimee made arrangements to return with her infant daughter to North America, where she joined her mother, now in New York working for the Salvation Army.

While there, Aimee met and married Harold Stewart McPherson. Together, they had a son, Rolf Porter Kennedy McPherson, born on 23 March 1913. The McPherson marriage was neither long nor happy. Sensing that her call to ministry had not ended, Aimee embarked on a preaching career in Canada and the United States. Harold joined in her evangelistic travels at first, but by 1918 he had filed for separation. His petition for a divorce was granted in 1921, on the grounds of abandonment.

McPherson had abandoned her husband to pursue her call to ministry, and when she set out on a cross-country preaching tour during the summer of 1918, automobile travel was not only a novelty but, because of the lack of developed highways, a very dangerous undertaking. As one biographer noted, "Aimee Semple McPherson may well have been the first woman to drive a car from New York to California without a man to fix flat tires" (Epstein 1993, 146). Preaching along the way, Aimee traveled in a party of five, including herself, her mother, the two children, and Louise Baer, who was employed as a stenographer to type McPherson's notes. The adventures of their travels in the gospel car, emblazoned with slogans such as "Jesus Is Coming Soon—Get Ready," are extensively documented (McPherson 1923, 144–60), and there is no doubt that this small band of travelers attracted a great deal of attention wherever they went. Arriving in Los Angeles in December 1918, more than ten years after the events of Azusa Street, McPherson brought renewed attention to the Pentecostal movement and drew crowds of curious seekers to her meetings where conversions, Spirit baptisms, and physical healings were commonly reported.

McPherson's most enduring legacy is her role as founder of the International Four Square, with its headquarters in Los Angeles at the famed Angelus Temple, a domed church building with a seating capacity of fifty-three hundred people built in 1923. From that one church, a denomination evolved, which boasts over fifty thousand congregations worldwide with a membership of over six million people (Sutton 2007, 276) based on the "foursquare gospel." While the four main tenets of this gospel include Christ as savior, baptizer, healer, and coming king, the term "foursquare" also had popular meaning because "One stood foursquare for Uncle Sam, one's values, or one's friends; in that context, it connoted loyalty, fidelity, firmness, strength. The foursquare gospel would be the whole gospel, true to the Bible, absolutely dependable for time and eternity" (Blumhofer 1993, 193).

In addition to this impressive doctrinal and organizational legacy, there is a more infamous side to Aimee Semple McPherson. A series of personal troubles led to her story being sensationalized through contemporary press coverage and subsequent fictionalized accounts of her life. Those popular culture renditions include books, periodicals, films, and plays based on aspects of her life story; the most well-known among them is Sinclair Lewis's character Sister Sharon Falconer in the 1926 novel *Elmer*

Gantry. The fact is that McPherson's life included some very dramatic episodes. In part because of her flamboyant personality but also because of her high profile in the media, the public followed her private life with great interest. The most controversial episode of her life occurred in May 1926 when McPherson mysteriously disappeared while on an outing to Ocean Park Beach and was presumed dead. Her mother, who was her partner in ministry, held a memorial service, having given up hope of ever seeing her daughter alive again. Almost one month later, McPherson suddenly reappeared, reporting that she had been kidnapped and narrowly escaped from her captors. Her story was complicated by the fact that, at the time of her disappearance, Kenneth G. Ormiston (the radio engineer she employed for her ministry and a married man) had also disappeared, and some believed the two had run off together. Because of reports that McPherson and Ormiston had been seen together at a cottage during the period of her alleged abduction, a grand jury was convened in July 1926—but citing lack of evidence to proceed, the jury adjourned after twelve days with the mystery surrounding her disappearance unsolved (Sutton 2007, 137–40). In 1931, McPherson got married again, this time to David Hutton, an actor and musician. This marriage was also short-lived; the couple separated in 1933 and were divorced by March 1934. The final controversial episode of McPherson's life centers around her own death, which included all the drama and pathos of a Hollywood celebrity whose passing engendered a great deal of public attention and scrutiny. Aimee Semple McPherson died from an overdose of sleeping pills on 26 September 1944, and while there was speculation about suicide, the coroner's report concluded that her death was accidental. She was buried in the Forest Lawn Memorial Park Cemetery in Glendale, California.

McPherson is a most intriguing figure for scholars of the Pentecostal movement, and although there may be countless ways to approach a study of her life and legacy, three particular approaches have received attention and hold promise for further inquiry. First, gender studies is a useful approach, because the important fact that Aimee Semple McPherson was a Pentecostal woman should not be overlooked or downplayed. Pentecostal theology makes much of the fact that both men and women are called of God to spread the gospel message, and when McPherson rose to prominence, society was dealing with the popular culture phenomenon of the "new woman," which called for greater freedoms for women in all aspects of public life. In that sense, McPherson was a product of her times because her adventures of traveling, performing, and leading a large organization drew public attention for their novel, avant-garde qualities. She did not downplay her own sexuality; indeed her physical attractiveness and her relationships with men, both in personal and ministry contexts, deserve more attention from scholars. While attention has been paid to the "scandalous" nature of her behaviors, a more useful line of inquiry might be to pay attention to the power she exerted in relationships, whether they were personal or public.

A second useful way to think about McPherson is to consider her relationship to media and how she portrayed herself. Recent approaches to biography highlight the idea of the "performed" self, and there is no doubt that Aimee Semple McPherson was a master performer. She adopted a dramatic mode of dress in her signature outfit, which included a long flowing white dress, sometimes covered with a black cape. She engaged with contemporary media in ways that set her apart from other religious figures. By some accounts, she was mentioned more frequently in newspapers than any other public figure of her time, and while those reports served to increase public awareness of her ministry, they were often highly critical, particularly surrounding the personal difficulties she experienced, her divorces, her mysterious disappearance and return to ministry, and her death. But on a positive note, McPherson herself was a master of media, well-known for her "illustrated sermons" in which she incorporated dramatic presentations and spared no expense in using theatrical props to create spectacles for her audiences. One well-known example was a meeting staged in a boxing ring, where McPherson wore a sign reading, "Knock out the Devil." In another oft-cited sermon, entitled "The Heavenly Airplane," she drew upon her own travel experiences, setting up two miniature aircraft on the stage of the church in front of a painted skyline in order to illustrate the choice between a life piloted by the devil, with sin for the engine and temptation as the propeller, and a life piloted by Jesus that would lead one to the Holy City. She was the first woman to preach a radio sermon, and with the opening of the Foursquare-owned radio station, KFSG, she became the first woman to be granted a broadcast license by the Federal Radio Commission. There is an irony in McPherson's enlisting the use of modern media to such a large extent while calling for a return to "old-time religion," because while she decried modernism, she did so by using the most modern means available.

A recent book about McPherson's life has paid particular attention to her engagement with American religious and political culture, and this is a third approach that gives great insight into the question of her enduring legacy. Matthew Avery Sutton's biographical work argues that, because of McPherson, there was a "resurrection" of Christian America as evangelicals followed her lead by rising up to address their concerns about modernism and to engage in politics during the interwar years—on issues ranging from opposing the teaching of evolution in schools, to opposing communism, to assisting the poor (Sutton 2007, 241–49). Sutton concludes that, "McPherson's integration of politics with faith established a model that subsequent Pentecostals have used to move themselves from the outer reaches of sectarian separatism to the inner circles of power, and her celebrity status, use of spectacle, and mass media savvy set precedents for modern evangelicalism" (ibid., 280). One thing is certain, Aimee Semple McPherson, the famed celebrity-evangelist with Canadian roots, was a complex individual whose life and enduring legacy are riddled with fascinating ambiguities.

References and Suggestions for Further Reading

Barfoot, Charles H. 2011. *Aimee Semple McPherson and the Making of Modern Pentecostalism, 1890–1926.* London: Equinox.

Blumhofer, Edith L. 1993. *Aimee Semple McPherson: Everybody's Sister.* Grand Rapids, MI: Eerdmans.

———. 1997. "'Canada's Gift to the Sawdust Trail': The Canadian Face of Aimee Semple McPherson." In *Aspects of the Canadian Evangelical Experience*, ed. G. A. Rawlyk, 387–402. Montreal and Kingston: McGill-Queen's University Press.

Epstein, Daniel Mark. 1993. *Sister Aimee: The Life of Aimee Semple McPherson.* New York: Harcourt Brace.

McPherson, Aimee Semple. 1923. *This Is That: Personal Experiences, Sermons, and Writings.* Los Angeles: Echo Park Evangelistic Association.

Sutton, Matthew Avery. 2007. *Aimee Semple McPherson and the Resurrection of Christian America.* Cambridge, MA: Harvard University Press.

Native American Pentecostalism

According to some accounts of the Azusa Street revival, Native Americans were among the mix of people who experienced the "modern day Pentecost" that occurred in the old livery stable on Azusa Street. Sustained outreach to Native Americans did not really begin in the United States, however, until a missionary named Clyde Thompson established a mission among Northern California Native peoples in 1918. Thompson was an Assemblies of God (AG) missionary, and while some evidence exists that other Pentecostal groups did sporadic missionary work among Native Americans, AG is the only documented Pentecostal denomination that undertook extensive missionary work among Native peoples in the United States. Thompson and other white Pentecostal missionaries were the forerunners to the AG's Home Missions program, which eventually extended across the United States to a multitude of reservations. In Canada, the AG's Canadian counterpart, the Pentecostal Assemblies of Canada (PAOC), led the way among Native peoples (although other groups such as the Church of the Foursquare Gospel and independent Charismatic churches also evangelized Native peoples). In Alaska, the AG also launched a large missionary program targeting Inuit and Alaskan Natives. Additionally, Canadian Pentecostals established a mission among Native Americans at the Six Nations Indian Reserve near Brantford, Ontario, as early as 1910 under the leadership of Arthur Brant (Stewart 2010, 27).

Although white missionaries reached Northern California Natives in 1918, nationally coordinated and funded AG missionary efforts to Native peoples were not undertaken until the 1940s, because the Department of Home Missions (which became responsible for the AG's missions to Native peoples) was not established until 1937. The first nationally appointed Home missionary of any sort was recorded in 1952. This was Charlie Lee of the Navajo nation. Lee was a graduate of the AG's Central Bible Institute who returned to his home reservation in the Shiprock area of New Mexico and began preaching in Navajo. Lee was an anomaly in this era, however, for most missionaries were white Pentecostals who did not speak Native languages. These missionaries spread out across the country to a variety of reservations in the Northeast, Southeast, West, and Southwest, and in the Plains states. AG missionaries had a national focus, but the missions became especially strong among the Mohawk, Lumbee, Apache, Navajo, Pima, and Papago tribes.

Native American converts emerged out of this early period to become leaders within the AG as missionaries, pastors, and Native elders. Charlie Lee (Navajo), George Effman (Klamath), Andrew Maracle (Mohawk), Rodger Cree (Mohawk), and John McPherson (Cherokee) were all early Native missionaries and leaders. Led by Lee, these early Native missionaries reintroduced the concept of the "indigenous principle" to early Native missionary work. In its modern form, the indigenous principle was articulated by the Latin American missiologist Melvin Hodges, who taught that missionaries should root Pentecostal Christianity in the culture of those being converted—thus a good missionary should work to plant a self-supporting, self-perpetuating, indigenous form of Christianity that was free of ethnocentrism and paternalism. Hodges was one of Charlie Lee's teachers while he was at Bible school, and Lee took his ideas and began to turn them into a reality.

By the 1960s, AG missionary work to Native peoples had expanded, and a Native leadership began to emerge to advocate for Native Pentecostals within the AG. In the late 1950s, a white female missionary to Arizona Natives, Alta Washburn, had opened up a local Bible school that would help prepare Native people for the ministry in downtown Phoenix. Her local Bible school was taken over by the AG in 1965 and became an official Bible college, dedicated specifically to training Native American Pentecostals for the ministry—it is now called the American Indian College of the AG. Other Native-focused AG Bible schools followed, but the American Indian College is the oldest and has long been one of the AG's centers for developing Native evangelists. Native leadership was further enhanced within the AG by the work of Charlie Lee, who managed to transform his mission into the first General Council–affiliated indigenous church in 1976. This means that Lee's church enjoyed indigenous (Navajo) leadership, was self-supporting, and existed specifically to meet the needs of Navajo Pentecostals. In doing this, Lee showed that the indigenous principle worked, and that there was hope for Native leadership within the AG.

Only three years after Lee's success, in 1979, John McPherson was elected the first national American Indian representative for the AG. Although it was (and remains) an unfunded position, this was the first national leadership post that served Native Americans in the AG. In the 1990s, the AG created the Native American Fellowship as an autonomous space where Native leaders could work together on Native-specific evangelistic needs. In 2008, John Maracle (Mohawk) was elected to the ethnic fellowship seat on the executive presbytery, the first Native person to hold an elected high office within the AG. Native American Pentecostals make up 1.5 percent of the overall AG population, and missionary work to various Native groups remains a focus of the AG in the continental United States.

The AG has also invested extensive missionary efforts among Alaska Natives, although less is known about the overall outcome of this missionary work because it is an understudied region. The AG, however, is not the only Pentecostal group that is active in Alaska. Scholarly work by the anthropologist Kirk Dombrowski shows that Charismatic and independent Pentecostal groups thrived among Alaskan Natives in the 1970s, and that many of these churches were led by Native leaders. Dombrowski posited that the growth in Pentecostalism mainly came from those who were on the economic margins of village life—meaning that Pentecostalism was especially appealing to Native people who were struggling financially.

In Canada, much of the work among Native peoples was undertaken by the PAOC as well as other Canadian Charismatic and Pentecostal groups. Historian Robert Burkinshaw has shown that, as in the United States, Pentecostalism grew among the Native peoples in Canada mainly during the 1950s and 1960s. Again, as in the United States, a Native leadership developed from the missionary efforts of the PAOC, and by 2001, about 3.4 percent of registered Canadian Natives described themselves as Pentecostals.

Among American and Canadian Native Pentecostals, a few similarities emerge from Dombrowski's, Tarango's, and Burkinshaw's studies. One is the development of a Native leadership—often in the most difficult of circumstances. Native peoples found autonomy within Pentecostalism, even when they had to face institutionalized racism, ethnocentrism, and paternalism. The second major similarity is the use of the Pentecostal camp meeting as the main tool for evangelism among Native peoples. Native leaders and Native evangelists frequently emerged out of the camp meeting "circuit," often to rise to regional and sometimes national prominence. Camp meetings provided Native Pentecostals an avenue to connect with fellow Native Pentecostals and their leaders and proved to be one of the main social events of the year—whether they took place among Apaches in Arizona or Inuit peoples in Alaska. Finally, and perhaps most important, Native people found healing and power within Pentecostalism. Sometimes this was physical healing, but it is also clear from testimonials and interviews that racial reconciliation remained an important aspect of this healing—belief in the Holy Spirit and in the power of the Holy Spirit gave some Native people the power to stand up and address the wrongs that historically have been done to them by both Canadian and American governments.

References and Suggestions for Further Reading

Burkinshaw, Robert K. 2009. "Native Pentecostalism in British Columbia." In *Canadian Pentecostalism: Transition and Transformation*, ed. Michael Wilkinson, 142–70. Montreal and Kingston: McGill-Queen's University Press.

Dombrowski, Kirk. 2001. *Against Culture: Development, Politics, and Religion in Indian Alaska*. Lincoln: University of Nebraska Press.

Stewart, Adam. 2010. "A Canadian Azusa? The Implications of the Hebden Mission for Pentecostal Historiography." In *Winds from the North: Canadian Contributions to the Pentecostal Movement*, ed. Michael Wilkinson and Peter Althouse, 17–37. Leiden and Boston: Brill.

Tarango, Angela. 2009. "Choosing the Jesus Way: The Assemblies of God's Home Missions to American Indians and the Development of an Indian-Pentecostal Identity." Doctoral dissertation, Duke University.

Neo-Pentecostalism

ANDREW K. GABRIEL

✄ Sometimes referred to as the Neo-Charismatic movement, Neo-Pentecostalism is a transdenominational renewal movement that includes all Pentecostals (as broadly understood) who do not fall under the category of classical Pentecostalism or the Charismatic movement. Originally the term "Neo-Pentecostalism" was used synonymously with the Charismatic movement. Although many continue to use the term in this manner, the term is increasingly used with the more narrow definition employed here. Reciprocal historical and theological influences often blur the lines between classical Pentecostalism, the Charismatic movement, and Neo-Pentecostalism. No doubt many churches and individuals in the so-called classical Pentecostal denominations would fit into the description of Neo-Pentecostalism. Neo-Pentecostalism includes the "Word of Faith" movement, the "third wave" of renewal that arose in the mainstream evangelical churches in the 1980s, as well as the renewal churches, networks, and groups around the world that are not tied to traditional Pentecostal or mainline Charismatic groups. Given the wide and growing spectrum of this group, today Neo-Pentecostalism is the largest of all renewal movements.

Neo-Pentecostalism shares many of the emphases and practices of the wider Pentecostal movement, including an emphasis on the immediate presence of God, an experience of the Holy Spirit, divine intervention in life, speaking in tongues, the receiving of spiritual gifts, and healing. In comparison to classical Pentecostals, Neo-Pentecostals tend to place less emphasis on the baptism of the Holy Spirit and speaking in tongues as well as less emphasis on holiness (which is understandable, given that much of classical Pentecostalism in North America arose out of the Holiness tradition). Apart from these characteristics, Neo-Pentecostalism is exceptionally diverse, both doctrinally and in practice, because it includes such a broad range of Christians. While some Neo-Pentecostal groups teach historic evangelical doctrine, others do not. For example, some of the African Neo-Pentecostal independent churches mix Pentecostal spiritual experiences with their traditional beliefs in ancestor spirits and witchcraft.

Among individuals, Oral Roberts played the most significant role in the growth of Neo-Pentecostalism. In 1968 Roberts left the Pentecostal Holiness Church and joined the United Methodist Church to foster a firm connection with the Charismatic movement. Roberts had previously launched his healing ministry in 1947 in Enid, Oklahoma. His various book, magazine, and devotional publications helped make him the most famous Pentecostal in the world. However, nothing made as much impact as Roberts's television ministry (started in 1955), which caused the exposure Americans had to Roberts's revival meetings and healing crusades to proliferate.

In 1951 Roberts backed the formation of one of the most influential Neo-Pentecostal groups in the world—namely, the Full Gospel Business Men's Fellowship International (FGBMFI). Originating in Los Angeles, this organization included men from both mainline churches and Pentecostal churches and served to advance the Pentecostal experience to men who would not have otherwise encountered it. Unlike the meetings of early Pentecostals in tents and storefronts, the FGBMFI met in restaurants and hotel ballrooms. Eventually, the FGBMFI helped finance Oral Roberts University in Tulsa, Oklahoma, which opened in 1965. The university served to advance the teaching of many Neo-Pentecostals through its classes and conferences. Today the FGBMFI is active in 160 nations.

The advent of Christian television networks also aided the spread of Neo-Pentecostalism. The two largest are the Christian Broadcasting Network (CBN, started in 1959) based in Virginia Beach, Virginia, and Trinity Broadcasting Network (TBN, started in 1973) based in Phoenix, Arizona. These networks have helped make famous many Neo-Pentecostal faces such as Kenneth Copeland, Benny Hinn, Rodney Howard-Browne, and T. D. Jakes. Many would also consider Jimmy Swaggart and Jim Bakker, both coming out of a classical Pentecostal denomination (the Assemblies of God), as representatives of Neo-Pentecostalism. Among print media, first published in 1975, *Charisma* magazine has become one of the most important means for Neo-Pentecostals to market their conferences, books, videos, and CDs.

One significant Neo-Pentecostal movement includes the Shepherding or Discipleship movement. Arising out of Fort Lauderdale, Florida, the movement lasted from 1970 to 1986 and emphasized that people must submit every area of their life to the church leaders (the "shepherds"). Although the movement had a hundred thousand members at its height, other Neo-Pentecostals, including Pat Robertson (founder of CBN) and Demos Shakarian (founder of FGBMFI), criticized the movement for exploiting the members.

The Word of Faith movement is a well-known subsection within Neo-Pentecostalism. The movement is sometimes critically described as teaching the "prosperity gospel," otherwise known as the "health and wealth" gospel. These titles arise because the Word of Faith movement teaches that if people practice a "positive confession" of the Word of God as they exercise their faith, there is a predetermined law of divine principles that assures they will live a healthy and successful life. Baptist pastor E. W. Kenyon, along with Oral Roberts, provided an early impetus within the movement, but the movement really emerged in the 1970s under the leadership of "faith preachers" Kenneth and Gloria Copeland, Frederick Price, and the movement's elder statesman, Kenneth Hagin, Sr. The movement is particularly strong in the Bible Belt of the United States (the mid and southeastern states), although its teachings can be found in Pentecostal churches around the world.

Neo-Pentecostalism spread quickly with the emergence of the "third wave" of Pentecostalism in evangelicalism in the 1980s and into the 1990s. C. Peter Wagner (1988) described this third wave in historical contrast to the first wave of Pentecostalism (classical Pentecostals and the resulting denominational Pentecostalism) and second wave of Pentecostalism (the Charismatic movement in the historic established mainline denominations). In general, adherents within the third wave of Pentecostalism taught that the baptism in the Spirit occurred at conversion (unlike the teachings of the classical Pentecostals, who taught that it was an experience subsequent to conversion), and third wave advocates also viewed tongues as a gift that a Spirit-filled believer might or might not receive. They also had an emphasis on "power evangelism," which referred to the use of the gifts of the Spirit (or "signs and wonders") in evangelism.

The third wave is most associated with the leadership of John Wimber, who in 1977 cofounded the Vineyard Christian Fellowship in Anaheim, California. This network included five hundred churches in the United States by 1998. Wimber also taught a class with Peter Wagner at Fuller Theological Seminary entitled "Signs, Wonders, and Church Growth." The Toronto Blessing, which began in 1994, is also part of the third wave. This refers to the meetings held at the Toronto Airport Christian Fellowship (originally part of the Vineyard Association), which is led by John Arnott. By 1995 an estimated six hundred thousand people visited the Toronto church. The meetings were known for the "holy laughter" that occurred, and for people falling, shaking, or making animal noises (such as roaring like lions or barking like dogs) while "under the power" of the Spirit (Poloma 2003).

The largest Pentecostal group in the United Kingdom consists of the Neo-Pentecostal networks of house churches known as the New Churches. The movement began as the "restoration" movement in the late 1950s. This movement proposed a restoration of the "fivefold ministry" of apostles, prophets, evangelists, pastors, and teachers (Eph 4:11). By the year 2000, over four hundred thousand people were affiliated with these house groups, many of which were part of church networks including New Frontiers, Covenant Ministries International, Salt and Light Ministries, Pioneer People, Cornerstone Ministries, and Ichthus Christian Fellowship.

In North America, some of the independent Pentecostal churches resulted from the resistance to the Charismatic renewal within the established denominations, including conservative denominations such as the Southern Baptist Convention and the Church of the Nazarene. These Neo-Pentecostal churches typically resist denominational structures, although sometimes they will plant churches that remain connected to the mother church. Neo-Pentecostalism also includes the vast number of African independent churches and much of the House Church movement in China.

Africa and Latin America hold some of the largest Pentecostal churches in the world. Many of these independent churches have no historical connection with North American Pentecostalism. This is true of Winners Chapel in Nigeria, which started in 1981. This church now has seating capacity for fifty thousand people in their main sanctuary. It has over four hundred branches in Nigeria, and it has spread to over fifty countries in Africa, Europe, and North America. Some of the independent churches in Africa have been charismatic since the 1860s, many years before the Azusa Street revival. It seems that some forms of Neo-Pentecostalism are, therefore, actually older than the so-called classical Pentecostalism arising out of North America.

REFERENCES AND SUGGESTIONS FOR FURTHER READING

Anderson, Allan. 2004. *An Introduction to Pentecostalism: Global Charismatic Christianity.* Cambridge: Cambridge University Press.

Burgess, Stanley M., and Eduard M. van der Maas. 2002. "Introduction." In *The New International Dictionary of Pentecostal and Charismatic Movements.* Revised and expanded edition, ed. Stanley M. Burgess and Eduard M. van der Maas, xvii–xxiii. Grand Rapids, MI: Zondervan.

Hollenweger, Walter J. 1972. *The Pentecostals.* London: SCM Press.

Poloma, Margaret M. 2003. *Main Street Mystics: The Toronto Blessing and Reviving Pentecostalism.* Walnut Creek, CA: AltaMira.

Quebedeaux, Richard. 1976. *The New Charismatics: The Origins, Development, and Significance of Neo-Pentecostalism.* Garden City, NY: Doubleday.

Synan, Vinson. 1997. *The Holiness-Pentecostal Tradition: Charismatic Movements in the Twentieth Century.* Second edition. Grand Rapids, MI: Eerdmans.

Wagner, C. Peter. 1988. *The Third Wave of the Holy Spirit: Encountering the Power of Signs and Wonders Today.* Ann Arbor, MI: Vine Books.

North American Pentecostalism

MARGARET M. POLOMA

⚜   Reflecting the adage that Pentecost is an experience not a denomination, North American Pentecostalism can be characterized as a
big tent that houses religious believers from a wide variety of Christian
allegiances. Pentecostals are actually a family of denominations (some
would say a highly fragmented family), comprised of scores of separate
denominations, followers within mainline denominations, and overlap-
ping network organizations that represent an undetermined—but growing—number of independent congregations. For the most part, North
American Pentecostals are evangelical Christians who adhere to a biblical
orthodoxy, and who tend to be conservative on moral issues (especially
same-sex marriage and abortion).

While some contend that glossolalia, or the ability to pray in tongues, is
the defining feature, many Pentecostals are not glossolalic. What they do
share is a worldview that embraces an alternate reality in which the seemingly supernatural is natural. They contend that believers can walk and talk
with God as surely as biblical men and women of old—they can hear from
God and they can prophesy God's Word as an encouragement to others.
They believe they can do the things that Jesus did through the power of his
Spirit, including healing and miracles (including financial "miracles"), and
on occasion even witness resurrections from the dead.

The Pentecostal movement is by far the largest and most important
religious movement to originate in the United States. Its origins are commonly traced to a Bible school in Topeka, Kansas, in 1901, where glossolalia was first linked theologically to a second (or third) Spirit baptism, and
to the Azusa Street revival (1906–1909) in Los Angeles, California, from
where Pentecostalism quickly spread across North America and beyond.
As its presence has increased, Pentecostalism has been called Christen-
dom's "fourth force," alongside Catholicism, Protestantism, and Orthodox
Christianity—a force that has swept beyond its permeable experiential
boundaries to intertwine with other major Christian forces.

Pentecostalism in North America has experienced at least three major waves of revival that have saved this experiential religion from morphing into denomination, doctrine, or ritual where paranormal religious experiences are buried in history or retained only as personal secrets. The first wave began in the early twentieth century. It launched the movement and marked the birth of the major Pentecostal denominations, including the Church of God in Christ, the Assemblies of God, the Pentecostal Assemblies of Canada, the Pentecostal Assemblies of the World, the Church of God (Cleveland, Tennessee), and the International Church of the Foursquare Gospel. In 1916 the movement experienced a major split in which some of the leaders began to deny the doctrine of the Trinity that professed three persons in one God, arguing instead that the name of God is Jesus alone, and believers must be baptized in his name only. The United Pentecostal Church is the largest North American "Oneness" denomination. A precursor of the second wave began in 1947 with the revival in North Battleford, Saskatchewan, at a time when many Pentecostals were concerned about the decline of the gifts of the Spirit (including healing, prophecy, and miracles). The New Order of the Latter Rain saw the rise of new healing ministries and the emphasis on relational networks over the social structures that had developed in Pentecostalism. Latter Rain soon experienced opposition and charges of heresy from many Pentecostal leaders. In this somewhat amorphous movement it remains difficult to determine direct influence of Latter Rain on the second (often called the Charismatic movement) and third waves of revival that continue to influence the shape of Pentecostalism in North America.

The Charismatic movement marked the crest of the second wave. It is commonly traced to the 1950s and 1960s, at a time during which Pentecostalism filtered into the mainline Protestant, Catholic, and even Orthodox churches in North America. The Charismatic movement peaked in the late 1970s, leaving a legacy that, together with the Latter Rain, provided the materials for the so-called third wave of the movement. The approach of the third wave differs somewhat from that of the first two waves in its rejection of the belief that glossolalia is the only evidence of Spirit baptism.

John Wimber, a former rock musician who experienced conversion during the Jesus movement in California, began his ministry by embracing teachings of the Charismatic movement. He soon became an international spokesman for a new form of Pentecostalism in the 1980s and 1990s—albeit one that often eschewed Pentecostal and Charismatic labels.

While accepting the alternate worldview that is the heart of Pentecostalism, Wimber emphasized that glossolalia was but one of the "signs and wonders" or spiritual gifts found in the Bible, and these gifts were essential for what he called "power evangelism." Wimber would later reject a revival movement that erupted at the Toronto Airport Vineyard in 1994 and swept into other churches that formed part of Wimber's Association of Vineyard Churches. Many of these once Vineyard churches have been joined by former denominational Pentecostals and remnants of the Charismatic movement in forming new networks that are now at the heart of this third phase of Pentecostalism. Networks like Global Awakening, Iris Ministries, and Partners in Harvest are in the forefront of living out a Pentecostalism that counters a modernist Christianity known to deny and debunk the paranormal experiences that were integral to early Christianity.

The boundaries between North American Pentecostals and non-Pentecostals, however, are growing increasingly fuzzy. Not only is there a "Pentecostalization of evangelicalism," where conservative Christian churches are embracing facets of the Pentecostal worldview and its practices, but there is also an "evangelicalization of Pentecostalism," where Pentecostal experiences become less common as Pentecostal churches adapt to the language and practices of a less experiential "seeker-sensitive" Protestantism. There is not and never has been a single Pentecostalism in North America but, rather, many Pentecostalisms that are often affected by race, ethnicity, social class, and denominational differences. Although they may wear different masks, to remain Pentecostal in practice as well as in name all face a dilemma that the sociologist Max Weber called the "routinization of charisma." There is always the danger of enshrining doctrine based on once common but unpredictable experiences while becoming predictable and structured in ways that are inimical to paranormal experiences. Throughout its one-hundred-year history, the Pentecostal religious culture has always had pockets of believers that made room for fresh revitalization and revival with rumors of angelic activity that brought the possibilities of the supernatural to ordinary mortals.

REFERENCES AND SUGGESTIONS FOR FURTHER READING

Patterson, Eric, and Edmund Rybarczyk, eds. 2007. *The Future of Pentecostalism in the United States.* Lanham, MD: Lexington Books.

Poloma, Margaret M. 1989. *The Assemblies of God at the Crossroads: Charisma and Institutional Dilemmas.* Knoxville: University of Tennessee Press.

Robeck, Cecil M., Jr. 2006. *The Azusa Street Mission and Revival: The Birth of the Global Pentecostal Movement.* Nashville, TN: Nelson.

Wacker, Grant. 2001. *Heaven Below: Early Pentecostals and American Culture.* Cambridge, MA: Harvard University Press.

Oneness (Apostolic) Pentecostalism

DAVID A. REED

Oneness Pentecostalism is the third stream to emerge from the early twentieth-century Pentecostal revival. It was the result of a schism in 1916 within the newly formed organization Assemblies of God (AG), because some rejected the doctrine of the Trinity and the insistence on water baptism in the "name of the Lord Jesus Christ." Two major influences gave rise to the "New Issue," as it was initially called.

The first influence focused on the Name of God. To defend the deity of Christ against the liberalism of their day, early evangelicals turned to a study of the names and titles of God in the Old Testament to show that Jesus fulfilled all the qualities of deity. This led some biblical teachers to find the key to Jesus' divine identity in his own name. Preferences varied from the title "Lord" to the "Lord Jesus Christ," and the preferred name by early Oneness Pentecostals, "Jesus."

The second influence caused the first schism within the Pentecostal movement, called the Finished Work Controversy. William Durham, an early Pentecostal leader in Chicago, touched off the crisis in 1910 with a sermon titled, "The Finished Work of Calvary." Polemically, it was a frontal attack on the whole Pentecostal movement, which had taught from its beginning the inherited Wesleyan Holiness doctrine of entire sanctification. The nascent Pentecostal movement was also at that point becoming unstable, with slow growth and the strain of internal conflicts. Growing theological discontent was brewing over what seemed to be excessive attention given to—and confusion over—Pentecostal experiences, especially in sorting out the three crisis experiences of conversion, sanctification, and baptism in the Spirit. Durham's challenge was in effect a call to return to the centrality of Jesus Christ and his atoning work on the cross.

Durham's message and his forceful personality produced a dramatic shift both theologically and demographically. Between 1910 and his untimely death in 1912, he singlehandedly redirected the majority of the Pentecostal movement to his Finished Work of Calvary teaching. In 1914, many leaders who had followed his direction formed the AG fellowship. But the vacuum created by Durham's death also produced a more radical alternative within the new organization.

The catalyst had occurred serendipitously a year earlier, in 1913, at a Worldwide Camp Meeting in Arroyo Seco, California, on the edge of Los Angeles. During the camp meeting, a Canadian Finished Work evangelist, Robert E. McAlister (1880–1953), was asked to preach at a baptismal service, and it was one point in particular that became the seed of the new movement. McAlister noted the inconsistency between Jesus' commission to baptize in the triune name of Father, Son, and Holy Spirit (Mt 28:19) and the apostolic practice of baptizing in some form of the name Lord Jesus Christ (Acts 2:38). His explanation was that Jesus was speaking parabolically about himself, a statement that would be understood by only his disciples.

An Australian evangelist and friend, Frank Ewart (1876–1947), meditated over McAlister's interpretation for a year. On 15 April 1914, he left his work at Victoria Hall in Los Angeles and with a coworker, Glenn Cook, set up a tent in nearby Belvedere. In a rented tank of water, they baptized each other in the name of the Lord Jesus Christ.

The New Issue spread like wildfire through the ranks of the AG, moving quickly east to the Midwest and north to Indianapolis through networks of churches, camp meetings, and magazines. By 1915 the movement had attracted such prominent leaders as Garfield T. Haywood, an African American pastor and popular preacher from Indianapolis, and Franklin Small from Winnipeg, Canada. The most controversial crisis was the re-baptism of E. N. Bell, one of the most influential leaders in the AG and editor of its papers the *Weekly Evangel* and the *Word and Witness*. It became clear that, while Bell found great spiritual benefit in being baptized in the name of the Lord Jesus Christ, he had never considered abandoning his Trinitarian faith.

The theology of the new movement began to develop quickly. As its first doctrinal architect, Ewart built a twofold platform for the practice of baptizing in the name of Jesus. The first was that, since there is only one baptism, its justification must be based on God's name being one (Zec

14:9). In the Christian era, that name is Jesus. The second—flowing from the first—is that, since God's name is one, God's being must be radically one. This became the logic for Ewart's rejection of the traditional doctrine of Trinity in "three persons." His preferred term was three "manifestations."

By 1915, Haywood, Small, and others were contributing to the new teaching, especially concerning the doctrine of salvation. Haywood taught that spiritual life begins at conception, but that the new birth of which Jesus spoke in John 3:5 is the threefold process set forth in Acts 2:38: repentance, water baptism in the name of Jesus Christ, and the gift of the Holy Spirit. This new birth interpretation was embraced by Andrew Urshan (1884–1967) in 1919, who then became the fourth key leader to join the new movement and contribute to the formulation of its doctrine.

Small and Ewart, on the other hand, taught that one is born again at conversion, while baptism in the name of Jesus and Spirit baptism according to Acts 2:38 are essential to the believer's full provision for the Christian life. These two interpretations of Acts 2:38 have continued throughout the history of the movement. Small stands alone as the one early pioneer who understood and consistently upheld Durham's Finished Work of Calvary teaching throughout his ministry.

Oneness publications also began to appear, which further accelerated the new teaching but also intensified the conflict within the AG. The Third General Council of the AG met in 1915 to press for tolerance and unity within the fellowship. But failure to resolve the differences resulted in a confrontation at the 1916 Fourth Council meeting. In the end, a final vote led to the expulsion of 156 of the 585 ministers, largely because of their rejection of the doctrine of the Trinity and their insistence upon baptizing believers in the name of Jesus.

This began the organizational story of Pentecostalism's third stream. The first corporate body, the Pentecostal Assemblies of the World, was multicultural until 1924, when the strain of race took its toll. Following the schism and two failed attempts to reunite, the two largest white groups finally merged in 1945 to form the United Pentecostal Church (UPC). In 1971 the Apostolic World Christian Fellowship was formed as a worldwide alliance to promote fellowship and coordination of ministries among the various groups. Except for the UPC, which did not join, there are currently 135 member organizations.

Oneness doctrine continues to be a barrier to official fellowship with Trinitarians. Its distinctive doctrines center primarily on God, Christ, and salvation. God in his eternal being is without distinction. Therefore, Oneness Pentecostals reject the language of "persons" because it hints of tritheism, even if Trinitarian theology intends otherwise. The historical reason can be traced to the shift in Durham's Finished Work doctrine from pneumatology to christology. It sealed the impression among Oneness Pentecostals that traditional Trinitarian language undermines the centrality of Jesus Christ. Oneness Pentecostal theology is best described as a form of modalism which teaches that God reveals himself in three modes or manifestations—Father, Son, and Holy Spirit.

Oneness christology affirms the full divine and human natures of Christ. But his deity is that of the Father or the one God without distinction, not God the Son, the Second Person of the Trinity. The Son is the human person, Jesus of Nazareth. The Holy Spirit is the one Spirit of God, not the Third Person (Jn 4:24). While the divine Father and human Son remain inseparable in Jesus throughout his life and death, the nature of the union is "God and man in one person." In contrast, the traditional Trinitarian doctrine of the Incarnation is that God, as the divine logos, has so fully entered into union with humanity that the human and divine in Jesus are inseparable in the one "God-man."

Requiring baptism in the name of Jesus is based on a distinctive theology of the Name. As God made himself known in the Old Covenant through his Name, so Jesus is the name that God has given for salvation in the New Covenant. When the Name is invoked in baptism, its significance is more than "The Bible says so." It is the means whereby Christian identity is established. Since "Father, Son, and Holy Spirit" is regarded as a threefold generic term of relationship, it does not attain the status of God's proper, revealed Name for New Covenant salvation.

Oneness Pentecostals are complex and diverse. They share a common Pentecostal heritage but hold teachings considered by many to be heterodox. They vary widely in their relations with Trinitarians, from strict exclusivity to open fellowship. Some views, like baptism in the name of the Lord Jesus Christ, are agreeable to many Trinitarians. Others, like their rejection of the doctrine of the Trinity, are not. Oneness Pentecostals are not part of a cult, but they represent an ecumenical challenge within the wider Christian community for greater mutual understanding and fraternal bonds of affection.

REFERENCES AND SUGGESTIONS FOR FURTHER READING

Boyd, Gregory A. 1992. *Oneness Pentecostalism and the Trinity.* Grand Rapids, MI: Baker Book House.

French, Talmadge L. 1999. *Our God Is One: The Story of the Oneness Pentecostals.* Indianapolis, IN: Voice and Vision.

Fudge, Thomas A. 2003. *Christianity without the Cross: A History of Salvation in Oneness Pentecostalism.* Parkland, FL: Universal.

Norris, David S. 2009. *I AM: A Oneness Pentecostal Theology.* Hazelwood, MO: Word Aflame Press.

Reed, David A. 2008. *"In Jesus' Name": The History and Beliefs of Oneness Pentecostals.* Blandford, UK: Deo.

Origins

ALLAN HEATON ANDERSON

✄   Pentecostalism began at the beginning of the twentieth century; there is agreement about that among most contemporary scholars. There is less agreement about where and how the movement began and spread. It has multiple roots, which include the radical evangelical missionary movement, the African-based slave religion in the United States, and the healing and Holiness movements of the Western world in the late nineteenth century. But by far the most widely publicized theories on the origins of Pentecostalism have it as a "made in America" religion. The beginnings of Pentecostalism are placed in nineteenth-century American radical evangelicalism, especially in the fringe groups within the Holiness movement and among disenchanted Methodists. Depending on the position of the particular historian or hagiographer, global Pentecostalism according to these theories was born either in the Church of God movement in the North Carolina Appalachian hills in the 1890s, in Charles Parham's Apostolic Faith in Kansas in 1901, or (the most popular theory) in the Azusa Street revival in Los Angeles during 1906–1909. Walter Hollenweger, in particular, wrote of the need to determine the origins of Pentecostalism from a theological or ideological perspective. He and others began to assert the important role of this predominantly African American church as the generator of Pentecostal churches throughout the world. More recently, Cecil M. Robeck, Jr., has definitively recorded the significance of Azusa Street and its leader, William Seymour, in global Pentecostal history. The rise of Pentecostalism in this revival in Los Angeles gave a certain authenticity to African American holistic Christianity. Outward manifestations of Pentecostalism's flexibility in different cultures and religions did not always satisfy Westerners, who were drawn by their own sense of cultural decorum toward promoting a more cerebral and less emotional expression of Pentecostal practice. This also occurred in early American Pentecostalism, when the founder of the "initial evidence" doctrine, Charles Parham, recoiled in horror at Azusa Street when he saw the intermingling of races in manifestations of ecstasy. Histories of Pentecostalism usually begin with American pioneers such as Parham and Seymour and then emphasize the beginnings of Pentecostalism in other countries with reference to missionaries sent from the United States or other Western countries.

Despite the importance of the Azusa Street revival in global Pentecostal origins, due recognition should also be given to places in the world (including other centers in the United States and Canada) where Pentecostal revival broke out independently of the Azusa Street revival and in some cases even predated it. The Korean revival began among missionaries in Wonsan in 1903 and soon spread to thousands of Korean people. This predated the 1904 Welsh Revival and quickly took on a Korean character of its own. The "Korean Pentecost" in Pyongyang in 1907 continued the earlier revival, affected other revivals in China such as the Manchurian Revival of 1908, and irrevocably changed the face of East Asian Christianity. Korean Pentecostals unanimously acknowledge the contribution of this revival to their movement. The Korean revival greatly influenced the present dominance of the Charismatic movement in the Presbyterian and Methodist churches there, many of whose characteristic practices have been absorbed by classical Pentecostal churches like Yonggi Cho's Yoido Full Gospel Church (by the 1970s the largest congregation in the world). Furthermore, although strictly speaking the Korean Pentecost was not a classical Pentecostal revival, early Korean revival leaders in the Presbyterian and Methodist churches were much more "Pentecostal" than the American missionaries might have wanted them to be, and their characteristic revival practices persist in Protestant and Pentecostal churches in Korea today.

In the case of China, the influence of Pentecostalism accelerated the development of indigenous churches, particularly because Pentecostals were closer to traditional folk spirituality with its sense of the supernatural than other churches were. Most of the grassroots Chinese churches today numbering millions of believers are Pentecostal either in explicit identity or in orientation. Pentecostalism in China, because of its egalitarianism and belief in the priesthood of all believers, also facilitated the development of churches independent of foreign missions. This was equally true of Pentecostalism in Africa and Latin America—something the early Pentecostal missionaries from the North could not have anticipated and probably would not have encouraged. Chinese evangelists crisscrossed that vast nation and beyond with a Pentecostal message similar to—but distinct from—its Western counterpart, resulting in many thousands of conversions to Christianity. A Chinese preacher, Mok Lai Chi, was responsible for the early spread of Pentecostalism in Hong Kong and South China and started a Pentecostal newspaper in 1908. The Methodist evangelist John Sung (Song Shangjie) with his healing and evangelism meetings in the 1930s and 1940s (he also spoke in tongues) was responsible for the spread of Pentecostal ideas throughout China and South East Asia.

The 1905–1907 revival at Pandita Ramabai's Mukti Mission in Pune, India, in which young women baptized by the Spirit had seen visions, fallen into trances, and spoken in tongues, began before the Azusa Street revival. This revival was understood by Ramabai herself to be the means by which the Holy Spirit was creating an Indian Christianity. Pentecostal missionaries worked with the Mukti Mission for many years, and Ramabai received support from the fledgling Pentecostal movement in North America and Britain. The Mukti revival had other far-reaching consequences that penetrated parts of the world untouched by Azusa Street. In 1907, American Methodist missionary Willis Hoover heard of this revival through a booklet written by his wife's former classmate Minnie Abrams, Ramabai's associate worker. Later, Hoover enquired about the Pentecostal revivals in other places, especially those in Venezuela, Norway, and India among his fellow Methodists. The revival in Hoover's church in 1909 resulted in his expulsion from the Methodist Church in 1910 and the formation of the Methodist Pentecostal Church, the largest non-Catholic denomination in Chile.

All over the world untold thousands of revivalists with no known Western connections were responsible for the spread of the Pentecostal gospel. In the Ivory Coast and the Gold Coast (now Ghana), a Liberian Grebo called William Wade Harris spearheaded a revival in 1914 that was quite distinct from the Western Pentecostal movement but with many phenomena including healing and speaking in tongues. This revival resulted in 120,000 conversions in a year, the largest influx of Africans to Christianity the continent had ever seen. We may never know whether Harris had any encounter with American missionaries from Azusa Street working in Liberia in his home region of Cape Palmas, but there were certainly no connections thereafter. In the 1930s, the Yoruba healing evangelist Joseph Ayo Babalola began revival meetings in southern Nigeria that swept many thousands into his Christ Apostolic Church. These various Pentecostal revivals were not primarily movements from the Western world to "foreign lands" but more significantly mass movements of conversion to Christianity within these continents themselves and independent of Western Pentecostal origins.

Although there were connections to Azusa Street through those missionaries who directly or indirectly went from there to different continents, due recognition must be given to those places where Pentecostal revivals broke out independently of this event, led by local leaders whose role has often not been featured prominently in Pentecostal historiography. Pentecostal origins are complex and varied, polycentric and diffused. A theory of origins in Los Angeles in 1906, while certainly having merit as far as some parts of the world are concerned, must be balanced by the equally convincing case of multiple, often unconnected religious and cultural origins. Seen from this perspective, Pentecostalism is neither a movement with distinct beginnings in the United States or anywhere else nor a movement based on a particular theology. It is a movement or, rather, a series of movements that took several years and several different formative ideas and events to emerge. The historical roots of Pentecostalism in the radical fringes of "free church" evangelicalism—together with an emphasis on "freedom in the Spirit"—render it inherently flexible in different cultural and social contexts and made the transplanting of its central tenets in different parts of the world more easily assimilated. With the passing of a century, the historical roots are not as easily recognizable.

It may be argued that the revivals independent of Western Pentecostalism in Korea, China, India, Chile, Nigeria, Ghana, and Côte d'Ivoire were not specifically Pentecostal revivals. It all depends on how we define the term "Pentecostal." If we consider the practices of healing, prophecy, speaking in tongues, other physical manifestations, and emotional prayer meetings to be characteristics of Pentecostalism, then we have to acknowledge the multiple origins theory. This more nuanced view will help us dispel the premise of treating American forms of Pentecostalism as normative.

It will maximize our understanding of the impact and influence of local leadership in comparison to that of Western missionaries, and it will enable us to better comprehend the contextualization of the Pentecostal gospel in different cultures, nations, and contemporary contexts.

REFERENCES AND SUGGESTIONS FOR FURTHER READING

Anderson, Allan. 2007. *Spreading Fires: The Missionary Nature of Early Pentecostalism.* Maryknoll, NY: Orbis.

Dayton, Donald W. 1987. *Theological Roots of Pentecostalism.* Peabody, MA: Hendrickson.

McGee, Gary B. 2010. *Miracles, Missions, and American Pentecostalism.* Maryknoll, NY: Orbis.

Robeck, Cecil M., Jr. 2006. *The Azusa Street Mission and Revival: The Birth of the Pentecostal Movement.* Nashville, TN: Nelson.

Charles Fox Parham

ALLAN HEATON ANDERSON

✣   Many, but by no means all, classical Pentecostals (and certainly those first associated with the Azusa Street revival) hold a belief that the baptism in the Spirit is invariably accompanied by the initial evidence of speaking in tongues. Charles Fox Parham (1873–1929) is the person credited with discovering the doctrine of initial evidence, but as we will see, his teaching of "missionary tongues" (the ability to speak in a previously unknown foreign language for the purpose of evangelism) did not endure in later Pentecostalism. Parham was an independent Kansas healing evangelist who resigned from the Methodist Church in 1895, experienced healing from the consequences of rheumatic fever, and began his own healing ministry thereafter. He moved to Topeka, Kansas, in 1898 where he opened a healing home and began publishing *The Apostolic Faith* in 1899, which propounded his views on healing in the atonement of Christ (accompanied by abundant testimonies by people claiming healing), premillennialism with the belief in a worldwide revival (the "latter rain") to precede the imminent coming of Christ, and a "third blessing" beyond conversion and "entire sanctification" called "baptism with the Spirit."

There is evidence that Parham came to believe in "missionary tongues" in 1899 through the testimony of one of Frank Sandford's disciples. Parham cannot be understood without reference to Sandford (1862–1948), an influential revivalist and healer. A former Baptist pastor in Maine who came to an experience of sanctification through the Holiness movement and a belief in divine healing through contact with A. B. Simpson, Sandford received an experience of Spirit baptism in 1894, which he described as an enduement of power. He founded the Holy Ghost and Us Bible School in 1895, where several future Pentecostal leaders were trained. Here, speaking in tongues as known foreign languages was believed to be a sign of the imminent return of Christ and the means by which the world would be evangelized—an idea that Pentecostals would pursue with vigor. Sandford lacked John Alexander Dowie's ethnic inclusiveness and pacifism, adding emphases on the imminent premillennial return of Christ; "spiritual warfare," a form of intercessory prayer; and Anglo-Israelism, the racist theory that the white Anglo-Saxon Protestant nations (especially Britain and the United States) were descended from the lost tribes of Israel. Sandford also later advocated circumcision, observance of Saturday as the Sabbath, and abstinence from pork. "Israel" was to be a blessing to all nations, which reinforced his missionary zeal. Although he was opposed to Pentecostalism, his main impact was the formative influence he had upon Parham, who imbibed many of his teachings, especially those of "missionary tongues" and Anglo-Israelism.

In February 1900 Parham met some of Sandford's followers from Sandford's Shiloh community in Maine, and Sandford himself came to Topeka in June that year. Parham was so impressed that he decided to accompany Sandford to Shiloh and enroll in his Bible school. He accepted Sandford's views including Anglo-Israelism, and the possibility of foreign tongues given by Spirit baptism to facilitate world evangelization remained with Parham for the rest of his life. En route to Maine, Parham visited Dowie's Zion City and Simpson's Bible and Missionary Training Institute, among other places. After six weeks of attending Sandford's lectures, hearing speaking in tongues for the first time, and accompanying Sandford on a preaching trip to Canada, Parham returned to Topeka convinced that God had called him to enter a new phase of ministry. He opened Bethel Gospel School in a newly leased building known as Stone's Folly and enrolled thirty-four students in a short-term school to train for world evangelization, where the only textbook was the Bible. Before leaving on a three-day preaching trip, Parham gave the students the assignment to discover in the book of Acts "some evidence" of the baptism with the Spirit. He convinced them that they had yet to receive the full outpouring of a second Pentecost, and he called them to seek this with fasting and prayer. They reached the conclusion that the biblical evidence of Spirit baptism was speaking in tongues, which they told Parham on his return. New Year's Eve 1900 was set aside for praying for this experience. A watch-night service was held with great expectation. Throughout New Year's Day of 1901 they prayed and waited until finally at 11 o'clock at night, Agnes Ozman asked Parham to lay hands on her to receive the gift of the Spirit. She was the first to speak in tongues, described later by Parham as "speaking in the Chinese language," and followed by others including Parham "in the Swedish tongue" three days later. Although this revival attracted the skeptical curiosity of the local press, for two years there was little acceptance of it. Leading Holiness and healing periodicals were either unaware of it or did not consider it of any significance.

After the death of the Parhams' son and their move to Kansas City, Parham preached at Holiness missions in Kansas and Missouri in 1903–1904, where there were again experiences of tongues and healings. By 1905, several thousand people were said to have received Spirit baptism in this new movement known as the Apostolic Faith. Parham's theology (unlike that of Dowie or Sandford) was in the "Third Blessing" framework. He formulated the "evidential tongues" doctrine, which became the hallmark of white American classical Pentecostalism, but unlike that of later classical Pentecostals, his theology insisted on the belief that tongues were authentic languages (xenolalia or xenoglossa) given for the proclamation of the gospel in the end times. These tongues were the second Pentecost, which would usher in the end, achieve world evangelization within a short period, and seal the Bride of Christ, the church. This was the doctrine that was proclaimed by William Seymour at Azusa Street, motivating scores of early Pentecostals to go out immediately as missionaries and begin to speak in the tongues of the nations to which they had been called.

We must acknowledge Parham's role in this all-important early motivation for frantic missionary migrations in early Pentecostalism; this was primarily and fundamentally a missionary movement from its beginnings to the present day. But it is also necessary to see Parham's role in the light of earlier precedents—especially that of Sandford, Dowie, and the healing movement—and to ask how effective he was in actualizing the outflow of these missionaries. He was most interested in tongues-speech as an experience of a deeper spirituality, although his wife later said that he aimed to train "Apostolic Faith" missionaries in Topeka "to go to the ends of the earth." Indications are that he did not succeed in taking the missionary potential of his doctrine beyond an initial evidence theory and that his Anglo-Israelism may have contributed to his lack of enthusiasm for "foreign" missions. After his break with Seymour, his differentiating between "true" and "false" tongues in fact stopped any flow of missionaries from his movement altogether. This left Azusa Street and other centers of Pentecostalism to spearhead the American missionary advance.

Although some writers consider Parham to be the founding father of Pentecostalism, he was ultimately refused this status by almost the entire North American Pentecostal movement. Thomas Junk, missionary in Shandong, China, rejected his leadership claims in 1909, and E. N. Bell, former Baptist pastor associated with Parham and later first chairman of the Assemblies of God, wrote a repudiation of Parham's leadership in October 1912. He warned "all Pentecostal and Apostolic Faith people of the churches of God" to "take notice and be not misled by his claims" (Bell 1912, 3). Parham's doctrine of xenoglossa for the proclamation of the gospel was quite different from the doctrine of evidential unknown tongues that later emerged in classical Pentecostalism. Some of Parham's other beliefs—such as Anglo-Israelism, "soul sleep," and the "annihilation of the wicked" doctrines—were also at variance with generally accepted Pentecostal doctrine.

Unlike his predecessors Dowie and Sandford, Parham did not actively engage in world evangelization. His efforts did not constitute the driving force that resulted in Pentecostalism's quick transformation into an international missionary movement. That role was filled by his onetime disciple William Seymour. After his failure to gain control of either Zion City or the Azusa Street revival in 1906 and his arrest in an unproved homosexual scandal in 1907, Parham lost most of his supporters. He spent the last two decades of his life in relative obscurity in Baxter Springs, Kansas, from where he led his Apostolic Faith movement. He continued to embrace Anglo-Israelism and became increasingly racist in his views, supporting racial segregation. He also had the ignominy of speaking to gatherings of the Ku Klux Klan, who he thought had "high ideals for the betterment of mankind" (Parham 1927, 5). Most Pentecostals in North America distanced themselves from him, especially his claim to be the sixth angel of the book of Revelation. But despite his many failures, there can be no doubt that it was probably Parham more than anyone else who was responsible for the theological shift in emphasis in early American Pentecostalism to tongues as the "evidence" of Spirit baptism, given for the evangelization of the nations.

REFERENCES AND SUGGESTIONS FOR FURTHER READING

Anderson, Robert Mapes. 1979. *Vision of the Disinherited: The Making of American Pentecostalism.* New York: Oxford University Press.

Bell, Eudorus N. 1912. *Word and Witness,* October 20.

Blumhofer, Edith L. 1993. *Restoring the Faith: The Assemblies of God, Pentecostalism, and American Culture.* Urbana: University of Illinois Press.

Faupel, D. William. 1996. *The Everlasting Gospel: The Significance of Eschatology in the Development of Pentecostal Thought.* Sheffield: Sheffield Academic Press.

Goff, James R., Jr. 1988. *Fields White unto Harvest: Charles F. Parham and the Missionary Origins of Pentecostalism.* Fayetteville: University of Arkansas Press.

Parham, Charles F. 1927. "Leaves by the Wayside: Ku Klux Klan." *The Apostolic Faith,* March.

Wacker, Grant. 2001. *Heaven Below: Early Pentecostals and American Culture.* Cambridge, MA: Harvard University Press.

Prophecy

MARGARET M. POLOMA

✄   Although prophecy is commonly understood as a prediction of future events, most would agree with Gerald T. Sheppard who in writing on prophecy insists that "prophecy does not typically predict the future, but gives assurance, confirmation, warning, or spiritual encouragement" (Sheppard 2001, 64). Prophecy is better described as a "forth-telling" of God's word than a foretelling of future events. There are some well-known men and women regarded in Pentecostal history as having had a special prophetic gift, and there is a contemporary prophetic movement afoot in Neo-Pentecostalism that insists on the restoration of the "office of prophet" (along with the offices of evangelist, healer, and apostle). Even those who acknowledge there is a special office of prophets would agree, however, that prophecy is a spiritual gift in which all believers can participate. According to the Pentecostal worldview, prophecy is thus not a gift relegated to a class of spiritually elite; it is available to men as well as women, young as well as old, children as well as adults, rich as well as poor.

Keeping in mind this broad definition of prophecy, there is a wide range of activities that may be referred to as "prophetic" by Pentecostals. Prophecy may take the form of "interpretation," given by a person in a familiar language as a response to incomprehensible tongues (or glossolalia). This is a common ritual for proclaiming a prophetic word to a corporate gathering of traditional Pentecostals. Neo-Pentecostal rituals are less likely to predicate a prophetic vernacular word with speaking in tongues; the word believed to be spoken by God is commonly proclaimed without an utterance in tongues. Prophecy is also used to designate other variations in which a word from God is proclaimed, including "anointed preaching," when the preacher feels like a channel of the Holy Spirit and words seem to flow in an effortless manner. Prophecy can be coupled with prayer for healing, where a healing evangelist might prophetically proclaim ailments for which or persons for whom divine healing is forthcoming. Similarly, it can be spoken by a lay minister who might receive prophetic insights about a person who is seeking healing prayer. When an intuited prophetic word of encouragement, confirmation, or warning is given by one individual to another, it is sometimes referred to as a "word of knowledge." Prophecy operates both on the collective level of church ritual and on the interpersonal level where two or more persons are engaged in prayer or even in secular activities.

Descriptions of the commonly accepted practices associated with prophecy differ widely, thus sounding a note of caution about any simple definition of the phenomenon. Definitions of prophecy that attempt to capture its breadth have been said to be vacuous, while those that simplistically limit prophecy to foretelling are usually ill informed. Prophecies notably reflect varied content, form, and style of deliverance as well differences in the self-description of the one delivering a prophetic message. Characteristic profiles of prophecy bear strong resemblance to other phenomena listed as "gifts of the Holy Spirit" as found in the New Testament (see especially 1 Cor 12–14), including glossolalia ("tongues and interpretations"), discernment of spirits, words of wisdom, and words of knowledge, as well as related practices of prophetic intercession and prophetic healing. All require "hearing from God"—whether through an intuited impression, a vision, a dream, a divine coincidence (serendipity), or verbal proclamation—and then speaking forth or acting upon God's word. All these forms are recognized as functioning to edify, encourage, and comfort, to provide correction and warning, to direct and guide, and to inspire intercessory prayer.

Putting aside theological distinctions about prophecy that seek to identify spiritual relatives of the prophetic family, it is possible to demonstrate a relationship between prophecy as forth-telling God's word and contemplative or intuitive forms of prayer. Social scientific surveys have reported that the majority of those who pray, Pentecostal as well as non-Pentecostal, claim to have heard God speak to them, directing them to say or do something specific. Prophecy, hearing, and responding to the voice of God thus may be regarded as an extension of simple prayer experiences commonly reported by the American public, especially by those who profess to be evangelical Christians. Prayer and prophecy, in theology and as found in survey reports, are inextricably linked. Prophecy involves intuitive prayer in which the person praying "listens" to God before speaking or taking action.

Prophecy, however, is more than a personal mystical experience through which God speaks to and through humans. Research has demonstrated that prophecy is a leading religious predictor of benevolent activities. In biblical terms, this finding reflects the Apostle Paul's admonition "Pursue love and strive for the spiritual gifts, and especially that you may prophesy" (1 Cor 14:1). While glossolalia is for "self-edification," Paul continues, prophecy is meant "for the church." The prophetic is not limited to human interaction with the divine; it also serves as a catalyst for "divinely inspired" interpersonal interaction. It is two-way interaction with God—described elsewhere in this volume as a basic component of Godly Love—that empowers charismatic interaction with others.

REFERENCES AND SUGGESTIONS FOR FURTHER READING

Grudem, Wayne A. 2000. *The Gift of Prophecy in the New Testament and Today.* Revised ed. Wheaton, IL: Crossway Books.

Poloma, Margaret M. 2003. *Main Street Mystics: The Toronto Blessing and Reviving Pentecostalism.* Walnut Creek, CA: AltaMira.

Poloma, Margaret M., and Ralph W. Hood, Jr. 2008. *Blood and Fire: Godly Love in a Pentecostal Emerging Church.* New York: New York University Press.

Sheppard, Gerald T. 2001. "Prophecy from Ancient Israel to Pentecostals at the End of the Modern Age." *The Spirit and the Church* 3(1): 47–70.

Pandita Sarasvati Ramabai

ALLAN HEATON ANDERSON

✄ Pandita ("Scholar") Sarasvati Ramabai (1858–1922) was a famous Indian Christian reformer, Bible translator, and social activist. Ramabai is significant both in the origins of Pentecostalism and in the acceptance of its phenomena among some in the wider Christian community. Ramabai was a converted Brahmin who had earlier rejected Hindu social propriety and married out of her caste. She was widowed with her baby daughter, Manoramabai, after less than two years of marriage. She became a Christian during her almost three-year stay in England, where she studied education, Greek, and Hebrew, and was baptized in 1883. From England she traveled to the United States, where she spent two and a half years studying education systems and publicizing her planned mission in India. A Ramabai Association was founded to pledge financial support for her school for the next ten years. Like most educated Indians, Ramabai believed in Indian nationalism, stimulated by the repression and arrogance of the British toward Indian social structures that had resulted in determined Indian resistance. She commented favorably on women's rights in American society, although not without fair criticism of shortcomings there.

She returned to India in 1889 and started a home for widows near Bombay (now Mumbai), which moved to Pune after a year. In 1895 she established a mission on a farm she had bought at Kedgaon near Pune, and her work shifted from a religiously neutral charity to an overtly evangelical Christian organization. This mission was given the name Mukti (salvation), and its main purpose was to provide a refuge for destitute girls and women, particularly those who had been the victims of child marriages and had become widows and those rescued from starvation in famine areas. The mission had forty-eight residents in 1896, but by 1900 there were almost two thousand. For some years the mission struggled to make ends meet, and funds coming in only covered bare necessities. Ramabai, however, believed that Hindu women could only find complete freedom by converting to Christianity, and her mission aimed to facilitate this and provided a total environment for its large community trained in income-generating skills.

Ramabai and her daughter, Manoramabai, had a team of seventy, including twenty-five volunteer workers from overseas. One of these was Minnie Abrams, a deaconess missionary in the Methodist Church since 1887 who joined Ramabai as an independent faith missionary in 1898 and took care of the mission during Ramabai's trip that year to the United States. Abrams was a significant contact person between Ramabai and the emerging global Pentecostal network. In 1904, Ramabai began her translation of the Bible into Marathi from Hebrew and Greek, a process that took her eighteen years (almost to the end of her life), a most remarkable achievement. She arranged for a musician to set her translation of the Psalms to Indian chant tunes, in order to change the over-Westernized Indian Christian liturgies that she disliked.

Much of the Christian half of Ramabai's life resonated with Pentecostal images and experiences. She identified increasingly with the radical evangelicals, the Keswick "higher Christian life" and Holiness movements, and D. L. Moody. Many revivalist networks began to promote her work in their publications. Ramabai attended and addressed the Keswick convention in England in 1898, where she asked for prayer for an outpouring of the Spirit on Indian Christians and pleaded for "1,000 Holy Ghost missionaries" (Adhav 1979, 216). After hearing of a revival conducted by R. A. Torrey in Australia, she dispatched Manoramabai and Abrams there in 1904, and they returned with the conviction that prayer and "pouring out your life" were required for revival. In January 1905, Ramabai instituted a special, daily, early morning prayer meeting, when seventy women would meet and pray, in her own words, "for the true conversion of all the Indian Christians including ourselves, and for a special outpouring of the Holy Spirit on all Christians of every land." The number at this daily prayer meeting gradually increased to five hundred. In July 1905, as she wrote two years later, "the Lord graciously sent a Holy Ghost revival among us, and also in many schools and churches in this country" (Dongre and Patterson 1963, 78). The revival lasted for a year and a half and resulted in eleven hundred baptisms at the school, confessions of sins and repentances, prolonged prayer meetings, and the witnessing of some seven hundred of these young women in teams (called Praying Bands) into the surrounding areas, about a hundred going out daily, sometimes for as long as a month at a time. The revival was reported in the Western evangelical and Pentecostal press soon after it occurred. References to the revival are plentiful and clearly situate it within the emerging Pentecostal movement. The first report of the revival in India entitled "Pentecost in India" was carried in the third issue of *The Apostolic Faith* in Los Angeles:

> News comes from India that the baptism with the Holy Ghost and gift of tongues is being received there by natives who are simply taught of God. The India Alliance says, "Some of the gifts which have been scarcely heard of in the church for many centuries, are now being given by the Holy Ghost to simple, unlearned members of the body of Christ, and communities are being stirred and transformed by the wonderful grace of God. Healing, the gift of tongues, visions, and dreams, discernment of spirits, the power to prophecy and to pray the prayer of faith, all have a place in the present revival." Hallelujah! God is sending the Pentecost to India. He is no respecter of persons. ("Pentecost in India" 1906, 1)

This report states that speaking in tongues occurred in the Bombay area before news of Azusa Street had reached India, and the first missionaries to India from Azusa Street, Albert and Lillian Garr, only reached Calcutta (Kolkata) a month after the report. There were several occasions of tongues speaking in different parts of India in the months before the Azusa Street revival was heard of. Two months after a visit by a Praying Band from Mukti to an Anglican mission station in Aurangabad in April 1906 (the month the Los Angeles revival began), tongues were evident among those who had been present—in June in Manmad, and in July 1906 in Bombay. It is unlikely that Los Angeles had any influence on what happened at Mukti. Abrams's own account of revivals in various parts of the world specifically links the Mukti revival with those in Wales and northwest India, sees the Korean and Manchurian revivals as issuing from these same sources, and the Los Angeles and European Pentecostal revivals as connected but separate movements. Both the Mukti and the Azusa Street revivals were formative events contributing toward the emergence of Pentecostalism.

Ramabai herself was a sympathetic and involved participant in a Pentecostal revival, who staunchly defended the spiritual gifts manifested there—including speaking in tongues—against prominent critics. The importance of this Indian revival for the Pentecostal missionary movement, not only in India but also much further abroad, cannot be underestimated. There were at least four far-reaching consequences. First, it is clear that the Azusa Street leaders saw the Indian revival as a parallel to the one in which they were involved. Second, women played a more prominent role in the Indian revival than in the American one. The revival was preeminently a revival among women, led by women, motivating and empowering those who had really been marginalized and cast out by society. This was another case of Pentecostalism's early social activism, empowering the oppressed for service and bestowing dignity on women. In this, the Mukti revival and Ramabai herself were pioneers within global Christianity and without precedent. The revival movement was also to result in an unparalleled missionary outreach of Indian Christian women into surrounding areas and further abroad. Third, both Ramabai in her ministry and the revival she led demonstrate an openness to other Christians, an ecumenicity and inclusiveness that stand in stark contrast to the rigid exclusivism of subsequent Pentecostal movements. Fourth was its impact on Latin American Pentecostalism. Abrams contacted May Louise Hoover, her friend and former Bible school classmate in Valparaiso, Chile, with a report of the revival in Mukti contained in a booklet she wrote in 1906 titled *The Baptism of the Holy Ghost and Fire*. As a result of Abrams's booklet and her subsequent correspondence with the Hoovers, the Methodist churches in Valparaiso and Santiago were stirred to expect and pray for a similar revival, which began in 1909 and constituted the beginning of Chilean Pentecostalism.

The various revival movements in Mukti, Valparaiso, and Los Angeles were all part of a series of events that resulted in the emergence of global Pentecostalism. The Mukti revival can legitimately be regarded with Azusa Street as one of the most important early formative centers of Pentecostalism. The legacy for Indian Pentecostalism of the Mukti revival continued well into the twentieth century through Indian leaders trained there and through missionaries who had been associated with Mukti. After the death of Pandita Ramabai in 1922, a year after her daughter, Manoramabai, died from heart failure, the overseas Pentecostal press continued to reflect on her life and work. As far as they were concerned, Ramabai and the Mukti revival were an essential part of their heritage.

REFERENCES AND SUGGESTIONS FOR FURTHER READING

Adhav, Shamsundar Manohar. 1979. *Pandita Ramabai*. Madras: Christian Literature Society.

Anderson, Allan. 2007. *Spreading Fires: The Missionary Nature of Early Pentecostalism*. Maryknoll, NY: Orbis.

Dongre, Rajas K., and Josephine F. Patterson. 1963. *Pandita Ramabai: A Life of Faith and Prayer.* Madras: Christian Literature Society.

Kosambi, Meera, ed. and trans. 2000. *Pandita Ramabai through Her Own Words: Selected Works.* New Delhi: Oxford University Press.

Mair, Jessie H. 2003. *Bungalows in Heaven: The Story of Pandita Ramabai.* Kedgaon, India: Pandita Ramabai Mukti Mission.

"Pentecost in India." 1906. *The Apostolic Faith,* November.

Revival

MARGARET M. POLOMA

✂   Revivals have given birth to major Protestant denominations and have spawned countless Christian sects over the centuries. They have been especially significant in American history, their by-products woven into the warp and woof of the American religious mosaic. Revivals have functioned to revitalize spiritual fervor, to reawaken apathetic believers, to renew existing religious structures, and to reform others. Pentecostalism, garbed in its playful spiritual worldview of possibilities that is antithetical to the dominant naturalistic dress of objectivities, was birthed in one such revival. It presents a worldview that embraces the miracles and mysteries that permeate the Bible, one in which affect plays an important role, and its loosely knit, weblike structures provide a milieu where revivals are actively sought. In North America, the decade immediately preceding the arrival of the third millennium was riddled with revival fires, largely sparked by revivals in Latin America, which in turn fueled other global revivals in countries of the former Soviet Union, Africa, Asia, and Latin America.

Although a revival is ultimately judged by its ability to revitalize and spread Christianity, the immediate sign that often draws believers and curious alike is its embodied worship. These physical signs include speaking in tongues, prophesying, jerking, shaking, resting in the Spirit ("going down under the power"), uncontrolled laughter and/or weeping, and even rolling on the floor (the probable reason Pentecostals are sometimes called "holy rollers"). What historian Ann Taves describes as "fits, trances, and visions" have commonly been part of the American revival scene and bring with them controversy, criticism, and critique (Taves 1999). The debate surrounding religious "enthusiasts" and "intellectualists" has a long history in America, going back to the transatlantic awakening of the 1730s and 1740s, during which there were bodily agitations not unlike those later seen in Pentecostal revivals around the globe. The early debate brought criticism from various sectors, including from the Congregationalist minister Charles Chauncy, who was concerned with social order and commitment to an established church. Moderate defense of the bodily agitations, trances, and visions came largely from revivalists, including the cautious Jonathan Edwards and the more accepting John Wesley. The enthusiasts (from the Greek, literally "filled with God") believed that God could be encountered with an individual's whole being while the intellectualists were convinced that any encounter with God was one of the mind, and the defenders differed in their judgments of authenticity of the various bodily demonstrations. Pentecostals became the newest enthusiasts, whose theology in theory, if not always in practice, made room for ongoing revivals.

Thus it was against a background of American religious revivals that Pentecostalism was born, giving rise to a network that would soon spread across the continent and around the world. Although several independent sightings of early Pentecostalism have been noted by historians of religion in places other than Los Angeles, many scholars argue that the Azusa Street revival led by the African American son of a sharecropper William Seymour (1906–1909) was the event that launched this global religious movement. In 1900 there were no Pentecostals as we know them today; present global estimates of Pentecostal believers count over one half billion. Whatever else it represented, the Azusa Street revival clearly flowed in the pietistic stream of American Christianity (itself birthed in earlier Methodist and Holiness revivals), where religious affect was at least as important as cognition. As such, the movement developing out of the Azusa Street revival has demonstrated an ongoing need for revitalization in order to weather the tendency for the charismatic to morph into routine and institutionalization. To paraphrase the famed psychologist Abraham Maslow, religions are born of peak experiences but soon become filled with non-peakers who teach other non-peakers about those early experiences. Ongoing intense religious or "peak" experiences found in revivals are needed for Pentecostalism to maintain its affective faith where doctrine and membership are secondary to firsthand experiences of the divine. This need for fresh revival rains, wind, and fire has not gone unmet.

The years from the late 1940s to the close of the twentieth century were accompanied by periodic revivals that modified the course and forged new tributaries for the worldwide Pentecostal movement that at one time or another has touched even mainline streams of Christianity. These include the healing revivals of the late 1940s and the Latter Rain movement of the 1950s, which popularized Pentecostal healing practices; the Charismatic movement of the 1960s and 1970s, which brought Pentecostal beliefs and practices into mainline churches, including Roman Catholicism; the renewed democratization of Pentecostal power, influenced by the late John Wimber and the newly founded Association of Vineyard Churches in the 1980s; and the countless revival sites that dotted the globe during the 1990s, which spread to the American continent. Scores of revivals ebbed and flowed during the last decade of the old millennium, with some enduring to provide revival waters for the new millennium. Perhaps the most significant North American site for revitalizing the multifaceted Pentecostal movement at the turn of the third millennium was the Toronto Airport Christian Fellowship (TACF) in Ontario, Canada, an epicenter of the latest wave of the Spirit movement. From its humble beginnings as a Vineyard church of some three hundred persons located in a small strip mall just outside the Pearson International Airport, TACF—the Toronto Blessing, as the revival was called—quickly became internationally known as the place where the "river" (a popular renewal metaphor) was flowing. It was a mere matter of months before tributaries of the Toronto Blessing developed around the world. The nightly renewal meetings at TACF (originally scheduled for 20–24 January 1994) continued uninterrupted through 2004, giving rise to Neo-Pentecostal networks that strive to keep revival fires burning through local conferences, networked schools of the supernatural, and remote mission trips to sites where revival is ongoing (Poloma 2003).

It is important to note that Pentecostal revival activity is not a simple example of neo-religious colonialism or Western expansion but, rather, a complex system of reciprocal effects and countereffects. The Toronto Blessing, for example, was ignited in part by a South African evangelist (now a U.S. resident), Rodney Howard-Browne, who prayed for a relatively unknown Missouri pastor, Randy Clark, who in turn ministered the outbreak of the Toronto revival. Clark, in time, would establish a revival network known as Global Awakening, which works together with other revival networks both nationally and internationally. John Arnott, the pastor of

TACF and its renewal, had a personal link to the Argentine revival, which began in 1982 and continues to impact the global Pentecostal-Charismatic community, often through the ministries of its globe-trotting evangelists. American missionaries Heidi and Rolland Baker launched a revival in Mozambique, while South African evangelist Rodney Howard-Browne ignited revival in America. From Pentecostalism's earliest Azusa Street revival days, pilgrims came from afar to experience the revival and took revival fires back with them, while American missionaries went forth to other lands with fresh revival zeal. From its inception, Pentecostalism has been a global religion. Revivals in other parts of the world once nurtured through the work of American missionaries and evangelists now play a significant role in rekindling revival fires on American soil.

REFERENCES AND SUGGESTIONS FOR FURTHER READING

Blumhofer, Edith L., and Randall Balmer, eds. 1993. *Modern Christian Revivals.* Urbana: University of Illinois Press.

McClymond, Michael, ed. 2007. *Encyclopedia of Religious Revivals in America.* Vols. 1–2. Westport, CT: Greenwood Press.

Poloma, Margaret M. 2003. *Main Street Mystics: The Toronto Blessing and Reviving Pentecostalism.* Walnut Creek, CA: AltaMira.

Taves, Ann. 1999. *Fits, Trances, and Visions: Experiencing Religion and Explaining Experience from Wesley to James.* Princeton, NJ: Princeton University Press.

Salvation

KENNETH J. ARCHER

✖   Pentecostals believe that salvation is the work of God for the restoration of all creation and especially the redemption of humanity (Gn 3:15; Dt 26:5–9; Lk 4:18–19; Mk 10:45; Eph 1:4–10; Rv 21:1–7). Salvation cannot be separated from creation or the consummation of creation. God's merciful judgment upon human sinfulness to restore creation makes redemption possible. Salvation, like creation, is born out of God's love (Jn 3:16). God's righteous judgment upon human sinfulness should be understood as God taking upon himself the full gravity of human sin in order to put humanity back into a right relationship with God and creation. For this reason, salvation has occupied a privileged place in Christian theology.

Salvation provides opportunity for a sinful and alienated people to enter into a dynamic covenant relationship with God (Heb 10). The believer is brought into a union with God and participates in the life of God (Jn 15:4–6, 17:20–26, 20:22). A person becomes a new creature in Christ Jesus through the Holy Spirit (Ez 11:19–20; 2 Cor 5:17). Therefore, the purpose of salvation is to reconcile humans back into a right relationship with God, which enables them to participate in a new community (1 Pt 2:4–12). Salvation is also concerned about the cosmic realm, which ultimately culminates in a new heaven and new earth (Rom 8:20–24; 2 Pt 2:13). Salvation enables creation and humanity to enjoy the life for which they were originally created (Jn 10:10). The final act of salvation is the glorification of the redeemed and the consummation of creation. Creation and the redeemed community enter into a glorified existence with the living God, which supersedes original creation (Is 11:4–9; Rv 21:1–4).

The basic definition of salvation is the act of saving, delivering, and making whole. Salvation embraces all dimensions of embodied life, including restoration of the image of God in humanity, healing, deliverance from demonic bondage and sin, and material provisions for sustaining life. Salvation, then, is a comprehensive term that addresses the full range of the effects of human sinfulness.

The theological breadth and depth of salvation cannot be captured by one or two words. It is expressed by diverse words, which coalesce into a rich matrix of meanings associated with salvation. Biblical words and theological concepts such as redemption, new birth, liberation, reconciliation, ransom, conversion, justification, adoption, faith, assurance, sanctification, glorification, union with Christ, perseverance, deliverance, rescue, safety, healing, soundness, and peace all reinforce that salvation is the story line of the Bible. God is the savior, and the predominant role of redeeming humanity falls upon Jesus Christ (Ps 27:1; Mt 1:21; 1 Tm 1:1; 2 Tm 1:10).

Salvation is God's merciful response to the problem of sin. Salvation cannot be understood fully unless we recognize the reality of the human condition. The need for redemption and deliverance is a result of the catastrophic consequences of the great rebellion of Adam and Eve (Gn 3), and the evil influence of rebellious created spirit-beings (fallen angels or demons). Humans have ingested the deadly virus called sin and transmitted it to all of creation (Is 53:6; Rom 5:12–14). Only God, into whose image we have been created, can save us from our sins and restore us to right relationships. The Son of God assumes human nature without losing his divinity and provides for our atonement (Lk 1:26–35; Phil 2:4–11; Heb 1:14, 2:14, 4:14–16). Through his incarnation, ministry, substitutionary death on the cross, resurrection, and ascension, God provides, assures, and secures our salvation. Jesus is the primary agent of salvation for there is no other name under heaven by which we are saved (Acts 4:12). As a result of the incarnation, we can be united to God. As a result of the shedding of his blood on the cross, we can be forgiven of our sins, reconciled to God, and liberated from the demonic kingdom (Rom 3:25; Heb 9:12–14; 1 Pt 3:18). As a result of the resurrection, we have one who sits at the right hand of the Father and intercedes for us (Heb 7:25). As a result of Pentecost, the Holy Spirit has been sent to abide with us (Acts 2:33). Jesus is the means for our redemption and shows us the way of salvation. All the redemptive benefits are provided for us because of the atoning work of Jesus Christ. The redemptive benefits are applied to us through the mission of the Holy Spirit.

Salvation is full and whole. Salvation addresses the whole embodied person (body, soul, spirit) and is extended to all of creation (Rom 8). Jesus saves us from sin (Lk 7:47–48), provides for our material needs, heals us from sickness (Mt 4:23) and death (Jn 11:25), sanctifies us from the power and penalty of sin (1 Cor 1:2), delivers us from Satan and the demonic realm (Mk 1:39; Lk 10:18–19), and baptizes us in the Holy Spirit (Acts 1:5). Through the Holy Spirit, Jesus restores us to a right fellowship with God, others, and creation. We are set free from captivity so that we can live loving, just, and holy lives for the glory of God.

Salvation emphasizes the personal, relational, corporate, and experiential dimensions. If one is not careful, salvation might be seen as individualistic. Salvation is personal, but it is lived out in community. God has graciously acted in space-time to bring about his one plan and purpose. The living God's purpose is to have one covenant community. God will be our God and we will be his people (Ex 6:7; Mt 2:6; 2 Cor 2:16).

Pentecostals take sin seriously and believe that through the Holy Spirit God's grace comes to convict, convert, consecrate, and empower people to love and live with God. The Pentecostal understanding of salvation is based upon God's unmerited grace and human response of faith. God's grace comes from the Spirit and the Word to the unregenerate depraved person granting him or her an opportunity to respond. The person is given an authentic opportunity to choose freely to receive forgiveness and to enter into a salvific relation with God (Acts 2:21; Rom 10:13). People, however, must respond positively to God's salvific invitation through faith and repentance (Mt 4:17). A person may reject God's invitation to enter into salvation, thus resisting saving grace and grieving God (2 Pt 3:9). If a person persists in resisting saving grace, he or she will experience eternal damnation (Rv 21:8).

Pentecostals, like Arminians and Wesleyans, maintain a biblical synergistic view of salvation. A biblical synergism affirms that God always initiates the redemptive relationship that enables one to respond voluntarily. God is always the benefactor, and we are the beneficiaries. Humans in their present depraved condition cannot respond to God. God's prevenient grace enables the depraved person to respond positively through faith and repentance, and this response precedes regeneration and culminates in eternal life. Salvation is always by grace through faith unto good works (Eph 2:1–10). It is a priceless and precious gift from God (2 Cor 9:15). Following Christ calls for our cooperation with God's grace in receiving and maintaining personal salvation. This biblical view of synergism is contrary to the monergistic view of Augustine, Calvin, and Luther, who believed in a deterministic understanding of the working of grace, that is, God is active and humans are passive. In their view God solely does the work of regeneration or new birth. Grace is irresistible, and only those individuals who were elected (predetermined) to salvation will be saved.

The person who responds positively to the proclamation of the gospel through the calling of the Spirit enters into the process of salvation (Acts 2:38; Rom 10:12–15). The process or way of salvation follows a temporal order. Salvation is a past, present, and future series of events (1 Pt 1:3–5; Rom 5:1–2). The process begins with regeneration and culminates in the glorification of the resurrected body. The way of salvation also includes the redemptive experiences of sanctification and Spirit baptism as well as the possibility of healing. Signs and wonders testify that the future kingdom of God continues to break into the present (Mk 16:17–20; Acts 2:42; Heb 2:4). Such acts are important manifestations of God's grace, which point to and find ultimate fulfillment in the future events of salvation.

Salvation is a past event, in the sense that through Christ's substitutionary death we can be saved (Heb 9:28). The redemptive experience of initial conversion begins the process of salvation. Jesus' mission means that sin itself, its consequences, and our experiences with sin are all temporal. For those who have been saved (born again), they will not bear the ultimate consequence of sin, which is eternal separation from God (Rom 8:38–39). The experiences associated with initial conversion are repentance, justification, regeneration, and adoption. Conversion signifies that one has entered into a new relationship with God.

Conversion means turning away from the world and the sinful way of life by turning toward God (Acts 3:19). Repentance signals that conversion is taking place. Faith is confidence in God's promise to save us through Jesus Christ. By faith one repents of his or her alienated and hostile relationship with God through confession of personal sin. Repentance involves personal remorse for sin and willingness to embrace God's way of life. As a result of converting, one is justified by God. Justification involves the forgiveness of sin (Rom 4:25). God acquits us of sin and puts us into a right relationship with him. God's justifying grace impacts the believer with transforming power, which brings into being a new creation. In being regenerated, we become a new person in Christ Jesus. We are no longer to live as a depraved person wallowing in sin (Gal 5:22–25). As a result of becoming a new person, we also are adopted into the family of God (Gal 4:6). We belong to God because we have been ransomed. We have been translated from the dominion of Satan into the kingdom of God. Adoption brings a new relational and legal status with God. We are to live as the family of God in the fallen world.

Justification makes sanctification possible. Sanctification is initially experienced at regeneration, but it is not entirely perfected in the believer (Jn 1:9). Although we are justified, God requires us to press on and work out our salvation (Phil 2:12). Sanctifying grace addresses the power of sin and the influence of Satan upon the life of the Christian and community. Sanctification involves both an ongoing process as well as definitive moments of deliverance. At new birth we experience initial sanctification because we have been separated from a sinful demonic world and brought into a peaceful relationship with God (Rom 5:1). Sanctification is a process that develops from and builds upon regeneration. It involves the ongoing ontological changes in the believer as he or she is transformed into the image of Jesus Christ. Sanctification involves crises experiences that transpire as one is liberated from the bondages of sin and Satan. We can journey with God into perfecting love, which is a life of holiness and compassionate care for fallen humanity and corrupted creation. Thus, sanctification, like justification, is not a static position before God. It requires ongoing repentance and participation in spiritual disciplines as we look forward to full redemption. God imparts sanctifying grace so that we might be free to enjoy the fullness of abundant life in hopeful anticipation of eternal life (Gal 5:1; Jas 1:25, 2:12).

The baptism in the Holy Spirit is a redemptive experience that enhances our relationship with God. It follows regeneration and is poured out upon a cleansed heart (Acts 2:38; Rom 5:5). Spirit baptism is the gift of the Father and empowers us to continue the ministry of Jesus Christ for the sake of the world (Acts 1:8). Speaking in tongues (glossolalic speech) is the biblical sign closely associated with the experience of Spirit baptism (Acts 2:4), and when it accompanies Spirit baptism, it is a personal prayer language that enables deeper levels of intimacy and opens up greater ability to live as a witness of the gospel. Spirit baptism should also produce a deep longing for God and a compassionate commitment to the mission of God. Joy, praise, fruit of the Spirit, and tears accompany the ongoing Spirit-filled life.

Salvation is a past experience but never a static experience. We have been saved and sanctified, but not yet glorified. Our future experience of salvation is connected to the second coming of Jesus. The dead in Christ will be resurrected, and those who are alive will be transformed (1Thes 4:16–17). Our earthly bodies will be transformed into glorified bodies so that we can enter into the fullness of salvation (1 Cor 15). There will be a new heaven and a new earth. The separation between heaven and earth, and between God and redeemed humanity, will be permanently overcome through the glorification of creation. Indeed, God will be our God and we will be his people enjoying the beauty of creation and the intimacy of fellowship. God is and most certainly will be victorious over sin and Satan. We have victory in Jesus Christ our Lord.

In summary, salvation is made possible through the atonement of Christ, yet it is a proleptic experience that is ongoing in the life of God's community. Salvation is an experiential relational journey with God in which we are being transformed into the image and likeness of Christ. Salvation is a past event, grounded in regeneration and anticipating the future glorification of creation. The community, through the powerful presence of the Spirit, lives in the world and shares in God's mission of redemption for the world but is not of the world. During this journey we can experience healings, deliverance, and Spirit baptism. Salvation provides the possibility of living holy, peaceful, and loving lives. We are invited to follow Jesus Christ faithfully through the personal presence of the Spirit into the mission of God, which is the redemption of creation and the salvation of humanity.

References and Suggestions for Further Reading

Archer, Kenneth J. 2010. *The Gospel Revisited: Towards a Pentecostal Theology of Worship and Witness.* Eugene, OR: Pickwick.

Gause, R. Hollis. 2009. *Living in the Spirit: The Way of Salvation.* Cleveland, TN: CPT Press.

Green, Joel B. 2003. *Salvation.* St. Louis, MO: Chalice Press.

Kärkkäinen, Veli-Matti. 2004. *One with God: Salvation as Deification and Justification.* Collegeville, MN: Liturgical Press.

Yong, Amos. 2005. *The Spirit Poured Out on All Flesh: Pentecostalism and the Possibility of Global Theology.* Grand Rapids, MI: Baker Academic.

William Joseph Seymour

ALLAN HEATON ANDERSON

✖   The African American preacher William Joseph Seymour (1870–1922), the son of freed slaves, was a Holiness preacher who heard Charles Parham preaching in Houston, Texas, in 1905. He was allowed to listen to Parham's lectures at his short-term Bible school for about a month—through a half-opened door, in keeping with the segregation customs of the southern states. Seymour was persuaded by Parham's views on the baptism in the Spirit. He was invited by the preacher Julia Hutchins to pastor a small African American Holiness church in Los Angeles in April 1906—but his sermon saying that tongues was a sign of Spirit baptism caused Hutchins then to lock the church building against him. Members of this church, soon joined by the evangelist Lucy Farrow from Houston and others (including eventually Hutchins herself), continued meeting with Seymour in prayer in Richard and Ruth Asberry's house at 214 North Bonnie Brae Street, where the Pentecostal revival began. At the house where Seymour was staying, his host, Edward Lee, asked the preacher and Farrow to lay hands on him on 9 April 1906, after which he fell to the floor as if unconscious and began speaking in tongues. Later that evening and over the next three days, seven others including Seymour and his future wife, Jennie Moore, received the same experience. For three days and nights, the house was filled with people praying and rejoicing, continuously and loudly. A few whites joined this group of African Americans, and the house became too small for the rapidly increasing numbers.

Within a week, the new movement had rented and moved into an old wooden building used for storage at 312 Azusa Street, a former African Methodist Episcopal Church building, where the Apostolic Faith Mission began. The Azusa Street revival (1906–1909) in central Los Angeles was the best-known of the earliest centers of Pentecostalism in North America and immediately sent out missionaries to other parts of the world. The revival began in a relatively poor working-class neighborhood, in an interracial and intercultural church led by Seymour. Daily meetings commenced at about ten in the morning and usually lasted until late at night, completely spontaneous and emotional, without planned programs or speakers. Singing in tongues and people falling to the ground "under the power" or "slain in the Spirit" were common phenomena. By mid-July, between five and seven hundred people were in regular attendance. This revival in a rundown part of the city was instrumental in turning what was until then a fairly localized and insignificant new Christian sect into an international movement. Early Pentecostals like Seymour were convinced they would overcome all obstacles through the power of the Spirit and thereby defeat the enemy Satan and conquer his territory, the "world." *The Apostolic Faith*, the revival's periodical and Seymour's mouthpiece (he wrote many of its articles himself), printed in its first issue in September 1906 that the "power of God" now had Los Angeles "agitated as never before." As a result of the coming of Pentecost with "the Bible evidences," many were being converted, sanctified, and filled with the Spirit, "speaking in tongues as they did on the day of Pentecost." The daily scenes in Azusa Street and in other parts of the city were "beyond description." The periodical declared, "the real revival has only started, as God has been working with His children mostly, getting them through to Pentecost, and laying the foundation for a mighty wave of salvation among the unconverted." These Spirit-baptized saints were now "daily going out to all points of the compass to spread this wonderful gospel." This was the transnational, universal orientation that was an essential part of Pentecostalism from its beginnings.

Seymour's core leadership team was fully integrated, with black and white men and women responsible for various aspects of the work (more than half were women), but Seymour remained in charge. He was described as a meek and gracious man of prayer, even allowing his critics to speak to his congregation and advertising the meetings of his rivals. Such was the impression Seymour made on people that healing evangelist John G. Lake, meeting him for the first time in 1907, commented that Seymour had "more of God in his life than any man I had ever met" (Lake 1981, 19). Seymour was a spiritual father to thousands of early Pentecostals in North America. For the next three years, the revival in Azusa Street was the most prominent center of Pentecostalism, further promoted by *The Apostolic Faith*, which reached an international circulation of fifty thousand at its peak in 1908. People affected by the revival started several new Pentecostal centers in the Los Angeles area, so that by 1912 there were at least twelve in the city. Hundreds of visitors from all over the continent, and internationally, came to see what was happening and to be baptized in the Spirit. Many of these individuals in turn began centers in various North American cities and eventually further afield. Hostile local press reports helped publicize the revival with glaring headlines such as "Whites and Blacks Mix in a Religious Frenzy." A local white Baptist pastor said that Azusa Street was a "disgusting amalgamation of African voodoo superstition and Caucasian insanity" (Faupel 1996, 202–5). Parham traveled to Los Angeles in order to "control" this revival in October 1906 and was disgusted, particularly by the interracial fellowship and what he termed "hypnotism" and the "freak imitation of Pentecost." "Horrible, awful shame!" he cried. Years later, Parham referred to Azusa Street as making him "sick at my stomach . . . to see white people imitating unintelligent, crude negroism of the Southland, and laying it on the Holy Ghost" (Anderson 1979, 190). Among other things, these racist remarks at least made the correct assumption that Azusa Street's Pentecostalism owed much of its manifestations of the Spirit to the broader African American religious milieu. Parham was rejected by Azusa Street as overseer, was never reconciled with Seymour, and fell into relative obscurity. A year later Parham was arrested on unproved charges of sodomy and was disgraced. His role in the formation of the classical Pentecostal doctrine of baptism in the Spirit was all but forgotten as Pentecostal leaders dissociated themselves from him.

Under Seymour's leadership the new Pentecostal movement took on international dimensions never realized in Parham's work. Perhaps because of all the hurt Seymour had suffered from white Pentecostals, he later repudiated Parham's "initial evidence" doctrine and was himself later rejected as leader by white Pentecostals unable to allow a sustained role for black leadership. After Parham's foiled attempt to take over the work, in 1908 Seymour's workers Clara Lum and Florence Crawford left Azusa Street, objecting to Seymour's marriage and taking the mailing list of *The Apostolic Faith* with them to Portland, Oregon where Crawford subsequently commenced her own Apostolic Faith Mission. Several competing white missions in Los Angeles drew away members from Azusa Street. In 1911, Chicago preacher William Durham, who had received Spirit baptism at Azusa Street, came to Los Angeles and tried to take over the mission while Seymour was away on a preaching trip, until Seymour returned to lock the church against him. Seymour's business manager, Glenn Cook, left with Durham at this time, and they started a rival congregation nearby. By 1912 Seymour's Apostolic Faith Mission at Azusa Street had become a small black congregation, and a constitution ruled in 1915 that leadership of the movement was to remain with a "man of color." After Seymour's death in 1922 his wife, Jenny, became "bishop" of the church, until 1931 when the building was demolished. At least twenty-six different denominations trace their Pentecostal origins to Azusa Street, including the two largest: the Church of God in Christ and the Assemblies of God. In a real sense, William Seymour and the Azusa Street revival mark the beginning of classical Pentecostalism, which reached from there to many other parts of the world.

References and Suggestions for Further Reading

Anderson, Robert Mapes. 1979. *Vision of the Disinherited: The Making of American Pentecostalism*. New York: Oxford University Press.

Faupel, D. William. 1996. *The Everlasting Gospel: The Significance of Eschatology in the Development of Pentecostal Thought*. Sheffield: Sheffield Academic Press.

Lake, John G. 1981. *Adventures in God*. Tulsa, OK: Harrison House.

Robeck, Cecil M., Jr. 2006. *The Azusa Street Mission and Revival: The Birth of the Global Pentecostal Movement*. Nashville, TN: Nelson.

Wacker, Grant. 2001. *Heaven Below: Early Pentecostals and American Culture*. Cambridge, MA: Harvard University Press.

Snake Handling

AMARNATH AMARASINGAM

"And these signs will accompany those who believe: by using my name they will cast out demons; they will speak in new tongues; they will pick up snakes in their hands, and if they drink any deadly thing, it will not hurt them; they will lay their hands on the sick, and they will recover." (Mk 16:17–18)

The above passage from the book of Mark serves as motivation for what many may consider to be a rather strange practice performed by some contemporary Christians: the handling of poisonous serpents. Most snake-handling services begin like all other church services with greetings and initial prayers. At some point, the pastor announces that serpents are present in the specially crafted boxes near the front of the church. Following this, one of the members begins a song, which is accompanied by clapping, the beating of drums, and the clashing of cymbals. The service becomes elevated to a celebration of God's presence. "Suddenly, and without announcement, someone moves toward one of the special wooden boxes, unlatches the lid, and calmly extracts a venomous serpent." Worshippers gather around while more serpents are removed from the crates and passed among the congregation. As the celebration dies down, the serpents are returned to their crates, and "the sick, oppressed, and spiritually needy" are offered assistance through prayer. After further sermons, songs, and personal testimonies, the two- or three-hour service comes to a close as members leave one at a time (Hood and Williamson 2008, 4, 5).

The practice of snake handling is usually traced to the emergence of the Church of God (Cleveland, Tennessee) and its later transition to Pentecostalism. In the late nineteenth century, R. G. Spurling, Sr., a Baptist minister, became disillusioned with denominational creeds, and he established the Christian Union Church in Monroe County, Tennessee. However, the Christian Union, which dedicated itself to upholding a pure biblical Christianity, soon dissolved. Spurling's son Richard G. Spurling

Jr. (1857-1935) continued the teachings of his father in the mountains of Appalachia. He was also one of the main speakers at the Holiness revival in Camp Creek, North Carolina, and became the pastor of the first Church of God (Cleveland, Tennessee) congregation established in Camp Creek, on 15 May 1902 (Synan 1997, 73, 74).

Another important individual in the history of the Church of God is Ambrose Jessup Tomlinson (1865-1943). A.J. Tomlinson first came in contact with the revival at Camp Creek in 1896 and became the pastor of the Camp Creek church on 13 June 1903. In 1904, Tomlinson moved the church to Cleveland, Tennessee, where, at the Second General Assembly in 1907, it was officially given the name Church of God. This tied the organization, historically, to R. G. Spurling Sr.'s earlier Christian Union, which had also used the name Church of God. The Church of God's subsequent adoption of Pentecostal beliefs and practices—and particularly the notion that "supernatural signs," namely, speaking in tongues, healing, and casting out demons, would accompany the true church—contributed to its early success (Hood and Williamson 2008, 24; Synan 1997, 78).

Although most scholars agree that pinpointing a single point of origin for the practice of snake handling is impossible, George Went Hensley (1881-1955) was the individual largely responsible for popularizing the practice of snake handling throughout the Appalachia region. Some evidence suggests that there was lively debate across the Appalachian Mountains and the Ozarks as to whether snake handling was important. In these regions, snake handling predates Pentecostalism and had been a part of folk ritual practice for some time. Hensley's first contact with the Church of God seems to have occurred at the church in Owl Hollow just outside of Cleveland, Tennessee. As the story goes, in 1908 the community at Owl Hollow invited A.J. Tomlinson as the keynote speaker for the dedication of their small church. As Tomlinson was too busy, he sent his sixteen-year-old son, Homer, instead. While preaching in the afternoon, Homer invited anyone wanting to be saved to come forward. Five young men responded and came to the front. One of these men was Hensley. Initially, Tomlinson approved of the practice of snake handling, probably influenced by the fact that his daughter Iris handled serpents. However, Tomlinson eventually denounced the practice, and Hensely left the Church of God to establish his own denomination, the Church of God with Signs Following. On 24 July 1955, Hensley, who apparently had experienced over four hundred snakebites during his life, was bitten for the last time by a five-foot rattlesnake. His death was ruled a suicide by the authorities (Hood and Williamson 2008, 38; Synan 1997, 189).

The snake-handling tradition has had many detractors, with many states having banned the practice from the mid-twentieth century onward. As Hood and Williamson (2008, 210) have argued, "it is our contention that, given little factual knowledge about snake handling churches and the long history of media stereotyping, lawmakers were easily persuaded that snake handling needed to be banned." The first state to ban snake handling was Kentucky in 1940. With media stories of snakebites and deaths, states found it fairly easy to pass laws against the practice. Not much is known about the contemporary practice of snake handling; the actual number of snake-handling churches and the actual number of handlers can only be estimated. Part of the reason for this is because snake-handling churches are now independent and largely fragmented. As Hood and Williamson (2008, 229) note, "we have documented churches in abandoned gas stations in Alabama, in isolated trailers throughout Appalachia, and in homes deep within the many hollows of the Appalachians." Many churches are also fairly secretive because of the possible legal ramifications. While the practice of snake handling may persist only among small close-knit gatherings in the isolated back alleys of the United States and the western provinces of Canada, it is fair to say, as Thomas Burton (1993, 135) has argued, that it is "the eclectic result in varying degrees of a number of religious, socio-economic, psychological, and traditional factors in American culture." In other words, although it is a practice embraced by only a small group of people, it has the potential to teach us much about the culture and religious landscape of North America.

REFERENCES AND SUGGESTIONS FOR FURTHER READING

Burton, Thomas. 1993. *Serpent-Handling Believers*. Knoxville: University of Tennessee Press.

Covington, Dennis. 1995. *Salvation on Sand Mountain: Snake Handling and Redemption in Southern Appalachia*. New York: Penguin.

Hood, Ralph W., Jr., and W. Paul Williamson. 2008. *Them That Believe: The Power and Meaning of the Christian Serpent-Handling Tradition*. Berkeley and Los Angeles: University of California Press.

Kimbrough, David L. 1995. *Taking Up Serpents: Snake Handlers of Eastern Kentucky*. Chapel Hill: University of North Carolina Press.

Leonard, Bill J. 1999. "The Bible and Serpent-Handling." In *Perspectives on American Religion and Culture*, ed. Peter W. Williams, 228–40. Malden, MA: Blackwell.

Synan, Vinson. 1997. *The Holiness-Pentecostal Tradition: Charismatic Movements in the Twentieth Century.* Second edition. Grand Rapids, MI: Eerdmans.

Spiritual Gifts

KEITH WARRINGTON

Pentecostals strongly assert a belief in the existence and role of spiritual gifts, given not on merit but as a result of the grace of God. Their name is not derived from the fact that they are spiritual, as opposed to earthly, gifts nor that they are given to people who have achieved a certain level of Christian spirituality. Rather, their derivation is the Spirit. Most Pentecostals refer to these manifestations of the Spirit as spiritual (*pneumatikoi*; 1 Cor 12:1, 14:1) or charismatic (*charismata*; Rom 12:6; 1 Cor 7:7, 12:4, 28–31) gifts, where the word "gifts" is understood. The first term, "spiritual," emphasizes the fact that the gifts are related to the Spirit (*pneuma*), while the term "charismatic" probably associates them with the characteristic of grace (*charis*). It appears that Paul uses the different terms interchangeably (Eph 4:11 uses neither in referring to the gifts mentioned therein). The following principles concerning these gifts of the Spirit, which are acknowledged by most Pentecostals, may be gleaned from 1 Corinthians 12:4–11.

First, the gifts are associated with the words "service" (1 Cor 12:5) and "working" (1 Cor 12:6). Thus, they are not to be administered selfishly but selflessly, and not for personal gain but for the benefit of others (1 Cor 12:7; Eph 4:12). When the manifestation of a gift ceases to exalt the person of Jesus (1 Cor 12:3) or to edify or develop other believers (Rom 1:11; 1 Cor 12:7), it loses much of its value. When there is an absence of a manifestation of love, there is an absence of a complete manifestation of God through the gift (1 Cor 13:1–3). All gifts must, therefore, be subject to clinical and careful assessment and judgment.

Second, every Christian receives a manifestation of the Spirit (1 Cor 12:6, 11; Rom 12:4–6). For some, this may be a regular capacity to function in a particular way, though it is possible for all to function in any gift. Although the potential is that all may manifest any of the gifts, Paul is clear that not all should be expected to manifest any in particular (1 Cor 12:29–30). Pentecostals believe that the gifts are "on loan" from the Spirit, and Christians are, therefore, expected to use them in ways that are appropriate to his character and will. Even when individuals frequently manifest a particular gift, it is preferable to understand this as a manifestation of the Spirit through them, and not that they are using the gift of their own volition.

Third, the gifts are intended to portray harmony in diversity. They are intended to reflect a dynamic relationship with the Spirit, resulting in beneficial relationships among each of the gifts (1 Cor 12:4–31).

Fourth, the gifts are described as being manifested according to the will of the Spirit (1 Cor 12:7, 11). The fact that these gifts are given by the Spirit increases the sense of responsibility on those who administer them, in particular that they do so appropriately, as indicated by the nature of the giver of the gifts.

Fifth, the gifts are varied (1 Cor 12:4–6). Paul provides five major lists of gifts in (a) Rom 12:6–8, (b) Eph 4:11, (c) 1 Cor 12:8–10, (d) 1 Cor 12:28, and (e) 1 Cor 12:29 (cf. 1 Cor 13:1–3, 14:6, 26). None of these is intended to be comprehensive, but merely representative. One of the main purposes of these lists is to demonstrate the diversity of gifts available to believers. Sometimes these terms refer to people who function as gifts to the Christian community (Eph 4:8). On other occasions they define a particular individual ability (1 Cor 12:8–10) or lifestyle calling (1 Cor 7:7).

Sixth, many Pentecostals acknowledge that the Spirit can empower believers to function in ways that are beyond their normal powers, and also that he may enable them to utilize the gifts they have already been granted as part of their personality as created by God. After salvation, these gifts and sensitivities may be enhanced and spiritually energized so as to achieve a higher potential of benefit for others. Thus, the abilities of individuals prior to their conversion may be used by the Spirit for the benefit of others. There is also the possibility of irregular or frequent manifestation of gifts that were not present in their lives prior to their salvation.

Seventh, the manifestation of the gifts in a public context must be subject to careful assessment. Sanctified common sense, the shared wisdom of the Christian community, a comparison of the content and manner of operation with the teachings located in the Bible, and receptivity to the Holy Spirit, all will help to confirm or reject the validity of the manifestation.

The gifts are intrinsically equal to each other. An authentic manifestation of any gift is determined by the appropriateness of its context of use. Thus, Paul identifies prophecy as having greater value than tongues without interpretation, because the former benefits those present while tongues that are not interpreted do not (1 Cor 14:1–6). It is not that prophecy is intrinsically superior to the gift of tongues, since both are manifestations of the Spirit, but the former is more valuable to the community since it is understandable and, therefore, beneficial.

Eighth, gifts may be manifested in association with others. Thus, in healing, it is appropriate to expect the gifts of faith and discernment also to be operative. Similarly, the exercise of the gift of administration would anticipate the presence of the gift of wisdom.

REFERENCES AND SUGGESTIONS FOR FURTHER READING

Kydd, Ronald A. N. 1984. *Charismatic Gifts in the Early Church: An Exploration into the Gifts of the Spirit during the First Three Centuries of the Christian Church.* Peabody, MA: Hendrickson.

Lim, David. 1991. *Spiritual Gifts, a Fresh Look: Commentary and Exhortation from a Pentecostal Perspective.* Springfield, MO: Gospel Publishing House.

Petts, David. 2002. *Body Builders: Gifts to Make God's People Grow.* Mattersey, UK: Mattersey Hall.

Schatzmann, Siegfried S. 1987. *A Pauline Theology of the Charismata.* Peabody, MA: Hendrickson.

Warrington, Keith. 2008. *Pentecostal Theology: A Theology of Encounter.* New York: T&T Clark.

Spirituality

PETER D. NEUMANN

To understand Pentecostal spirituality, it is necessary first to define "spirituality" more broadly in the Christian context. Daniel E. Albrecht helpfully identifies Christian spirituality as "*the lived religious experience of the Christian faith*" (1999, 14; original emphasis). Spirituality, then, does not refer to articulated theological doctrines, although it shapes and is shaped by such. Nor does the term refer simply to particular practices or rituals performed in a given worship setting, although these are often a primary means of expressing and reinforcing spirituality. Spirituality, rather, is the way in which the "spiritual dimension" of the human being is expressed or lived out, in and through everyday life and religious experiences. It is the way, or approach, taken in life and worship by which people relate to God (Albrecht 1999, 23).

Spirituality is especially significant for understanding Pentecostalism, since it arguably serves as the primary means for differentiating Pentecostals from other Christian traditions and spiritualities—in contrast, for example, to examining Pentecostal theological beliefs and/or practices alone (Albrecht 1999, 23–24). The goal here, then, will be to identify certain features of Pentecostal spirituality that distinguish it from other Christian spiritualities. Admittedly, it can be a challenge to define Pentecostal spirituality because of the fact that there are variances in expression between the so-called three waves of Pentecostalism (classical Pentecostals, Charismatics, and Neo-Pentecostals) and also because of the tremendous and constantly evolving diversity of beliefs and practices within Pentecostalism globally. While the three waves do share similarities with regard to spirituality, what follows will first attempt to identify features of classical Pentecostal spirituality, while highlighting possible variances with the other two waves where appropriate. In brief, Pentecostal spirituality is (1) experiential, (2) biblical/revelatory, (3) holistic, and (4) missional/pragmatic.

Pentecostal spirituality should be understood first and foremost as experiential. This is perhaps best appreciated in contrast to other Christian traditions that (stereo)typically approach spiritual life from a starting point of rational assent to particular doctrines (Protestant evangelical, for example) or through participation in liturgy associated with a particular church tradition (Roman Catholic, for example). It is not that Pentecostals do not assent to doctrines, or that they do not have traditions and forms of worship (see Albrecht). Charismatics, in particular, would view spiritual life as being worked out within and through a given ecclesiological and liturgical tradition. For Pentecostals, however, experience of God, by the Holy Spirit, is the point of departure for spirituality.

So, what is it that Pentecostals mean by "experience of God"? In short, Pentecostals believe that the Holy Spirit is intimately involved in creation and especially in the lives of believers, personally, in a way that can be palpably experienced or "felt." For this reason Steven Land, among others, argues that Pentecostal experience of God should be understood as being located primarily in the affective dimension of the human being (Land 1993, 13). Such experiences with the Spirit serve (potentially and hopefully) to effect radical transformation within the lives of believers, which can be expressed in various ways. Experience of God for Pentecostals, then, is best understood as encounter with the Spirit—with the transcendent God who is "Other." This is in contrast to other ways of speaking about experience of God that accent God's immanent involvement in and through all creation. Pentecostal experience of God is better understood as a "transcendent-immanence"—a close encounter with the God who is able to interrupt the everyday course of life and history to empower and edify God's people.

This approach to experience of God should, for the most part, also be distinguished from mysticism (traditionally understood), since Pentecostals do not typically emphasize loss of consciousness or self in the divine. This is not to deny that Charismatics belonging to churches with a historical mystical tradition (such as the Roman Catholic Church) might view this somewhat differently (Spittler 1988, 146), or that Pentecostal worship sometimes has more "contemplative" moments (Albrecht 1999, 240). When Pentecostals speak of having an experience of God, however, it is probably best to understand this as a form of "religious experience," although profoundly shaped by particular theological beliefs and practices (and, therefore, not "generic" religious experience).

Pentecostals, then, expect and emphasize encounters with the Holy Spirit that radically transform their broader Christian experience and spirituality. Such encounters with God are often described using the nomenclature of "Spirit baptism" (borrowing the metaphor from the book of Acts), emphasizing a sense of being "immersed" in or overwhelmed by the Holy Spirit. Charismatics and Neo-Pentecostals would not necessarily articulate the experience of Spirit baptism in quite the formulaic way as do classical Pentecostals (that is, as a "stage" within Christian experience), but nevertheless, such experiences are radically transformational and very personal—the Spirit being "felt" by and affecting the overall spiritual disposition of the individual.

While acknowledging the personal (even individualistic) emphasis on such experience, this Spirit-focused expectancy works itself out in both personal and communal expressions. Such experiential expectancy explains why Pentecostals emphasize prayer as central to spirituality (since God is close and will respond). It also accounts for why corporate worship is usually quite celebrative and invites an array of spontaneous and tangible expressions, including the variety of manifestations of spiritual gifts (for example, prophecy, tongues, healings, and so on), as worshippers respond to the Spirit's presence and activity. It is important, then, to appreciate the priority of experience within Pentecostal spirituality, and as Russell P. Spittler notes, only by doing so will the other features of Pentecostal spirituality make most sense (Spittler 1988, 147).

Given the weighty emphasis on experience in Pentecostalism, what is it that grounds Pentecostal experience(s) of the Spirit? Put another way, what keeps such encounters from being "free-floating," generic "religious experiences," open to a multitude of interpretations? The second major feature of Pentecostal spirituality, especially in its classical form, is its biblical/revelatory nature. Pentecostal spirituality finds its anchor in the Bible (especially the book of Acts) and is furthermore shaped by an intuitive desire to see a restoration of New Testament apostolic activity (including signs and wonders) in today's world. It is no coincidence that the official periodical of the 1906–1909 Azusa Street revival was entitled *The Apostolic Faith*—since such language expressed early Pentecostal restorationist attitudes. The point here is that Pentecostal experience of God is self-consciously understood as experience of the Jesus and Holy Spirit identified by and recorded in the pages of Scripture.

This restorationist biblicism also explains why Pentecostals are quite comfortable in their expectancy for the manifestation of the variety of spiritual gifts, including more extraordinary types such as healings, tongues, prophecy, and miracles. Since these manifestations are mentioned in the New Testament, Pentecostals are certain that the Spirit will make such available to believers today. After all, Jesus the Spirit baptizer is "the same yesterday and today and forever" (Heb 13:8). In this way Pentecostal spirituality is deeply rooted in the biblical Christian tradition. Charismatics and Neo-Pentecostals would also share the assumption that all the gifts of the Spirit are available today. However, they (particularly Charismatics) are less likely to adhere to classical Pentecostal primitivistic restorationism, since there is more openness to also appreciating the Spirit's work in and through the historical church tradition (which classical Pentecostals have frequently viewed with deep suspicion).

Also associated with and grounded in the biblical revelation is the belief in the Spirit's ongoing revelatory activity, in such gifts as prophecy, and so-called words of knowledge and wisdom (1 Cor 12:7–11). Since these prophetic-type gifts are mentioned in the New Testament, it is assumed that the Spirit will use such means to continue to speak to believers today. Such revelation is generally understood as not being equivalent in authority to the biblical canon and as needing to be evaluated by Scripture. With regard to Pentecostal spirituality, however, this belief in ongoing revelation again highlights the Pentecostal assumption that the Holy Spirit of the Bible is tangibly active within the church, speaking to and through believers.

Third, because Pentecostals are expectant that the Holy Spirit can be encountered in radical and transformative ways, their preparation for and response to such encounters is expressed holistically. Spirituality, in other words, involves the entire human person in all its dimensions—physical, emotional, social, mental, and so on. This is perhaps nowhere better exemplified than in the Pentecostal corporate worship setting (Albrecht 1999, 237–51). Pentecostals frequently enter into worship with exuberant celebratory praise, upraised hands, singing, shouting, clapping, dancing, laying on of hands in prayer for healing or Spirit baptism, anticipating that God will palpably meet his people (especially) in the midst of such an environment. Although Pentecostal spirituality is often identified as being individualistic, the fact that the communal worship setting plays such a central role in Pentecostal experience of the Spirit should nevertheless not be overlooked; Pentecostal holistic spirituality relies on this social dimension.

The response of worshippers to the "felt" presence of the Spirit is also expressed holistically in physical and emotional ways—in tears, laughter, tongues, healings, dance, singing, shouting, testimony, and the like. The affinity for oral expression within Pentecostal spirituality is a point not to be missed here. It helps underscore why Pentecostals are often better understood through their preaching, testimonies, and worship activities than by what they write in books. This holistic feature of Pentecostalism helps contrast their spirituality to that of other Christian traditions, which might approach spirituality more cerebrally or rationally. In sum, then, Pentecostal spirituality involves the whole person in its anticipation of and in response to encounter with the Spirit (Cartledge 2007, 19–32).

Finally, Pentecostal spirituality is missional and pragmatic. Pentecostals understand that experience of the Spirit will—in fact, should—result in personal transformation that radically affects the way one's Christian life is lived out in the world. In other words, encounter with the Spirit comes with a goal or purpose—it is missional and vocational. This is explicitly clear in the classical Pentecostal understanding of Spirit baptism, in which the believer is empowered for the purpose of service, primarily evangelism. With Charismatics and Neo-Pentecostals, this "mission" might be interpreted somewhat differently, perhaps emphasizing personal or church "renewal." In any case, encounter with the Spirit, as personal as it might be, is ultimately intended for more than simply the spiritual benefit of the individual. The Spirit touches the lives of believers in powerful ways, calling them to participate in the mission of God in the world.

This missional feature is tied to a pragmatic disposition among Pentecostals, which is intertwined with the above-mentioned experiential and holistic features of their spirituality. Not only are Pentecostals confident that the Spirit calls and enables believers to participate in the divine mission, but they also assume that there should be tangible evidence of the Spirit's presence and activity in and through the lives of believers. Pentecostals, then, tend to be results-oriented; they look for the "cash value" in any spiritual endeavor and seek perceptible confirmation of the Spirit's work. Such pragmatism is not without its weaknesses. The lack of tangible (and almost immediate) evidence of the Spirit's activity may give some Pentecostals reason to doubt whether the Spirit is really active at all in a given situation. But confidence in the Spirit's power and expecting to see results of the Spirit's work (and quickly!) have had the benefit of leading Pentecostals often to adopt a bold entrepreneurial attitude and a willingness to initiate new missional endeavors in creative ways (Albrecht 1999, 250; Wacker 2001, 9–14).

Pentecostal spirituality, then, while expressed diversely in its global context, can largely be identified as being experiential, biblical and revelational, holistic, and both missional and pragmatic. Furthermore, it should be evident that all these characteristics are interwoven, in that they mutually inform and support one another. It is this combination of features that makes Pentecostal spirituality unique within the broader Christian tradition.

REFERENCES AND SUGGESTIONS FOR FURTHER READING

Albrecht, Daniel E. 1999. *Rites in the Spirit: A Ritual Approach to Pentecostal/Charismatic Spirituality.* Sheffield: Sheffield Academic Press.

Cartledge, Mark J. 2007. *Encountering the Spirit: The Charismatic Tradition.* Maryknoll, NY: Orbis.

Land, Steven J. 1993. *Pentecostal Spirituality: A Passion for the Kingdom*. Sheffield: Sheffield Academic Press.

Spittler, Russell P. 1988. "The Pentecostal View." In *Christian Spirituality: Five Views of Sanctification*, ed. Donald A. Alexander, 133–54. Downers Grove, IL: InterVarsity Press.

Wacker, Grant. 2001. *Heaven Below: Early Pentecostals and American Culture*. Cambridge, MA: Harvard University Press.

Suffering

KEITH WARRINGTON

✖   Scholars of Pentecostalism have largely ignored the concept of suffering. Regardless of this scholarly lacuna, Pentecostal practices such as divine healing and deliverance from demonic influences, as well as the preponderance of Pentecostalism among the poor in both the West and all segments of the Global South, mean that suffering is a central theological and experiential concept within the global Pentecostal movement. Even though many Pentecostals have experienced various forms of suffering, the suspicion that suffering may be inappropriate for believers who exist in relationship with an omnipotent God lingers in the minds of some. Traditionally, few Pentecostals have considered the possibility that suffering may be embraced as the path intended by God for Christians, for his glory and for their good. However, moves toward the development of a Pentecostal theology of suffering have been made in recent years. The 1989 General Presbytery of the Assemblies of God in the United States, one of the major Pentecostal denominations, declared that the notion that suffering should not be viewed as an appropriate experience for believers was erroneous and elitist. Self-afflicted suffering or conditions caused by unhealthy lifestyles are not to be affirmed as offering positive consequences. Although some suffering may be caused by personal sin (Acts 5:1–11; Jas 5:15–16), much global suffering results from often inexplicable, though sometimes human-made, disasters.

At first sight, it may be assumed that a basic aspect of the ministry of Jesus was to remove suffering. However, not all suffering was remedied by

Jesus, nor is there evidence to suggest that this was an important part of his agenda. In his ministry there is little reference, if any, to the removal of slavery, the oppression of the Roman empire, the crippling poverty of the people, or the many other aspects of life that called for a radical solution to establish justice. Indeed, rather than causing all suffering to flee, he forecast suffering for his followers (Mk 10:38–45). As in the Old Testament (Jer 20:2), persecution was to be the normative experience of followers of God (Rom 8:17).

Similarly, although Jesus functioned with authority, he himself suffered. The path of the Messiah was one that commenced with a manger and concluded in the nakedness of a cross and the burial cloths of a tomb. The book of Acts and the lives of the apostles demonstrate that suffering continued as a normal experience of believers. As Jesus' mission was born and ended in suffering, so also the mission of the early church was conducted in the context of suffering.

Suffering is part of life; it does not sidestep the Christian. It is part of life in a world that has been harmed by sin. However, in all contexts of suffering, God has committed himself to be present. This means that his supportive resources are available and directed to believers whenever they are suffering. It is significant to note that Paul writes more about suffering than he does about restoration from it or its removal. Instead, he speaks about its presence in the life of a believer as being normative, a point echoed elsewhere in the New Testament (Jas 1:2, 3, 12, 5:10, 11; 1 Pt 1:6, 2:19–25).

Suffering can have positive benefits for those suffering and their communities. Because of a physical weakness, which resulted in his not being able to travel, Paul remained and preached the gospel to the Galatians (4:13). Although not all suffering is intended to provide lessons for suffering believers and those around them, the testimony of Paul (2 Cor 12:7) provides encouragement to consider such a possibility. For Paul, suffering had potential value, and so he removes the assumption that it is only associated with the displeasure of God. Instead, he associates suffering with positive benefits.

Occasions of suffering can result in God refining, transforming, or correcting his followers (1 Cor 11:29–32; Jas 1:2–4). Although suffering will not be present in heaven and is not intrinsically good, God occasionally uses it for his purposes nevertheless. Suffering may provide an opportunity to better contemplate God, depend on God, or hear from God. It also provides a context for demonstrating love for others (2 Cor 1:3–5). Although suffering is part of life in a fallen world that affects all, at the same time it provides opportunities for supporting and praying for one another.

Suffering also has the potential for being a valid context for reflecting God, and being understood as a pathway of personal positive development as much as a supernatural restoration. This is often the case in contexts where non-Christians (and Christians) have the opportunity to see a believer reflecting God in adversity as well as where a person has had that adversity removed.

The Holy Spirit is related not only to miracles, signs, and wonders but also to suffering and weakness. It is not the case that life lived in the shadow of the cross and life lived in the power of the Spirit are mutually exclusive. Thus, when Paul describes his sufferings (2 Cor 2:14–16), which resulted in people hearing the gospel, he concludes that the Spirit was part of the enterprise (2 Cor 3:3). Similarly, he associates suffering with being led by the Spirit (Acts 14:22). Luke writes with a similar agenda, identifying Paul's journey to Jerusalem to suffer as not only being prophesied by the Spirit (Acts 21:11) but also resulting from the leading of the Spirit (Acts 20:22).

However, in this suffering, the power of God is made manifest. The weakness of Christians, referred to in Romans 8:26, results in the unilateral involvement of the Spirit, in order to support them in their time of powerlessness. When the pressure of one's situation results in despair edging ever closer, Paul describes the presence of the Spirit as enabling Christians to retain the belief that their suffering is the prelude to something better (Rom 5:3–5). The Spirit thus enables the suffering Christian to abound in hope (Rom 15:13). Paul, therefore, encourages his readers to believe that their sufferings are not resulting from the superior power of the enemies of God. On the contrary, God is supreme, the Spirit affirms this fact (Rom 8:28), and the glory of the future will wipe out the apparent contradictions of the present.

In the context of the weakness of Christians, Paul also refers to the fact that the Spirit feels for them with groans that are too deep for words (Rom 8:26). Paul is not identifying the occurrence of the Spirit's intercession on their behalf but, instead, specifying that he is doing so, and that they may depend on the fact that such intercession is full of sincerity, even though they may not hear it. Thereafter, the Spirit is presented as operating practically on their behalf (Rom 8:26), helping them. Here, Paul uses a rare verb for "help" and prefaces it with another word that emphasizes the intensity of the help offered. Not only does the Spirit help, but he also significantly helps those who are weak and suffering.

Furthermore, Paul refers to the fact that the Spirit prays for believers in their weakness (Rom 8:26, 27). The picture offered is of the divine Spirit, so intimately relating to Christians that, for a moment, it is as if his closeness to them is greater than it is to God, enabling him to pray for them. This concept of the Spirit demonstrating this quality of empathy with Christians is remarkable. Even though they may not know how to pray, they are encouraged to recognize that the Spirit who affirms them (Rom 8:16, 17) himself prays for them (8:26) in accordance with God's will (8:27) and purpose (8:28).

Christians are not exempt from the suffering experienced in the world; in reality, they participate in its pain (Rom 8:18–23), and so does the Spirit. The suffering experienced by humanity is not the fault of the sufferers; rather, it is sin that is at fault, and both creation and humanity suffer as a result. However, both creation and humanity will be redeemed from this situation when God resolves the issue of sin, while the expectation of Paul is that Spirit-empowered Christians should positively impact the suffering world whilst being individually and corporately supported by the Spirit. Suffering must be viewed in the context of eternity, where all our questions may be answered in the knowledge that the God who directs the lives of Christians does so, not callously and uncaringly, but authoritatively and lovingly.

REFERENCES AND SUGGESTIONS FOR FURTHER READING

Brand, Paul, and Philip Yancey. 1993. *Pain: The Gift Nobody Wants.* New York: HarperCollins.

Carson, D. A. 2006. *How Long, O Lord? Reflections on Suffering and Evil.* Second edition. Grand Rapids, MI: Baker Academic.

Dunn, Ronald. 1994. *When Heaven Is Silent.* Waco, TX: Word.

Warrington, Keith. 2005. *Healing and Suffering: Biblical and Pastoral Reflections.* Carlisle, UK: Paternoster.

Yancey, Philip. 1998. *Where Is God When It Hurts?* London: Pickering and Inglis.

Televangelism

CALVIN L. SMITH

✂ Religious broadcasting is not an exclusively Pentecostal phenomenon. For example, the Catholic priest Charles Coughlin's weekly radio broadcasts in the 1930s reached audiences of millions, while more recently, Jerry Falwell and Robert Schuller are firmly outside the movement. Nonetheless, from the outset of the movement, Pentecostal preachers were quick to recognize the opportunities offered by religious broadcasting in all its facets. Clearly, there are doctrinal reasons for this. Already strongly conversionist by virtue of its revivalist roots, early classical Pentecostalism's eschatological interpretation of its pneumatology and pneumapraxis, associating the movement's inauguration with the "last days," contributed considerably to a sense of evangelistic urgency. Thus, it was a logical step for revivalist Pentecostal preachers such as Oral Roberts and Aimee Semple McPherson to exploit radio in order to reach wider audiences than could be accommodated only in buildings or tent meetings. With the arrival of television, Pentecostals quickly embraced the new medium, so that even by the early 1950s Rex Humbard—one of the pioneers of televangelism (a term coined by Jeffrey Hadden and Charles Swann; 1981)—was broadcasting church services weekly, and just a few years later, Oral Roberts had developed the infrastructure necessary to reach most of the American television audience.

To this driving evangelistic motivation we might add other reasons that Pentecostalism has embraced wholeheartedly—and indeed, monopolized—the electronic media. Given the association between old-style Pentecostalism and a culture of orality, religious broadcasting has proved attractive to the Pentecostal masses. More generally, sociologist Steve Bruce argues that televangelism is conducive to conservative and fundamentalist expressions of Protestantism (including Pentecostalism), which eschew liturgy in favor of "hearing the Word." Bruce also highlights the entrepreneurial drive exhibited by Pentecostal ministers and organizations, which contributes to the success of the Pentecostal televangelists (1990). It may also be argued that Pentecostalism's belief in the miraculous is prime territory for exploitation by what televangelism commentator Quentin Schultze refers to as the "new sorcery," where the televangelist's showmanship, entertainment, and miracle-working is directly compared with the slick "snake oil" salesmen and quacks of yesteryear (1991). Aside from this focus on healing and the miraculous, the medium's unashamed culture of soliciting donations from viewers lends itself particularly effectively to the dissemination of that other component of the so-called health and wealth gospel—prosperity.

From its very inception, televangelism and money have been inseparable bedfellows. Bruce details how, in 1961, Pat Robertson purchased a defunct UHF television station and raised finances for a single broadcast just long enough to solicit further donations. Later, Robertson's telethon—requesting seven hundred people to pledge ten dollars a month to cover ongoing broadcasting costs—gave rise to his famous 700 Club talk show, hosted by Jim Bakker (Bruce 1990, 38–39). Bakker, who later left Robertson's Christian Broadcasting Network (CBN) and eventually formed his own Praise the Lord (PTL) network, was at the center of one of the first major televangelist scandals. At first it was a sex scandal that forced Bakker to ask Jerry Falwell to act as caretaker of his network until he was seen by the public to have undergone a suitable period of penance and restoration. Then financial irregularities and details of extravagant expenditure subsequently emerged, which shocked American Pentecostals. Bakker ultimately had to serve time in prison.

Away from the financial irregularities and opulent lifestyles associated with some of the better-known televangelists, scandals have not been limited to the financial sphere. Sexual scandals have periodically made the news, which is all the more poignant given the fundamentalist moralizing and celebrity status of some televangelists in question. A notable example was the downfall and unforgettable televised confession of the Pentecostal televangelist Jimmy Swaggart, for his involvement with a prostitute. Swaggart was previously well-known for his aggressive promotion of a strict and ascetic moral lifestyle in his regular broadcasts.

Yet, although the idea of televangelism invariably evokes scandal in many people's minds, the medium raises other important issues as well. Not least among these is the second word of the portmanteau "televangelism." Despite a clear market demand for religious broadcasting as evidenced by a plethora of programs, channels, and networks expanding worldwide, the evidence is that, ironically, the medium actually wins very few converts and is completely ineffective as an evangelistic tool. Instead, religious broadcasting is primarily aimed at and viewed by Christians, so that, together with talk shows and church services, American Christian networks such as CBN broadcast family-orientated secular programming as a wholesome alternative to television's normal fare. It can be argued, then, that televangelism contributes to a sectarian mind-set and to separation from the world. Meanwhile, the Christian networks such as CBN and Trinity Broadcasting Network exercise an important hegemonic role, providing (but also controlling) broadcasting outlets for individual ministries and televangelists across the United States.

Another important issue is the social and political impact of televangelism. The cult of celebrity can directly contribute to enhancing a televangelist's public profile and political aspirations. More important, though, is the way in which ownership of a television channel or network can provide a power base and important launch pad for political activity. For example, Pat Robertson famously sought to garner support for the Contras waging a civil war against the leftist Sandinistas in revolutionary Nicaragua. He sought the Republican Party nomination for the 1988 presidential election. More recently, John Hagee's strong Christian Zionism (a position that, until recently, commanded considerable sympathy among classical Pentecostals) has keenly sought to mobilize support for the modern state of Israel, even seeking to bring pressure to bear on successive Washington administrations to back the Jewish state (though the extent to which his activity has actually directly contributed to American foreign policy is open to debate and challenged by some political observers).

What of televangelism's social impact? Focusing on different expressions of Pentecostalism represented by three highly successful black televangelists (T. D. Jakes, Eddie Long, and Creflo Dollar), Jonathan Walton (2009) explores the extent to which black televangelism serves as a role model for African Americans. He questions whether it reinforces cultural myths and anaesthetizes viewers against the need for structural change. Whether or not readers agree with Walton's analysis, nonetheless, his academic treatment demonstrates the need for further study into televangelism's social and cultural impact.

So far, this brief paper has focused primarily on televangelism in the United States, with good reason. Focusing on the British milieu, William Kay discusses how relaxed regulations in North America helped ensure that religious broadcasting developed more widely, freely, and powerfully than in the United Kingdom, where a much more regulated broadcasting industry severely curbed the rise of televangelism until recent years (2009). Even with the advent of satellite television and the deregulation of broadcasting, the negative portrayals of American televangelism resulted in strict rules concerning solicitation of donations. This situation is now beginning to change.

Elsewhere across the world, televangelism is a growing—and predominantly Pentecostal—phenomenon. In some regions such as Latin America, where the last three or so decades have witnessed an explosion of Pentecostalism, use of the electronic media has been widespread for some years. The preacher Luis Palau, for example, has broadcast across the continent for decades. Latin American Pentecostals are increasingly exhibiting a strong preference for local rather than North American programming. Nonetheless, despite the recent explosion of televangelism across the globe, North American religious broadcasting represents a powerful player and an important trendsetter within the medium.

References and Suggestions for Further Reading

Bruce, Steve. 1990. *Pray TV: Televangelism in America.* London: Routledge.

Hadden, Jeffrey K., and Charles E. Swann. 1981. *Prime Time Preachers: The Rising Power of Televangelism.* Reading, MA: Addison-Wesley.

Kay, William K. 2009. "Pentecostalism and Religious Broadcasting." *Journal of Beliefs and Values* 30(3): 245–54.

Schultze, Quentin J. 1991. *Televangelism and American Culture: The Business of Popular Religion.* Grand Rapids, MI: Baker Book House.

Walton, Jonathan L. 2009. *Watch This! The Ethics and Aesthetics of Black Televangelism.* New York: New York University Press.

Ambrose Jessup Tomlinson

DAVID G. ROEBUCK

A.J. Tomlinson (1865–1943) was the most influential leader of Pentecostal denominations that use some variation of the name Church of God in their titles and are connected to a movement that emerged out of eastern Tennessee and western North Carolina around the turn of the twentieth century. Tomlinson served as the primary pastor and first general overseer of the Church of God (Cleveland, Tennessee) from 1903 until 1923 when he separated from the denomination. He then served as general overseer of what came to be known as the Church of God of Prophecy. Significantly shaped by his influence, the Church of God movement remains a major part of the Pentecostal movement. In 2010 the Church of God (Cleveland, Tennessee) claimed more than thirty-four thousand churches and nearly seven million members in 180 countries and territories. Other denominations that claim Tomlinson as their founder add to these numbers.

Ambrose Jessup Tomlinson was born near Westfield, Indiana, on 22 September 1865. In addition to farming, his father constructed roads and railroads and participated in numerous business ventures. Originally members of the Westfield Society of Friends, Tomlinson's family parted with that Quaker congregation because of the family's support of abolition and civil marriage. By the time Ambrose was born, his parents, Milton and Delilah, were relatively affluent, disaffected with Quakerism, and politically active.

Weak and small at birth, A.J. overcame his limitations. He excelled academically, participated in school athletics and local drama, and was intensely political. Membership in the Populist Party introduced him to the ideals of an egalitarian society that included the working class, blacks, and women. These ideals later shaped his understanding of the church and mission.

Soon after his marriage to Mary Jane Taylor in 1889, Tomlinson's encounter with a severe thunderstorm encouraged him to examine his spiritual condition. In his vivid style he later wrote, "Nothing much was accomplished that night, but I never let up until I got a real experience of salvation. My cards were soon cremated, and I was soon attending Sunday School" (Tomlinson 1913, 202). This experience initiated his search for the "Bible Church," and he joined the Chester Meeting of the Society of Friends where he began to teach and preach. This congregation was both evangelical and Holiness, and Tomlinson sought sanctification as a second work of grace following justification. He described his seeking sanctification as a "tremendous conflict with an 'old man'" and a "violent contest" that lasted several months until with God's help the old man laid dead at his feet (ibid., 203–4).

Searching for spiritual understanding and experience characterized Tomlinson's life. He reportedly visited numerous ministries such as

Dwight L. Moody's in Chicago; that of A. B. Simpson in Nyack, New York; Martin Wells Knapp's God's Bible School in Cincinnati; and Frank W. Sandford's Holy Ghost and Us Bible School at Shiloh, near Durham, Maine. Forsaking his Quaker heritage, Tomlinson submitted to water baptism by Sandford in 1897.

Acquaintance with J. B. Mitchell further influenced Tomlinson's radical Holiness ideas of mission and solidified his permanent departure from Westfield, both geographically and theologically. Mitchell was a convert of Charles Finney and Oberlin College theology. Oberlin's Holiness theology was endued with a social emphasis shaped by godly compassion, a theology in which a heart full of God's love responds to human needs. Such compassion moved Tomlinson toward ministry to the whole person.

In 1894 Tomlinson and Mitchell formed the Book and Tract Company as a means of financing home missionary work in the mountains of Appalachia. In 1899 Tomlinson relocated his family to Culberson, North Carolina, where he operated a school, established an orphanage, distributed clothes to the poor, and published *Samson's Foxes* (1901–1902) as a means of raising support for his ministry. He later edited *The Way* (1904–1905) with M. S. Lemons, *The Church of God Evangel* (1910–1923), *The Faithful Standard* (1922), and *The White Winged Messenger* (1923–1943).

W. F. Bryant and R. G. Spurling were among Tomlinson's acquaintances in the mountain communities of North Carolina and Tennessee. In 1886 Richard Green Spurling with his father, Richard Spurling, had established the Christian Union at the Spurling mill site in Monroe County, Tennessee. The Christian Union was a protest against the rigid Landmark movement, which had swept the Baptist congregations in that region, and is considered the beginning of the Church of God (Cleveland, Tennessee). William Franklin Bryant, who lived in nearby Camp Creek, North Carolina, had come into the Holiness movement in 1896 as the result of a revival. Following several years of persecution and uncertainty among those who followed Bryant, Spurling had organized a congregation in Bryant's home in 1902, which they called The Holiness Church. After much consideration, Tomlinson joined The Holiness Church on 13 June 1903, and the congregation selected him as pastor.

Tomlinson's organizational skills and vision propelled him toward establishing other congregations in Georgia and Tennessee. By late 1904, success in Bradley County, along with the good schools and a railroad there, caused him to relocate to the small community of Cleveland, Tennessee, where the headquarters of the Church of God remains (2011). At least four congregations began an annual General Assembly in 1906, which selected Tomlinson as general overseer in 1909.

Under Tomlinson's leadership the movement grew and evolved. The Holiness Churches adopted the name Church of God at their second General Assembly in 1907. Among the developments he encouraged was the publication of a periodical entitled *The Church of God Evangel* (1910), appointment of state overseers (1911), selection of an elders' council (1917), establishment of a Bible training school (1918), and construction of an assembly auditorium (1920).

Although there are earlier reports of speaking in tongues and miraculous healings at Camp Creek, the Church of God did not develop a Pentecostal theology until after Tomlinson's personal Spirit baptism experience. Already actively seeking the experience in 1908, Tomlinson invited G. B. Cashwell to preach in Cleveland. Cashwell had left his home in North Carolina to visit the famous Azusa Street Mission and returned to the southeastern United States as an apostle of the Pentecostal doctrine and experience. Following Cashwell's sermon on 12 January, Tomlinson had an extraordinary Spirit baptism experience. Along with shaking, rolling, and a sense of levitation, he later wrote, "great joy flooded my soul. The happiest moments I had ever known up to that time. . . . Oh, such floods and billows of glory ran through my whole being" (Tomlinson 1913, 212). His joy was accompanied by a vision in which he traveled the globe speaking in the languages of the countries he visited. Tomlinson's Pentecostal experience transformed him and the Church of God. In less than two years, the movement spread throughout much of the southern United States and to the Church of God's first international mission in the Bahamas.

Along with the successes, however, differences developed between Tomlinson and other leaders regarding the nature of the church and church government. In 1923, the elders council removed Tomlinson from the office of general overseer amid charges and countercharges of leadership, financial, and copyright irregularities. Believing he had been elected general overseer for life, Tomlinson countered that the General Assembly had forsaken theocratic government. He continued his claim to be general overseer of the Church of God, but in 1927 the Tennessee Supreme Court ruled that Tomlinson and his followers could no longer use the name Church of God. They became known as The Church of God, Over Which

A.J. Tomlinson Is General Overseer until a later court case ended with their adoption of the name Church of God of Prophecy.

Under Tomlinson's leadership, the Church of God of Prophecy claimed a unique place as the bride of Christ. Near the end of his life, Tomlinson returned to the W. F. Bryant home place in North Carolina and initiated the development of Fields of the Wood as a biblical theme park and witness to the last days Church of God. In an age and region that accommodated cultural racism, Tomlinson taught that the church should be racially inclusive and appointed a number of black and Latino leaders.

Following Tomlinson's death on 2 October 1943, his youngest son, Milton (1906–1995), was chosen as general overseer. Then his oldest son, Homer (1892–1968), claimed to be the rightful general overseer and established the Church of God, with headquarters in Queens, New York. Thus began a series of separations with numerous denominations claiming supremacy in their efforts to be the Church of God. Some of these include the Church of God (Jerusalem Acres), founded in 1957 with an emphasis on Jewish customs, feast days, and Saturday worship; the Church of God (Charleston, Tennessee), founded in 1993 as the rightful advocate of theocratic government; and Zion Assembly Church of God, founded in 2004, with an emphasis on restoring God's house on earth.

References and Suggestions for Further Reading

Church of God Publications, 1901–1923. 2008. Cleveland, TN: Dixon Pentecostal Research Center. This DVD Rom includes many out-of-print primary sources written or edited by A.J. Tomlinson, including *The Last Great Conflict* and extant issues of periodicals he edited, such as *Church of God Evangel, The Faithful Standard, Samson's Foxes,* and *The Way.*

Conn, Charles W. 2006. *Like a Mighty Army: A History of the Church of God, 1886–1996.* Tribute edition. Cleveland, TN: Pathway Press.

Robins, R.G. 2004. *A.J. Tomlinson: Plainfolk Modernist.* New York: Oxford University Press.

Tomlinson, A.J. 1913. *The Last Great Conflict.* Cleveland, TN: Press of Walter E. Rodgers.

Women

ESTRELDA ALEXANDER

✂   Just before midnight at a New Year's Eve watch night service in 1900, a young student of Charles Fox Parham's, Agnes Ozman, asked her teacher to pray with her to receive Holy Spirit baptism with the gift of glossolalia as evidence. Just as a new day, year, and century dawned, Parham agreed to do so. As he prayed, Ozman reportedly began speaking in fluent Chinese, a language she had not learned, becoming the first person to claim this Pentecostal experience in direct response to seeking evidence of Holy Spirit baptism. One of several women students at Parham's Bible school, Ozman would become first among many women to hit the gospel trail, spreading a message that would eventually reach around the world. Indeed, the greater proportion of women than men who have historically participated in the Pentecostal movement has led some to characterize it as essentially a "women's religion." Its earliest period was marked by a radical egalitarian notion inherited from the Holiness movement out of which it sprang. Throughout its more than one-hundred-year history, women have played a significant, yet often overlooked, role. Early Pentecostals appeared to allow women unprecedented freedom, for they understood the revival as fulfilling the Joel 2:28 prophecy when God's Spirit would be poured out equally on men and women. They saw themselves as living in the last days before Christ's millennial reign and felt an urgency to enlist women as well as men to preach the soul-winning gospel in whatever venue they found themselves. Adherents regarded Holy Spirit empowerment and supernatural anointing above social constrictions, education, or formal preparation. Validation of one's call lay in the fruit of such empowerment rather than in any formal ecclesiastical system. This anointing was signified by preaching skill, charismatic gifts of divine healing and exorcism, and ability to win souls. Further, at least initially, these same adherents strongly disdained hierarchical structures and denominationalism, which reinforced the early movement's radical egalitarianism.

However, equality soon gave way to formal and informal restrictions on women's roles. On close examination, the position on the ground was often little different from that in other traditions. While official polity opened all levels of ministry to all qualified believers, unofficial tradition made room only for men in top positions, and women could not generally hope to be appointed to any positions of real authority such as pastors of viable congregations. This dichotomy came in part from competing theologies that complicated the situation of women leaders. Restorationist elements sought to return the church to "New Testament simplicity." While, for some, this restoration meant the "priesthood of all believers" including women, for others an essential element was to follow Pauline restrictions on women's involvement in the church. Pentecostals also sought to distance themselves from association with modernity and "worldliness," including ideas of the "new woman" in fashion as the movement took off. They sought by outward appearance, social constraints, and rhetoric to ensure a distinction from the modern, "unsaved" world. Many groups placed rigid proscriptions on women's appearance and apparel, to such an extent as to include dictating the appropriate length and style of women's hair, demanding hair covering in public worship, forbidding women to wear pants, dictating rules regarding the style and length of women's dress, and forbidding the wearing of cosmetics and jewelry.

More important, many leaders saw the push for women's rights as representing rebellion that threatened the God-ordained social order. These believers tended toward conservative understandings of women's familial and societal roles, which deepened as the movement aligned itself more closely with the broader evangelical community. Like other evangelicals, early Pentecostals saw women's proper place as being in the home. Married women were expected to be submissive supporters of their husband's work and ministry. Even more, there was an underlying ambivalence regarding women's public ministry, since many Pentecostals understood that a woman could be a "spiritual leader" at church, but she was to be under her husband's headship at home. Further, many understood that when God used a woman, she was God's second choice, because a man was not available. Nonetheless, like other segments of evangelicalism, the movement made a place for those few exceptional women whom God might choose to use in an extraordinary way.

The Azusa Street Mission and revival provided women freedom to preach, teach, counsel new converts, pray for individuals to receive Holy

Spirit baptism, and give and interpret messages in tongues. Lucy Farrow assisted Seymour in leading the congregation before embarking on a missionary trip across the United States and to Liberia. Florence Crawford oversaw the numerous Pentecostal missions springing up along the northwest coast and assisted Clara Lum and Seymour in editing the mission's *Apostolic Faith* newsletter before the two women broke with Seymour to establish their own mission in Portland, Oregon. Jennie Evans Moore came to the mission as a relatively new convert; within two years, she and Seymour were married, and from that time she worked with him to lead the mission, taking over as pastor after his death. Women went out from the Azusa Street revival as missionaries and evangelists, preaching the experience of Pentecost, baptizing new converts, and establishing congregations. Reports back to Azusa Street told of hundreds who experienced sanctification, the Pentecostal Spirit baptism, healing, and deliverance at their hands.

One of the best-known Pentecostal evangelists of the period was faith healer Maria Woodworth Etter, who had already gained prominence on the Holiness camp meeting circuit as she held evangelistic meetings that regularly drew thousands throughout the United States. Subsequently, she was the only one of the prominent Holiness faith healers to accept the Pentecostal message. By 1912 she was regarded by many Pentecostals as a prominent leader and speaker and held her largest revivals between 1912 and 1913, when she was nearly seventy years of age.

Carrie Judd Montgomery, whose ministry spanned more than sixty years, also influenced both the Holiness and Pentecostal movements. After the young Montgomery experienced a miraculous healing, she began writing and speaking on divine healing. Her first book, *The Prayer of Faith* (eventually translated into four languages), was published in 1880, when she was only twenty-two years old. A year later, she began *Triumphs of Faith: A Monthly Journal for the Promotion of Healing and Holiness*, which she published until her death in 1946.

Marie Burgess was baptized in the Holy Spirit in 1906 under the ministry of Parham, who sent her to New York City to evangelize in 1907. In that same year, she set up Glad Tidings Hall–Apostolic Faith Mission in Manhattan. After she married Robert Brown in 1909, the two guided that church to become Glad Tidings Tabernacle, for a long time the most prominent Pentecostal church in New York City and one of the most prominent on the East Coast. In 1917 the church affiliated with the

Assemblies of God, and Robert took on a leadership role in the denomination. After Robert's death in 1948, Marie continued as senior pastor until her death in 1971.

As the revival moved out from Azusa Street and new missions began to organize into more structured fellowships, and then denominations, women's roles became more complex. Almost from the beginning, most bodies placed some restrictions on their ministry and leadership. Limitations were placed on the titles they could receive, the ecclesial positions they could hold, and the level of ministry in which they could be involved. Some barred women from senior pastorates but allowed them to serve on staff under male leadership. Others banned women from the highest levels of ordination, leaving the position of bishop entirely reserved for men. As individual denominations evolved, no consensus developed regarding women's leadership. Some denominations, such as the Pentecostal Holiness Church and the Open Standard Bible Churches, granted women full clergy rights. Others, such as the Church of the Lord Jesus Christ of the Apostolic Faith, restricted women from almost all public roles. Most groups fell in between the two extremes, limiting women's institutional role in some way.

One of the most rigid gender demarcations was set in place by Church of God in Christ founder, C. H. Mason, who proscribed a dual structure that preserved the office of ordained pastor and title of preacher for men but allowed women to be licensed as evangelists or missionaries to minister to other women, raise funds for local and national programs, direct women's programs, and provide material support for leaders. Only women serving as military or institutional chaplains are fully ordained within the denomination. Yet, the Church of God in Christ's quasi-episcopal structure leaves room for a small number of bishops to grant jurisdictional ordination without denominational standing to some women. Further, some women serve with their husbands as co-pastors or inherit pastorates from their deceased husbands.

When the Assemblies of God was formed in 1914, the organization ordained women as evangelists or missionaries—but not in pastoral or other positions involving authority over men. Within three years, formal gender distinctions were dropped, though practical restrictions precluded women, other than missionaries, from performing ordinances until 1935. This move did not, however, materially improve ministry opportunities or reduce the predominance of male leadership at congregational and administrative levels. Although all formal restrictions have been removed, substantially fewer women have traditionally been appointed as senior pastors, and until recent years women have played little significant role outside their local congregations.

The Church of God (Cleveland, Tennessee) initially encouraged women to serve as evangelists and pastors, but limitations on their ministry and leadership quickly grew so that within a few years their roles were tightly proscribed. Over the decades, increasingly restrictive moves were enacted, and distinctions between the licensure of men and women were put in place. It was not until the late 1900s that most of these rights were restored, though the General Assembly vote and the privilege of serving in leadership roles outside the local congregation continue to be withheld, so that women today remain limited to the two lower of three ranks of ministry.

The issue of women's leadership has been as divisive as any within the relatively young life of the movement, causing repeated schism and creating new denominations. In the first quarter of the twentieth century, for example, Robert Lawson split from the Pentecostal Assemblies of the World to form the Church of Our Lord Jesus Christ, in part over his objections regarding the freedom women had to preach within the denomination, and their relative liberty regarding attire. Near the end of the century, the status of women was still problematic, when Robert Grayson split from the Church of God in Christ to form New Day Assembly, partly because of similar objections regarding the role and image of women.

Several women worked independent of male-dominated structures in order to establish their own congregations, some of which evolved into denominations of varying magnitude. Some, like Mary Tate's Church of the Living God Pillar and Ground of the Truth, which was founded in 1903 and became the parent body to at least six denominations, would become substantial. Tate, herself, would become the first woman to be consecrated as bishop of a U.S. denomination. Florence Crawford split from William Seymour's Apostolic Faith Mission to form a new body with the same name in the Pacific Northwest. Ida Robinson separated from the United Holy Church in response to its early stance regarding women's ordination, to form Mt. Sinai Holy Church of America to give women the opportunity to be involved in leadership at every institutional level. Rosa Artimus Horn founded Pentecostal Faith Church, Inc., in Harlem, Madeline Mabe Phillips founded the Alpha and Omega Church of God, Carrie Gurry established the King's Apostle Holiness Church, and Mozella Cook split with the Church of God in Christ to found the Sought Out Church of God in Christ. In Canada, Ellen Hebden founded the first Pentecostal church in that country in 1906 (the East End Mission or Hebden Mission, located in Toronto, Ontario), and Alice Belle Garrigus founded Bethesda Mission in 1911, which became the parent congregation of the Pentecostal Assemblies of Newfoundland and Labrador founded in 1930.

Perhaps the most noted Pentecostal woman of the entire twentieth century was the famed evangelist Aimee Semple McPherson, who founded the International Church of the Foursquare Gospel in Los Angeles, California, in 1924. Over the next three-quarters of a century, this body would grow to be the largest American denomination founded by a woman with a constituency of one and a half million. The flamboyant McPherson, known as much for her dramatic antics as for her prolific ministry, accomplished several firsts—including being the first woman in the United States to own a radio station, KFSG, which featured her weekly Angelus Temple broadcasts.

Mission has been a central focus of Pentecostal ministry from the movement's earliest days, in which women have played an important role. Florence Crawford, who was the first person to take the Pentecostal message to the Pacific Northwest, received her Pentecostal Spirit baptism at the Azusa Street revival, worked with Seymour, planting and overseeing new congregations. Julia Hutchins originally locked Seymour out of the church she pastored due to her objections regarding his theology of tongues speech as initial evidence of the baptism of the Holy Spirit. Later won over to Seymour's point of view and the Azusa Street revival, Hutchins (as well as Lucy Farrow) traveled as a missionary, preaching in several U.S. cities before taking the Pentecostal message to Liberia.

Ivy Campbell went to Ohio, and Rachel Sizelove to Missouri, working to evangelize those areas with the message of Pentecostal revival and to set up small congregations. Sizelove's ministry grew to have prominence in the Assemblies of God when a prophetic vision of a fountain of water in the center of Springfield, Missouri, served as a foundation for the establishment of the denomination's headquarters in that city. Lucy Leatherman traveled to Israel, Egypt, and Palestine and then, after joining the Church of God, moved to Chile and Argentina to help establish a denomination in that area.

Among the several husband-and-wife teams sent out from Azusa Street, Abundio and Rosa de Lopez held street worship services in the Hispanic sections of Los Angeles. Samuel and Ardell Mead returned to Liberia from Azusa Street to help spread the Pentecostal message in that country, accompanied by G. W. Evans and his wife, May. Also G. W. and Daisy Batman were missionaries to Liberia.

The 1906 Mukti (India) Mission revival rivaled the fervor of Azusa Street as young women saw visions, fell into trances, and spoke in tongues. There is no indication that this revival was precipitated by events in Los Angeles. Its leader, Pandita Ramabai, understood the Mukti Mission to be a vehicle for the Holy Spirit to create an independent Indian Christianity. An American woman, Minnie Abrams, worked with Ramabai, training hundreds of Indian women as evangelists. Alice Luce, a Holiness church planter in India, received her Pentecostal experience in 1910. After being ordained by the newly formed Assemblies of God, she established the Berean Bible Institute in San Diego to train Hispanic preachers and produced Bible school curricula, lessons for Sunday school quarterlies, several books, and regular contributions to the *Apostolic Light* magazine.

This strong missionary impulse would continue through such women as Lillian Thrasher, whose ministry in Egypt was so successful that both the Church of God and the Assemblies of God claim it as part of their missionary efforts. While Thrasher received only limited financial support from either body, she is credited with being the first Church of God foreign missionary. At first housing fifty orphans in her own home, she later built and operated a home for orphans and women, with support from wealthy Coptic Christians. By the time she died, the orphanage had expanded to thirteen buildings including a church, a clinic, and an elementary school, and Thrasher was also revered by the Egyptian leaders and community.

Another area in which women have continued to make significant contributions is education. Often, institutions that would eventually become Pentecostal colleges began because of the efforts of women who pushed reluctant leaders to invest resources in beginning Bible institutions to train young men and women for ministry. While some establishments remained small, unaccredited institutes, a number evolved into accredited Bible or liberal arts colleges. Aimee Semple McPherson clearly recognized the value of training for ministers and founded the LIFE (Lighthouse of International Foursquare Evangelism) Bible College almost simultaneously with opening the doors of Angelus Temple. Additionally, the Baker sisters founded Elim Bible College in upstate New York; Arena Mallory was tapped by C. H. Mason to take over the helm of Saints Bible College in Jackson, Mississippi, which she led for nearly five decades; and Bebe

Patten founded Oakland Bible Institute in Oakland, California, in the mid 1940s, which is today Patten University, a four-year liberal arts college affiliated with the Church of God.

Despite numerous restrictions, Pentecostal spirituality continued to attract women in large numbers. Women still make up the bulk of Pentecostal churches, bringing giftings and abilities that provide these congregations and denominations with a seemingly endless reservoir of lay talent to carry on extensive Christian education, congregational nurture, and outreach. To channel the spiritual enthusiasm and leadership skills of gifted women without disrupting the male power structure, Pentecostal denominations have established a number of auxiliaries designed specifically for this intent.

Over the century, judicatory bodies have wrestled with providing women with more conspicuous roles in the church's life and ministry. Some bodies have repeatedly given and rescinded women's rights to hold certain ministerial ranks or be involved in various areas of public ministry. The proportion of women in public ministry within the movement declined drastically after the Second World War. Women found other roles, establishing and involving themselves in gender-related groups such as women's auxiliaries and pastor's aid societies, as a way of maintaining some degree of autonomy and control over the areas of religious life that pertained primarily to women. Others took on areas of less interest to men, such as organizing missionary societies or prayer bands to support the spiritual needs of the church. Still others—buying into the central conservative arguments over women's roles—confined themselves to home responsibilities and gave up hope of undertaking meaningful leadership roles in the church. One of the ramifications of the continued ambiguity within the movement has been the exodus of highly gifted and educated women to denominations that are more open to their ministry and leadership.

At this writing, the movement's stance on women's roles remains ambiguous, and positions regarding women's leadership are almost as numerous as the denominations that comprise the movement. Women continue to make up Pentecostalism's major constituency, but the numbers and proportions of men within classical Pentecostalism is growing along with a renewed push for men to move into their "rightful" place of leadership in the church. Still the significant impact of women's involvement and leadership within the movement is undeniable.

References and Suggestions for Further Reading

Alexander, Estrelda. 2005. *The Women of Azusa Street.* Cleveland, OH: Pilgrim Press.

———. 2008. *Limited Liberty: The Legacy of Four Pentecostal Women Pioneers.* Cleveland, OH: Pilgrim Press.

Alexander, Estrelda, and Amos Yong. 2009. *Philip's Daughters: Women in Pentecostal-Charismatic Leadership.* Eugene OR: Pickwick.

Barfoot, Charles H., and Gerald T. Sheppard. 1980. "Prophetic vs. Priestly Religion: The Changing Role of Women Clergy in Classical Pentecostal Churches." *Review of Religious Research* 22:2–17.

Blumhofer, Edith L. 1993. *Aimee Semple McPherson: Everybody's Sister.* Grand Rapids, MI: Eerdmans.

Butler, Anthea D. 2007. *Women in the Church of God in Christ: The Making of a Sanctified World.* Chapel Hill: University of North Carolina Press.

Lawless, Elaine J. 1988a. *God's Peculiar People: Women's Voices and Folk Tradition in a Pentecostal Church.* Lexington: University Press of Kentucky.

———. 1988b. *Handmaidens of the Lord: Pentecostal Women Preachers and Traditional Religion.* Philadelphia: University of Pennsylvania Press.

Word of Faith Movement

AMARNATH AMARASINGAM

The Word of Faith movement is a relatively recent religious movement arising within the context of American evangelicalism, and particularly Pentecostal Christianity. It consists of denominationally independent churches, ministries, Bible colleges, volunteer organizations, and broadcasting networks. There is no formal organizational structure, but the movement is bound together by a "relational network" centered on the movement's doctrine, the Faith Message, and a shared understanding of the Bible (Harrison 2005, 5). As Milmon Harrison notes, the Word of Faith movement, in one way or another, "exhibits all of the characteristics of post–World War II religion in America" (1999, 26).

First among these characteristics is an aversion to denominationalism. According to the movement, denominationalism does a disservice to believers by reinforcing human-made divisions. Denominations separate Christians from each other, and neglect teaching them "what the Bible 'really' says (which, of course, they claim to be doing)" (Harrison 1999, 27). Second, the movement is also characterized by individualism. According to Milmon Harrison's research, decisions about which aspects of the Faith Message one accepts, questions about how to relate to the institution of the local church, and struggles surrounding how to implement doctrine in one's own life are largely matters of individual choice. Third, the movement also tends to engage in what Harrison calls "code-mixing," a kind of mix-and-match religiosity, in which elements of other religious or philosophical traditions are blended with Holiness-Pentecostal traditions. Fourth, the Word of Faith movement is also "heavily mass-mediated and culture-affirming in that it freely borrows from secular sources and media in the process of ongoing evangelism" (1999, 27). The leaders of the movement have no problem mining religious or secular resources in contemporary culture and using these to spread the Faith Message. Fifth, the movement also teaches that it is God's will for Christians to live fulfilled and materially prosperous lives. For the Word of Faith movement, success in this world does not foreclose salvation in the next.

The origins of the movement have often been traced to the late Kenneth Hagin, Sr. (1917–2003). Hagin, who was affectionately called "Dad" by followers, has influenced many contemporary Faith teachers including Frederick K. C. Price, Kenneth Copeland, Joyce Meyer, Benny Hinn, Creflo Dollar, and Joel Osteen. Since 1966, Hagin published numerous books and recordings in which the main tenets of the movement are set forth. His enormous influence means it is not surprising he is often considered the leader, if not the founder, of the movement. According to some recent scholarship, however, the original author of these teachings is thought, with some controversy, to be E. W. Kenyon (1867–1948). It was Kenyon who synthesized disparate ideological, philosophical, and theological elements circulating at the turn of the century into what is known today as the Word of Faith movement. Kenyon drew teachings from the Higher Christian Life movement, Pentecostalism, and New Thought metaphysics. According to Harrison (2005, 6), "Kenyon's synthesis of New Thought metaphysical philosophy, teaching that reality is actually created in the minds and affirmed in the speech of believers, gives today's Faith Message some of its most distinctive doctrinal and ritual characteristics."

The remarkable similarities between the writings of Kenyon and Hagin led some to charge Hagin with plagiarism, an accusation he adamantly denied. As Harrison (2005, 8) has written, "in light of the contribution of E. W. Kenyon to today's Word of Faith movement, it seems appropriate to characterize Hagin as the man who took Kenyon's teachings to a much broader audience than their original author was able to reach." In 1962, Hagin established what is now known as Kenneth Hagin Ministries, Inc., and severed his denominational ties with the Assemblies of God. In 1966, he moved to Tulsa, Oklahoma, where his colleague Oral Roberts had already established his headquarters. In Tulsa, Hagin began a radio ministry and started publishing his teachings in the *Word of Faith* magazine, which gives the movement its name (ibid., 7). Hagin also founded the Rhema Correspondence School (1968) and the Rhema Bible Training Center (1974), from which many new Word of Faith teachers have graduated over the years.

Harrison delineates three core beliefs and practices that animate the Word of Faith movement. First, there is the principle of knowing "who you are in Christ," which is "the key to living the higher Christian life that being born again will provide for all who will just accept it" (Harrison 2005, 8). It is believed that prosperity in this life is available to any who simply place their trust in Christ. Believers should never utter a negative word, should never waver in their faith that what they have asked for will be granted. The Bible is seen as a spiritual contract between God and the believer, which guarantees a better life full of material and immaterial benefits. Many believers in the movement will argue that intellectual training in seminaries or universities actually hinders an individual's ability to understand what the Bible is really telling them. Knowing who they are in Christ opens them up to this real knowledge, which is gained through direct revelation from God "through the reading of Scripture, prayer, or through the utterances of someone under the influence of the Holy Spirit" (ibid., 9).

A second core belief of the Word of Faith movement is the practice of positive confession. According to Harrison (2005, 10), "members are taught that once they know who they are in Christ, they can then speak the same words about themselves that God has spoken about them in the Bible. This allows them to access and exercise the power vested in them through their identification with Christ's finished work on the cross." In other words, just as God's Word can create, believers are taught, their words also have creative power. As born-again Christians, their words, when spoken, can put positive and negative forces in motion throughout the world. Thus, believers are encouraged to be especially vigilant about the words they choose to speak, as these may have far-reaching consequences. If an individual speaks negatively about his or her circumstances, it is thought to signify a lack of faith, which may have brought on such circumstances to begin with. In addition to being vigilant about the words they speak, believers are encouraged to be just as watchful over their thoughts and attitudes.

Third, the Word of Faith movement is characterized by an emphasis on prosperity, divine health, and material wealth. According to members of the movement, too many denominations falsely teach that Jesus was poor, and they teach Christians they should also be poor in order to identify fully with Christ. Such negative confession, according to Faith members, brings upon individuals lives void of the true riches God wants them to possess. "The idea that Jesus and his disciples were not poor but had houses and a common treasury from which Judas Iscariot embezzled funds is an important part of the Word of Faith movement's teaching on the subject" (Harrison 2005, 12). According to Faith teaching, individuals may remain poor even while they give tithes to their churches. Instead, as Oral Roberts has stated, offerings should be thought of as "sowing seeds," and if people "sow seeds of money, they should expect to receive a harvest of money in kind" (ibid.).

The Word of Faith movement, then, is a distinct subcultural movement within the larger landscape of Pentecostal Christianity. It is nondenominational and thus shows no sign of developing an organizational hierarchy to which member churches can be accountable. According to the movement, born-again Christians have direct access to God through Scripture and can become spiritually and materially wealthy through the proper application of scriptural principles. Television has played a significant role in helping to spread the Faith movement. All in all, the continuing popularity and reach of the movement seem to indicate that it will remain an indelible aspect of the American religious landscape for decades to come.

REFERENCES AND SUGGESTIONS FOR FURTHER READING

Harrison, Milmon F. 1999. "'Name It and Claim It!' The Word of Faith Movement, the 'Faith Message,' and the Social Construction of Doctrinal Meaning." PhD dissertation, University of California, Santa Barbara.

———. 2005. *Righteous Riches: The Word of Faith Movement in Contemporary African American Religion.* New York: Oxford University Press.

Lee, Shayne. 2005. *T. D. Jakes: America's New Preacher.* New York: New York University Press.

Lee, Shayne, and Philip Luke Sinitiere. 2009. *Holy Mavericks: Evangelical Innovators and the Spiritual Marketplace.* New York: New York University Press.

Simmons, Dale H. 1997. *E. W. Kenyon and the Postbellum Pursuit of Peace, Power, and Plenty.* Lanham, MD: Scarecrow Press.

Contributors

Estrelda Alexander is professor of theology in the School of Divinity at Regent University.

Peter Althouse is associate professor of religion at Southeastern University.

Amarnath Amarasingam is a doctoral candidate in religious studies at Wilfrid Laurier University.

Linda M. Ambrose is professor of history at Laurentian University.

Allan Heaton Anderson is head of the School of Philosophy, Theology, and Religion and professor of global Pentecostal studies at the University of Birmingham.

Kenneth J. Archer is professor of Pentecostal theology and Christian studies at Southeastern University.

Connie Ho Yan Au is director of the Pentecostal Research Centre at the Synergy Institute of Leadership.

Lewis Brogdon is director of the Black Church Studies Program at Louisville Presbyterian Theological Seminary.

Mark J. Cartledge is director of the Centre for Pentecostal and Charismatic Studies and senior lecturer in Pentecostal and Charismatic theology at the University of Birmingham.

Shane Clifton is director of research and head of theology at Alphacrucis.

Andrew K. Gabriel is assistant professor of Christian theology at Horizon College and Seminary at the University of Saskatchewan.

Stephen J. Hunt is reader in sociology at the University of the West of England.

Matthew T. Lee is associate professor of sociology at the University of Akron.

Martin W. Mittelstadt is associate professor of biblical studies at Evangel University.

Peter D. Neumann is assistant academic dean and professor of theology at Master's College and Seminary.

Margaret M. Poloma is professor emeritus of sociology at the University of Akron.

David A. Reed is professor emeritus of pastoral theology and research professor at Wycliffe College, University of Toronto.

David G. Roebuck is director of the Dixon Pentecostal Research Center and assistant professor of the history of Christianity at Lee University.

Calvin L. Smith is principal of King's Evangelical Divinity School at the University of Wales.

Adam Stewart is a lecturer in religious studies at the University of Waterloo and adjunct professor of theology at Master's College and Seminary.

Roger J. Stronstad is director of biblical theology and associate professor of theology at Summit Pacific College.

Angela Tarango is assistant professor of religion at Trinity University.

Keith Warrington is vice-principal and director of doctoral studies at Regents Theological College.

Michael Wilkinson is director of the Religion in Canada Institute and professor of sociology at Trinity Western University.